ROMANTIC PERIOD 1798–1832: AN ANTHOLOGY

While the 'Revolution Debate' of the 1790s has been extensively covered by scholars and critics, less attention has been given to the period which bridges the gap to the Victorian era. Yet this was a period of crucial social, economic, political and cultural change.

Romantic Period Writings 1798–1832 provides a valuable insight into the condition of Britain in the early part of the nineteenth century. It includes original documents from a range of disciplines and discourses. Among the material assembled in the anthology are writings by previously neglected or underrepresented women, working-class men, black radicals, and conservative and evangelical polemicists, as well as several unfamiliar texts by canonical writers. The writings are organised into sections on:

- Radical journalism
- Political economy
- Atheism
- Empire and race
- Nation and state
- Gender
- Literary institutions

Each section includes a scholarly introduction, select bibliography and annotations. Contributors include Ian Haywood, John Seed, Martin Priestman, Kate Teltscher, Simon Edwards, Susan Matthews, Catherine Boyle and Zachary Leader.

Zachary Leader and **Ian Haywood** both teach in the English Department of the Roehampton Institute, London.

ROMANTIC PERIOD WRITINGS 1798–1832: AN ANTHOLOGY

edited by

Zachary Leader and Ian Haywood

London and New York

First published 1998
by Routledge
11 New Fetter Lane, London EC4P 4EE

Simultaneously published in the USA and Canada
by Routledge
29 West 35th Street, New York, NY 10001

The right of Zachary Leader and Ian Haywood to be identified as the Authors
of this Work has been asserted by them in accordance with the Copyright, Designs
and Patents Act 1988

Typeset in Garamond by
Solidus Bristol Limited
Printed and bound in Great Britain by
Biddles Ltd, Guildford and King's Lynn

British Library Cataloguing in Publication Data
A catalogue record for this book is available from the British Library

Library of Congress Cataloguing in Publication Data
Romantic period writings 1798–1832 : an anthology / [compiled by] Zachary
Leader and Ian Haywood.
p.   cm.
Includes bibliographical references and index.
1. Great Britain–History–1800–1837–Sources.   2. Romanticism–
–Great Britain–Sources.   I. Leader, Zachary.   II. Haywood,
Ian, 1958–   .
DA535.R66   1998
941.081–dc21   97–48907
                                                                      CIP

ISBN 0–415–15782–X (pbk)
ISBN 0–415–15781–1 (hbk)

CONTENTS

CONTENTS

CONTENTS

PLATES

CONTRIBUTORS

Catherine Boyle is a research student at Roehampton Institute London, where she is completing a thesis on Shelley and radical publishing.

Simon Edwards is Principal Lecturer in English at Roehampton Institute London. He has written and spoken widely on Scott and Dickens, and is currently completing a book on the historical novel and the formation of nationalist politics.

Ian Haywood is Principal Lecturer in English at Roehampton Institute London. He is the author of *Faking It: Art and the Politics of Forgery* (1987), *The Making of History: A Study of the Literary Forgeries of James Macpherson and Thomas Chatterton* (1987), *The Literature of Struggle: An Anthology of Chartist Fiction* (1995) and *Working-Class Fiction: from Chartism to Trainspotting* (1997).

Zachary Leader is Professor of English Literature and Convener of the MA programme in 'Literature and Politics 1776–1832' at Roehampton Institute London. He is the author of *Reading Blake's Songs* (1981), *Writer's Block* (1991) and *Revision and Romantic Authorship* (1996).

Susan Matthews is Senior Lecturer in English at Roehampton Institute London. She is the author of essays and articles on the period, including a contribution to the Open University reader *Romantic Writings* (1996).

Martin Priestman is Reader in English Literature at Roehampton Institute London. His books include *Cowper's 'Task': Structure and Influence* (1983), *Detective Fiction and Literature: The Figure in the Carpet* (1990) and *Crime Fiction from Poe to the Present* (1998).

CONTRIBUTORS

John Seed is Senior Lecturer in History at Roehampton Institute London. He is author of numerous essays and articles on Unitarianism and middle-class culture in this period, including a book written with Janet Wolff, *The Culture of Capital* (1988).

Kate Teltscher is Lecturer in English Literature at Roehampton Institute London. Her book *India Inscribed: European and British Writing on India 1600–1800* was published in 1995.

ACKNOWLEDGEMENTS

This book has been produced by tutors from the English and History Departments of the Roehampton Institute, London. It grew, in part, out of work on Roehampton's interdisciplinary MA course 'Literature and Politics 1776–1832'. The editors would like to thank Isobel Armstrong, Marilyn Butler, John Lucas, Anne K. Mellor and Keith Nield, who offered crucial assistance at the planning stages of the anthology; Mark Storey, who helped in the deciphering of previously unpublished correspondence with Clare; Jane Pringle, of the Department of English at Roehampton, who helped in the preparation of the manuscript; and Talia Rodgers of Routledge, who has been a supporter of the anthology from its inception.

Thanks are due to Pickering and Chatto Publishers Ltd, for their permission to use William Godwin's essay 'Of Religion' from Mark Philp, ed., *Political and Philosophic Writings of William Godwin, Vol. 7: Religious Writings* (1993). The four letters of John Clare taken from *The Letters of John Clare* edited by Mark Storey, are reproduced by permission of Curtis Brown Ltd, London (copyright Eric Robinson 1985). Thanks to the staff at the British Library reproductions department who provided images for inclusion in this book.

EDITORIAL NOTE

The majority of extracts are taken either from the first edition or from a subsequent contemporary edition revised by the author. Full bibliographical details are provided at the head of each extract or in an initial endnote (when these details are complicated or need elaboration). The original spelling and punctuation have been retained throughout, except for obvious printing errors. Editorial emendations or interpolations are indicated by square brackets. Authorial footnotes, when retained, have mostly been included in the endnotes.

GENERAL INTRODUCTION

This book aims to provide an insight into the 'condition of Britain' in the first three decades of the nineteenth century. While the years after 1800 have no equivalent to the revolution debate of the previous decade, they were by no means years of stagnancy, or of retreat into a Burkean 'hearth and home' mentality.[1] Although the long war with Napoleonic France undoubtedly reinforced certain reactionary and quietist tendencies in British culture, the pressures for social, economic and political change remained. Some of these pressures were radical, embodied in campaigns for the abolition of the slave trade, for Catholic emancipation, or for parliamentary reform; other campaigns, such as the Evangelical movement, were decidedly conservative in their social outlook, even while they participated in some of the former causes.

Complications like these teach us the salutary lesson that contemporary labels such as 'radical' and 'reactionary' can be misleading or inadequate. A work may have radical potential at one level, but not at another. An enlightened attitude towards class, for instance, may be contradicted by a conservative attitude towards gender (on this score see Section 1). Moreover, a text may be formally challenging while its overt 'message' is not, or vice versa. For example, the rhyming couplets of Erasmus Darwin's scientific poem, *The Temple of Nature* (1803), excerpted in Section 3, would be regarded by Wordsworth as out of date, while its intellectual content was at the forefront of theories of evolution. In the light of such complications, the cut-off point of this anthology ought not to be read teleologically (or, to use an older parlance, Whiggishly).[2] Although the Reform Bill of 1832 can be interpreted as the delayed response of the British state to the demands for reform that first peaked so spectacularly in the 1790s – making it a sort of narrative closure for the revolution debate – its actual provisions were as notorious for their exclusions as their inclusiveness. The year 1832 may, indeed, mark a significant realignment of class forces in Britain, but it was hardly a major act of democratization. The propertied classes, for example, could think of themselves as having united against a common enemy, the still disenfranchised working class; women, Jews and colonized peoples also remained outside the magic circle of citizenship.

As several of the sections in the anthology suggest, the political implications of the multifaceted debate about modernity and civilization in the early decades of the nineteenth century were complex. The utilitarian 'science' of political economy, for example, was used to justify new poor laws which were to leave many working-class people in a far worse condition than under the older system of parochial patronage (see Section 2). The special civilizing role given to women by Evangelicals such as Hannah More depended on women not being 'contaminated' by public life (see Section 6). These complications are sometimes interpreted in terms of the Romantic period's shifting engagement with its Enlightenment past, but they can also be seen prospectively – as laying the foundations of that other historical and cultural bulwark, Victorianism.[3]

Such complexities are the inevitable outgrowth of recent trends in period study. Among historians and literary scholars there is now a widely held consensus that an understanding of the past must draw on a broad base of discursive sources. Since Gareth Stedman-Jones's groundbreaking 1983 essay 'Rethinking Chartism', for example, many historians (in particular, labour historians) have taken a 'linguistic turn' in their approach to historical documentation and interpretation. This has meant a new attention to literary and popular-cultural sources, and an awareness that all written documents are answerable to the techniques of 'literary' analysis.[4] While this development is still hotly debated by historians, it has coincided with the gravitation of literary studies to sources well beyond the traditionally defined field of Romanticism. Literary surveys of the Romantic period no longer confine themselves to the major male poets and the novels of Austen and Scott: room has been found for Jacobin, anti-Jacobin, Gothic, regional and sentimental fiction; for women and working-class poets; and for a variety of 'non-literary' texts.[5]

The most effective (and economical) way to teach the interconnections between the diverse discourses that comprise today's understanding of a period is through an anthology. The best of these to date are certainly more inclusive than their predecessors, but the space they devote to non-literary materials is often tantalizingly confined, and the rationale for inclusion often unclear.[6] *Romantic Period Writings* concentrates on non-canonical writings from the second 'half' or phase of the Romantic period: from 1798, the date of Malthus's essay on the *Principle of Population* and Godwin's *Memoirs of the Author of 'A Vindication of the Rights of Woman'* (and, of course, *Lyrical Ballads*), to 1832, the date of the passage of the Reform Bill. It has room, therefore, for longer and more thoroughly contextualized extracts than some other anthologies.

There are two areas in which the revolution debate resurfaced most conspicuously after its suppression in the 1790s. These are identified by Marilyn Butler as 'the working-class radical movement, and its press, of the post-Napoleonic era; and the more specialised, refined, but sometimes notionally radical body of literature known as the Romantic movement'.[7] While this book leaves 'the Romantic movement', and its extensively debated problems of definition, to other anthologies and critical studies,[8] it begins with the resurgence of popular radicalism in the post-war years. Section 1 looks at the role of the radical press as an agent of reform, and focuses its materials around a single key moment: the Peterloo Massacre of 1819.[9]

Though many radical causes had been forced underground by 1798, the issue of economic inequality remained a topic of mainstream controversy throughout the period. The figure which focuses this controversy, haunting the social consciousness of the period, is the rural pauper or vagrant. The years 1798–1832 saw a massive outflow of individuals and families from the countryside, forced out by pauperism and subsistence wages, an effect of the rationalization of agriculture along capitalist lines. Section 2 of the anthology documents some of the ways in which the newly evolving discipline or discourse of political economy sought to understand rural poverty in a period which witnessed extensive rural discontent, culminating in the Swing riots of 1830. It also demonstrates opposition to political economy in the writings of contemporary radicals such as William Cobbett and William Hazlitt.

The fate of the anti-religious strain of 1790s radicalism is the subject of Section 3 of the anthology. Though positive uses of the word 'atheism' were as rare in the early decades of the nineteenth century as they were in the 1790s, these decades saw a rising challenge not only to established faiths but to the deistic 'natural religion' of writers such as Tom Paine. The section begins with the deistic position, often a flag of convenience for more fully anti-religious and materialist views. Deism retained the concept of a broadly well-intentioned creator, one about whose precise nature it was unnecessary to quarrel. It was gradually challenged, though, by more openly sceptical views, including several uncompromising refutations of divinity *per se*. The relation of these challenges to wider controversies about political emancipation, individual freedom, and scientific or technological progress is striking.

The years 1798–1832 encompass significant phases not only of nationalist political activity and organization but of theoretical concern with nationhood, the subject of Section 5. The period separates the French Revolution from the European nationalist uprisings of the 1840s; in Ireland, England's oldest colony, it separates the 1798 rebellion, the 1800 Act of Union and the 1803 uprising of Robert Emmet from the Young Ireland movement of the late 1830s and 1840s. But as the extracts in this section show, these years were hardly, in terms of a developing sense of nationhood, a period of dormancy or quiescence. In both literary and non-literary writings, particularly new novelistic genres, questions of nationality continue to figure prominently. These are the years of the emergence of Irish and Scottish 'regional' fiction, including the historical romance and the historical novel. Issues of national reconciliation, modernization, and the professionalization of 'British' life (currently much debated by historians and critics, as in the controversy sparked by Linda Colley's *Britons: Forging the Nation*, 1992) are central to this fiction.[10]

Though issues of race and empire figure in Section 5 (the colonial 'Other', for example, was often used as a foil for 'Britishness'), they are addressed more directly in Section 4, which takes as its focus two key issues: the debate over slavery in the period between abolition (1807) and emancipation (1833), and the representation of India, largest of Britain's colonies. The extracts concerning slavery document the persistence of racial stereotypes and the growth of 'scientific' racism after the abolition of the slave trade, as well as the prominent role played by middle-class women in the emancipationist movement. The extracts on India document a comparable stereotyping, often by the very Evangelicals who championed the abolitionist cause. In these extracts, the supposed moral degeneracy of non-whites is seen as a product of culture and religion as much as of skull shape or comparative anatomy. The section also gives space to the dissenting perspectives of the black radical Robert Wedderburn and the 'polite' traveller Abu Talib.

The texts in Section 6 document the influence of gender ideology in a wide range of writing: on such subjects as education, the arts, the public sphere and the monarchy. This section traces both the reaction against explicit feminism which characterized the years of the war with France (1793–1815), and anxieties over definitions of masculinity. Though in practice the boundary between 'masculine' (public) and 'feminine' (private) sexual spheres was frequently transgressed, much of the writing of the period betrays an increasing nervousness about such transgressions. Women who entered the public sphere –from the feminist writer Mary Wollstonecraft to female royalty – challenged this distinction. Documents are included to contrast reactions to the deaths of Wollstonecraft in 1797 and Princess Charlotte in 1817, and to compare the debate over the morality of Wollstonecraft's life with that over the Queen Caroline affair of 1820. The period is also marked by a desire to reassert public images of strong masculinity, partly to counter more passive and feeling male images derived from Sensibility and Evangelicalism, and partly to characterize British public culture in opposition to a French culture often perceived as feminine.[11]

The last section of the anthology, 'Literary Institutions', documents important changes in the production of literature in the period, in the process questioning several Romantic (or 'Romanticist') presuppositions about writing, in particular those associated with a view of the author as autonomous genius. Chief among these changes is the emergence of a newly identifiable 'reading public', a conscious preoccupation of writers and publishers alike, even of the most 'elevated' of genres. These years also saw the rise of the journal or specialized literary review not only as a shaper of taste but as a tool of marketing. The relation of publisher, patron and periodical is examined in a series of extracts concerning the poet John Clare. The role of the circulating library in the increasing popularity of fiction is also documented, as is the influence of the literary annual in shaping the poetical tastes of the 1820s and early 1830s. This section also reflects the growing interest of recent criticism in the class and gender politics of literary forms and production.[12]

These are not, of course, the only pressing issues or topics in this period; the broadening base of both literary and historical studies has opened the way to a potentially dizzying range of relevant discourses. We believe that the materials we have chosen are not only interesting and important in their own right, but can also be used to shed new light on more familiar texts. For example, Percy Shelley's 'Mask of Anarchy' (1819) can be compared with radical accounts of Peterloo (Section 1); Wordsworth and Coleridge's vagrants in *Lyrical Ballads* (1798) with the writings on political economy (Section 2); Mary Shelley's *Frankenstein* with contemporary debates about atheism and science (Section 3), as well as representations of slavery and empire (Section 4); Scott's Waverley novels with non-fictional accounts of national difference (Section 5); and Austen's novels with the Evangelical repositioning of women's social roles (Section 6), and the proliferation of circulating libraries and literary annuals (Section 7).

1

RADICAL JOURNALISM

Ian Haywood

Forty-four thousand copies of No. 18 have been printed and sold. Let corruption *rub that out*, if she can.

(William Cobbett)[1]

It is the weekly paper which finds its way to the pot-house in town, and the ale-house in the country, inflaming the turbulent temper of the manufacturer, and disturbing the quiet attachment of the peasant to those institutions under which he and his father have dwelt in peace. He receives no account of public affairs ... but what comes through these polluted sources.

(Robert Southey)[2]

Ye are many, they are few.

(Shelley, 'The Mask of Anarchy')

The resurgence of English radicalism in the years 1816–20 is one of the most significant political and cultural developments in the period. In E. P. Thompson's words, these four years 'are the heroic age of popular Radicalism'.[3] Almost twenty years after the proscription of the London Corresponding Society, organized and co-ordinated mass protest against the unreformed political system moved once again to the centre of British political life. But 'monster' meetings and insurrectionary disturbances could not have taken place without the existence of a flourishing network of radical groups and organizers. Radical journalism was a crucial factor in building up this oppositional infrastructure. The radical press provided a medium for the rapid circulation of political news, propaganda and comprehensive accounts of radical events. The aim of radical papers was to enlighten and to inspire: to educate, mobilize and guide. Radical journalism did more than reflect contemporary events: it was an active agency of reform. Its discursive resources involved a rich variety of textual forms: announcements, detailed reports of meetings and trials, open letters, satirical verse and passionate editorials. Binding these diverse genres together was a profound, melodramatic sense that radicals were part of an historic and sublime confrontation between progress and reaction, good and evil, light and darkness.

6

It was the radical press which supplied to its readers a 'Radical martyrology and, more especially, a demonology'.[4]

No contemporary event manifested this mythic conflict so vividly as the Peterloo massacre of 16 August 1819, when a peaceful demonstration held at St Peter's Fields in Manchester was attacked by the local yeoman cavalry. Eleven people were killed, and many more injured. Peterloo provides the ideal focus for an exploration of radicalism in this period. In order to show how radical journalism functioned, most of the material in this section is drawn from one issue of a leading radical periodical, T. J. Wooler's *Black Dwarf*. Its impact and appeal cannot be fully understood unless we try to recreate the experience of reading close to an entire issue (see **extract 3**). While the readers of *Black Dwarf* would expect to be given a graphic account of the state's violence at Peterloo, they would also expect to be put in touch with the radical movement's response to the tragedy. Reading was the prelude to action; action was anticipated and articulated in reading.

In 1800 it was only possible for radicals to operate furtively. The Two Acts of 1795 had banned all political meetings of more than forty people (defiance of this order was punishable by death), and introduced the licensing of lecture halls. This unprecedented attack on civil liberties and free speech was highly effective in delivering its aim of repressing radical organizations and their publications. The London Corresponding Society, which pioneered working-class radical politics, organized its final mass meeting at Copenhagen Fields (now the site of Smithfield market, in east central London) in November 1795, with up to 200,000 protestors present. There would not be another such gathering for over twenty years. National political organizations were outlawed completely in 1799 after a government 'alarm' that some Corresponding Society leaders were in league with veterans of the United Irishmen rebellion of 1798.

At first sight, such measures may seem an unduly harsh response to the demand for political reform. After all, the essence of the radical programme which was first put forward by predominantly genteel-led groups in the 1760s and 1770s was constitutional rather than revolutionary: the British political system needed reforming to make it more representative of the whole (male) population, and to restore 'lost' democratic rights. In radicals' eyes, the oligarchical rule which had prevailed since the Glorious Revolution of 1688 had encouraged gross irresponsibility and 'Old Corruption' in the stewardship of the nation's resources. Wars had led to massive national debt and grotesque levels of taxation, which in turn reinforced huge economic inequalities. The unreformed electoral system, with its notorious 'rotten' boroughs of a few voters, allowed a ruling-class elite of aristocrats and landowners to control the political process by buying and selling political office. Once the political system was reformed, with universal male suffrage (though some reformers still preferred a property qualification), equal electoral districts, annual parliaments and secret ballots, these 'rotten' practices would be swept away and the moral and economic ills of society would be cured.[5] The state's resistance to such changes could therefore be seen as a simple case of self-interest, but the French Revolution gave the contest with reform a sharply ideological character. As Burke's *Reflections on the Revolution in France* (1790) demonstrated brilliantly, popular sovereignty could be smeared as un-British and unconstitutional, a dangerous and amateurishly theoretical concept. From the start of the war with France in 1793, the Pitt government embarked on a highly defensive domestic policy lasting more than thirty years. Naval mutinies in 1797 and the rebellion of the United Irishmen in 1798 confirmed the government's suspicion that Jacobin plotters were active throughout the realm. Spies, informers and *agents provocateurs* were deployed in large numbers. Jacobinism was the 'Red menace' of its time.[6]

Until the final defeat of Napoleon in 1815, therefore, the opportunities for radical campaigns were severely curtailed. Popular patriotic support for the war also weakened the radical case. But as Edward Royle and James Walvin note of the 1800–15 period, 'The popular demand for reform had never been entirely quelled by the legislation of the 1790s, and it was soon to re-emerge when favourable opportunities presented themselves.'[7] In 1803 Colonel Despard, a leader in the 1790s of the United Britons, was executed for high treason. E. P. Thompson has also argued that the Luddite machine-breaking disturbances of 1811–13 were politically motivated.[8] The re-emergence of constitutional political radicalism in these years revolved around the London borough of Westminster, which elected the Radical MP Sir Francis Burdett in 1807. The Westminster 'Committee' included veteran reformers and rising stars who were all to play a prominent role after 1815: Major John Cartwright (1740–1824), the 'Father of Reform', whose career stretched back to the 1770s; Jeremy Bentham (1748–1832), the utilitarian philosopher and penal reformer; Francis Place (1771–1854), the tailor and political organizer; Henry 'Orator' Hunt (1773–1835), the main speaker at Peterloo; and William Cobbett (1762–1835), the radical journalist.[9] In the war years Cobbett's *Political Register* (1802–36) carried the torch of the radical press single-handedly. It was Cobbett who kept alive in print the demonology of Old Corruption with its tax-eaters, boroughmongers (a popular abusive term for those who traded in parliamentary seats) and sinecures, though it was only in 1816 that Cobbett consciously addressed a working-class audience. His turn towards 'Journeymen and Labourers' was anticipated by Major Cartwright, who toured the industrial Midlands and North in 1813–15 to promote the setting up of provincial versions of his Hampden Club, first established in 1812. These Clubs provided the organizational basis for the post-war political Unions (or local radical associations) which organized mass rallies and petitions, including Peterloo. The Hampden Clubs also knitted together the regions and London into a national network. Radicalism began to reacquire the national identity it had wielded so powerfully in the 1790s.

In the wake of Waterloo the case for reform was boosted by the anger of thousands of demobbed soldiers who found themselves facing poor employment prospects and a bad harvest. The years 1816–20 witnessed a prodigous revival of radical meetings and radical journalism. The twin stars in this firmament were the demagogues Hunt and Cobbett. While Hunt revelled at the hustings, Cobbett preferred the slightly less spontaneous medium of print, but both men were masters of populist political analysis, hyperbole and the dramatic flourish. If Hunt was to find his apotheosis in the months surrounding Peterloo, as the extracts below show, Cobbett inaugurated the revival of radical journalism with his famous Address to 'Journeymen and Labourers' of 2 November 1816 **(extract 1)**. The innovatory quality of the Address was not its criticism of Old Corruption but its direct appeal to a working-class audience to become involved in the political process (ironically, Cobbett was not yet in favour of universal suffrage, though he changed his mind within weeks). In order to reach this constituency, Cobbett devised an ingenious new form of cheap publishing. He exploited a loophole in the law which imposed a 4d stamp duty on all newspapers. By printing only his leading article on an unfolded broadsheet (later a pamphlet form was used), Cobbett could avoid the stamp tax and publish the slimmed-down *Political Register* for only 2d (the normal cost was just over a shilling, well beyond the purchasing power of most working-class readers, though the *Political Register* was read aloud in taverns). This 'twopenny trash', a term Cobbett adopted from his enemies, sold in huge numbers: Cobbett claimed 200,000 copies were sold in two months, a testimony to the high levels of literacy in the working class.[10] Cobbett's popularity coincided with an intense period of mass political activity, including three meetings addressed by Henry Hunt at Spa Fields in London (at the meeting on 2 December 1816 a group of Spencean ultra-radicals, who believed in the use of insurrectionary tactics to secure the expropriation of the land, led an abortive attack on the Tower of London), and a national convention of Hampden Clubs in January 1817 which submitted a petition for reform with up to a million signatures. The government declared a state of 'alarm' and revived its 'Gagging' Acts of the 1790s. Cobbett saw the suspension of Habeas Corpus as directed primarily at himself and fled to America. His decision may have been a wise one. Later that year, at the treason trial of the ill-fated Pentridge rebel Jeremiah Brandreth, the defence attorney claimed that Brandreth had been deluded by reading Cobbett's Address.[11]

Cobbett inspired a flurry of cheap, weekly radical papers. Some of the better-known examples are Wooler's *Black Dwarf* (1817–24), *Sherwin's Political Register* (1817–19), Richard Carlile's *Republican* (1819–26), John Wade's *Gorgon* (1818–19), Thomas Davison's *Medusa* (1819) and the ultra-radical *Cap of Liberty* (1819). Legally, these papers could only provide a commentary on the news, not news itself, but the dividing line was a thin one. Cobbett had initiated a Golden Age of the radical press to meet the needs of the political situation. As E. P. Thompson notes, 'popular Radicalism took its style from the handpress and the weekly periodical', and Kevin Gilmartin emphasizes the fact that 'every radical weekly was to some extent involved in practical organization' and fostering a 'plebeian political culture'. In Gramscian terms, these weeklies were the voice of radicalism's 'organic' intellectuals. The government also had to face a thriving culture of demotic, scurrilous Regency satire. In an attempt to crack down on this 'radical counterpublic sphere', as Gilmartin calls it, the blasphemy, libel and sedition laws were invoked to prosecute radical publishers.[12] The year 1817 saw high-profile trials of Wooler and the caricaturist and publisher William Hone. But despite government pressure, juries acquitted both Wooler and Hone. The government's exasperation at this outcome led to more draconian legislation in 1819 and a more vigorous pursuit of its radical enemies. Richard Carlile was jailed for six years in 1819 for reprinting Paine's *Age of Reason*, though he continued to edit the *Republican* from inside prison.

In Cobbett's absence Thomas James Wooler's *Black Dwarf* became the leading radical weekly with a national circulation at its height of over 12,000.[13] Wooler (?1785/6–1853), a Yorkshire-born printer, was a close associate of Cartwright and in general supported the constitutionalist approach to reform. But Wooler's editorial style was far from high-toned or sombre. The popular appeal of the paper stemmed from its blending of satirical and melodramatic effects with serious political journalism. The paper's motto was taken from one of Pope's satires, and Wooler's cast of imaginary personae is reminiscent of the playful irony of the *Spectator*. The weekly letter from the Black Dwarf to the 'Yellow Bonze' (a Japanese priest) constituted a playfully posed editorial. Wooler's liberal use of Shakespearean quotations (a reflection of his training as a drama critic) assumes that a 'plebeian' readership would respond to the appropriation of high culture for radical ends. This theatrical tone gave the paper the imprint of Wooler's individual style, just as Cobbett's vituperative harangues and didactic flourishes stamped his identity on the *Political Register*. But the paper also had a democratic, 'practical' and educative function as a nexus for radical enlightenment and organization. Readers were invited to contribute items and to set up reading groups.[14] As John Wade enthused when launching the *Gorgon*, 'What a glare of light has been cast into every cottage and workshop of the kingdom!'[15] Readers could also see their own actions recycled in accounts of meetings and rallies. Radical weeklies were not simply platforms for print oratory; they were vital channels of communication for the radical movement.

Wooler in fact helped to create Peterloo, both as a journalist and an activist. In the columns of *Black Dwarf* he put forward the bold idea that radicals should elect their own MPs (or 'legislatorial attornies'), on the basis that the people were not constitutionally bound to recognize an unrepresentative parliament.[16] The government regarded any move towards a 'people's parliament' as dangerously Jacobin in tone and strictly illegal. In July 1819 Wooler was one of the organizers of the election of Sir Charles Wolseley (who stood bail for those arrested at Peterloo) as 'legislatorial attorney' for Birmingham, an act that earned Wooler fifteen months in prison in 1820. Peterloo was originally meant to elect an 'attorney' for Manchester, but the local magistrates declared the meeting, planned for 9 August, to be illegal. Rather than defy the law, the organizers postponed the meeting for a week and changed its function to the more traditional course of petitioning parliament. But as **extract 2** shows, Wooler believed it was the authorities, not the radicals, who were acting unconstitutionally. He throws the accusation of violent intent back at the government, which cannot accept the fact that mass radicalism is a peaceful and orderly process. This iconoclastic reversal of the constitutional roles of government and people was a hallmark of radical discourse in these years.[17] The radical emphasis on order, legality and patriotism ('Rule Britannia' was sung at Peterloo) was meant to show that what Burke called the 'swinish multitude' were rational citizens, while the ruling class were violent, irrational and paranoid. The semiotic power of 'open constitutionalism' was its emblematizing of democracy. The highly-disciplined monster meeting was a spectacle of the people's political agency, a Utopian image of the reformed body politic.[18] The policy of a consumer boycott of taxed commodities such as alcohol and tobacco also put power in the hands of the people.

There is a sense in which the Peterloo massacre was written into radical history before it happened. Wooler portrayed the state as ready to pounce at the slightest provocation, and it is clear from **extract 3** that he regarded the events of 16 August as inevitable. The bare details of the massacre are as follows: Henry Hunt had only just begun to speak when the magistrates ordered his arrest. This job was given to the inebriated Manchester and Salford cavalry, whose incompetent horsemanship in the confined space of a massed crowd caused a panic on both sides. Within ten minutes, ten protestors and one special constable lay dead. The extent to which the government colluded in the actions of the Manchester magistrates has been disputed by historians, but for Wooler and the radicals the true character of the unreformed state had finally been revealed, and the mask of power had fallen.[19] While the Regent praised the authorities for their 'prompt, decisive and efficient measures for the preservation of the public tranquillity',[20] radicals likened the intervention to that of an unruly mob or a foreign despotism. In his editorial 'letter' Wooler unleashes the full force of Gothic demonization against the bloodthirsty government, which he likens to a vampire. The Peterloo massacre became an instantly mythical slaughter of the innocents, as shown in the poem which closed this issue of *Black Dwarf* (and which bears some resemblance to Shelley's more famous poem, though the call for 'vengeance' is more extreme than either the 'The Mask of Anarchy' or Wooler).[21] The opportunity to single out women and children in the litany of casualties was rarely missed. The language of melodramatic excess and incredulity runs through Burdett's Address, Wooler's editorial and the report of the metropolitan delegate meeting at which Wooler is a speaker. At times the rhetoric veers towards open defiance, but the central appeal of the radical message remains constitutional, as typified by the Crown and Anchor meeting's 'general hiss' of condemnation at any suggestion of retaliatory violence, and the various resolutions passed. Wooler's personal outrage at the massacre is not the dominant text. The leading item is an Address from an elected MP, and the longest item is the report of the London meeting. The pyrotechnics of indignation are contrasted by Hunt's coolly sardonic prison letter, or restrained by the formal conventions of the political meeting. The immediate launch of a relief fund for the victims shows the important role of the radical press in publicizing such campaigns. Note also the inclusion of a reader's selection of learned authorities on the evils of drink, which was meant to support the recommended consumer boycott on taxable goods. Even in the midst of 'alarm', the educative purpose of the radical press continued. On the other hand, the carnivalesque pleasure of political satire is represented by a scene from a mock-dramatic sketch of the Manchester magistrates which appeared in the 8 September issue (**extract 4**).

In moral terms Peterloo was a victory for radicalism. Wooler saw the triumphal entry of Henry Hunt into London on 13 September 1819 as a regenerative counter-spectacle to the violation of Peterloo (**extract 5**).[22] At the end of the account of the procession and the subsequent meeting, Wooler pronounced 'So ends the *second act* of the grand, but *sanguinary* melodrama of the Manchester Massacre … the third act will close with due poetical justice being executed upon the offending parties'.[23] Unfortunately, the 'third act' was even more apocalyptic than Wooler imagined. The closure of the Peterloo narrative was the Six Acts of December 1819.[24] Once again 'seditious' meetings were banned, but there were also harsh new measures against the cheap radical press, including the closing of the stamp-duty loophole.[25] Almost overnight the price of most weekly radical papers went up to 6d, which made them too expensive for many working-class readers. It was not until the next decade that a new generation of radical publishers like James Watson and Henry Hetherington defied the law and revived the 'war of the unstamped'.[26] The Six Acts severed the organic link between mass radical activity and radical journalism. The popular radical support for the cause of Queen Caroline in 1820 was shortlived, and is most memorable for Hone and Cruikshank's satirical prints.[27] Insurrection and violent 'disturbances' resumed in the Cato Street conspiracy of 1820 (whose leaders claimed they were exacting revenge for Peterloo) and the Swing riots of 1830.[28] Even though in the 1820s 'reforming opinion in general was quietly seething',[29] the reform movement only partially regained its mass character in the Reform crisis of 1830. When the resurgent Whigs excluded the working class from the new franchise in 1832, both radicalism and radical journalism entered a new phase, though it was one deeply indebted to the 'heroic' post-war years.

Extract 1: from William Cobbett, *Cobbett's Weekly Political Register* 31 (18) (2 November 1816): 545–76

'To the JOURNEYMEN AND LABOURERS of England, Wales, Scotland and Ireland'

FRIENDS AND FELLOW COUNTRYMEN,

Whatever the pride of rank, of riches or of scholarship may have induced some men to believe, or to affect to believe, the real strength and all the resources of a country, ever have sprung and ever must spring, from the *labour* of its people; and hence it is, that this nation, which is so small in numbers and so poor in climate and soil compared with many others, has, for many ages, been the most powerful nation in the world: it is the most industrious, the most laborious, and therefore, the most powerful. Elegant dresses, superb furniture, stately buildings, fine roads and canals, fleet horses and carriages, numerous and stout ships, warehouses teeming with goods; all these, and many other objects that fall under our view, are so many marks of national wealth and resources. But all these spring from *labour*. Without the journeyman and the labourer none of them could exist; without the assistance of their hands, the country would be a wilderness, hardly worth the notice of an invader.

As it is the labour of those who toil which makes a country abound in resources, so it is the same class of men, who must, by their arms, secure its safety and uphold its fame. . . .

With this correct idea of your own worth in your minds, with what indignation must you hear yourselves called the Populace, the Rabble, the Mob, the Swinish Multitude; and, with what greater indignation, if possible, must you hear the projects of those cool and cruel and insolent men, who, now that you have been, without any fault of your own, brought into a state of misery, propose to narrow the limits of parish relief, prevent you from marrying in the days of your youth, or to thrust you out to seek your bread in foreign lands, never more to behold your parents or friends? But suppress your indignation until we return to this topic, after we have considered the *cause* of your present misery and the *measures* which have produced that cause.

The times in which we live are full of peril. The nation, as described by the very creatures of the government, is fast advancing to that period when an important change must take place. It is the lot of mankind, that some shall labour with their hands and others with their minds; and, on all occasions, more especially on an occasion like the present, it is the duty of the latter to come to the assistance of the former. We are all equally interested in the peace and happiness of our common country. It is of utmost importance, that in the seeking to obtain those objects, our endeavours should be uniform, and tend all to the same point. Such an uniformity cannot exist without an uniformity of sentiment as to public matters, and, to produce this latter uniformity amongst you is the object of this address.

As to the *cause* of our present miseries, it is the *enormous amount of taxes*, which the government compels us to pay for the support of its army, its placemen, its pensioners, &c. and for the payment of the interest of its debt. That this is the cause has been a thousand times proved; and, it is now so acknowledged by the creatures of the government themselves.... Indeed, when we compare our present state to the state of the country previous to the wars against France, we must see that our present misery is owing to no other cause. The taxes then annually raised amounted to about 15 millions: they amounted last year to 70 millions. The nation was then happy: it is now miserable ... there are few articles which you use, in the purchase of which you do not pay *a tax*.

On your shoes,
Salt,
Beer,
Malt,
Hops,
Tea,
Sugar,
Candles,
Soap,
Paper,
Coffee,
Spirits,
Glass of your windows,
Bricks and tiles,
Tobacco.

On all these, and many other articles, you pay *a tax*, and even on your *loaf* you pay a tax, because everything is taxed from which the loaf proceeds....

The *remedy* is what we have now to look to, and that remedy consists wholly and solely of such a reform in the Commons', or People's, House of Parliament, as shall give to every payer of *direct taxes* a vote at elections, and as shall cause the Members to be *elected annually*....

I have laid before you, with all the clearness I am master of, the causes of our misery, the measures which have led to those causes, and I have pointed what seems to me to be the only remedy – namely, a reform of the Commons', or People's, House of Parliament. I exhort you to proceed in a peaceable and lawful manner, but, at the same time, to proceed with zeal and resolution.... Any man can draw up a petition, and any man can *carry* it up to London.

Extract 2: from T. J. Wooler, *The Black Dwarf* 3 (32) (11 August 1819): 519–20[30]

Satire's my weapon; but I'm too discreet,
To run a-muck and tilt at all I meet:
I only wear it in a land of Hectors,
Thieves, supercargoes, sharpers, and directors. – Pope[31]

DEFENCE OF THE MANCHESTER MEETING ADVERTISED FOR THE 9TH INSTANT, AGAINST THE FOOLISH AND ILLEGAL CONDUCT OF THE MANCHESTER MAGISTRATES

The preparations for, and against the Public Meeting advertised to be held at Manchester on Monday, have created a degree of anxiety throughout the kingdom. The boroughmongers, having overcome their fears, seemed determined to begin the trial of *physical force*, having in vain hoped for the signal from the despair of the reformers. Their bayonets and cannon were ready; their cat's paw in the magistracy were willing to thrust their fingers into the fire, to rescue the chestnuts for their masters; and they believed the soldiers would lend a helping hand to set Manchester in flames, and consume all the reformers, in the conflagration. Every demoniac agent of the system seemed as eager as a vulture in quest of the blood which he hoped would flow; and the plunder that would ensue. The lines were closed around them; and it was doubtless hoped that not a reformer would live to detail the narrative of the murder of his fellow-citizen. What a day of rejoicing did the harpies anticipate for the ensuing day. The tenth of August would have been a perpetual jubilee, to celebrate the massacre at St. Peter's Church! But the *calm reason* of the *violent radical* reformers has again disappointed them. The troops may march quietly back to their respective barracks – the reformers are not *quite ready* to be cut to pieces. Sir John Byng may retire to York, to inspect, with the whiskered Lord Grantham, the growth of the hussar-mustachios[32] – and the Manchester magistrates go home, and write non-sensical orders for people to attend meetings, when they are wished to go away. The whole corps of blockheads may disperse to the tune of rogues march – the reformers are not in need of them, at present – when they are wanted, *they shall be sent for.*

The good sense of the immense bodies of people who assemble in the cause of reform absolutely maddens their enemies into the grossest folly. They cannot conceive how tens of thousands of the lower orders can meet together, deliberate dispassionately on the most important subjects, and quietly disperse without breaking their own heads, or their neighbours houses. There were no such quiet doings when these magistrates were young. Most of them were probably members of the *church and king mobs*, at the commencement of the French revolution;[33] and they sigh again

15

for the good times, when half a score of scoundrels, could, under the sanction of the magistracy, duck and pelt jacobins with impunity. A public meeting in favour of church and king, meant a glorious declaration of war against all the rational part of the community; and these magistrates are quite enraged that the *ignorant, impatient* multitude of *lower orders*, should behave so much better than the partizans of Mother Church and the boroughmongers.

As the battle between the legitimate plunderers and the people depends solely on the *discretion* of the latter, we highly approve of the postponement of the intended meeting.... Not that we are about to confess that it was *illegal*. On the contrary, we should have no hesitation to contend for its legality before any tribunal. But the *right*, and the policy of exercising the right, are separate things. The magistrates had declared the meeting illegal – the Regent had been taught to call the proceedings at Birmingham, 'a gross violation of the law!'[34] – the soldiers were said to be ready to cut to pieces all who should resist these declarations; and the people were invited to be slaughtered, by a peremptory mandate of nine magistrates, who were probably destined to be inspectors of butchery, and who warned all people, at their peril, to attend the meeting.[35] It is never policy to follow the suit of an adversary; and when the magistrates wanted the meeting, it was the business of the reformers to postpone it.

The meeting as originally proposed, notwithstanding the Regent and his proclamation,[36] and the magistrates and their ignorant handbill, was STRICTLY LEGAL – as legal as any meeting of the magistrates – as legal as any meeting of the cabinet – and infinitely more legal than any assembling of the House of Commons, since the enactment of the septennial bill.[37] We hesitate not to declare, in the face of the Regent, and his advisers, whether in Manchester or London, that the PEOPLE OF THIS COUNTRY HAVE A RIGHT TO MEET FOR ANY PURPOSE WHICH THEY PLEASE. There is no limit to their right of meeting, as to the subject of their deliberations. All power is theirs, or derived from them; and the right of assembling to express their opinions, cannot be taken from them until they are *formally* reduced to the condition of *abject slaves*. All that the law can do, is to *regulate* the meetings of the people. To prohibit them is beyond the power of the law; for the sovereignty of the people consists only of the assemblies of the people. Very far indeed below the RIGHTS OF THE PEOPLE, was the purport of the intended meeting at Manchester. The only part of the requisition objected to, was the clause which convened the meeting to 'consider the propriety of the unrepresented inhabitants of Manchester, electing a person to represent them.' It does not follow that the meeting should have determined to elect a representative; and until that were done, there could not be any shadow of illegality attached to the meeting.

The proposal might have been rejected. The meeting was convened to *consider* the subject; and are the people of England to be told they have NO RIGHT to take a subject into their consideration? Truly, gentlemen boroughmongers, you are growing very impudent in your behaviour. Charles James Fox[38] once declared the people had a right, if they thought proper, without assigning any reason, to say to a king, '*Go, we have no further use for you!*' And the boroughmongers of the present day, tell the *same people*, they must not meet even to consider what they shall do! The sovereignty of the people is reduced to a name, by the sovereignty of the boroughmongers, and the freeborn inhabitants of this realm are gravely told they have no right to consider; as a military officer would tell his soldiers they have no right to think! ...

Petitions have been disregarded, because unanswerable; and it becomes necessary to try some other experiment upon the metal of the seat-sellers. If the people are not to be represented, the reformers will do well to follow the example of the Quakers, as far as the payment of taxes is concerned; and to abstain in a body from the use of all articles subject to direct taxation, which can be dispensed with. We must stop the supplies, if we are not permitted to look after the disposal of them. There are five millions of reformers in the United Kingdom, who could depress the revenue ten millions by a little wholesome self-denial; and this may follow the refusal of the boroughmongers to admit the representatives of the people, into what should be the assembly of the people. And as we are fast adding to the numbers of reform, it is possible that nearly half of the revenue might be withdrawn from the grasp of the boroughmongers. . . . All is built upon the payment of the taxes, and the use and consumption of excisable articles. Lord Cochrane,[39] some time since, recommended the reformers to adopt this mode; but the numbers then enlisted in the cause bore no comparison to the overwhelming army that is now placed against the boroughmongers. The gathering snow-ball has become a mighty mountain; and still rolls, gathering to its already enormous bulk with too much velocity to be checked, and too much magnitude to be resisted.

THE BLACK DWARF.

A London Weekly Publication,

EDITED, PRINTED, AND PUBLISHED BY T. J. WOOLER, 5e, SUN STREET, BISHOPSGATE.

Communications (post paid) to No. 4, Catherine-street, Strand.

| No. 34, Vol. III.] | WEDNESDAY, AUGUST 25, 1819. | [PRICE 4d. |

Satire's my weapon; but I'm too discreet,
To run a-muck and tilt at all I meet:
I only wear it in a land of Hectors,
Thieves, supercargoes, sharpers, and directors.—POPE.

SIR FRANCIS BURDETT'S ADDRESS TO THE ELECTORS OF WESTMINSTER.

GENTLEMEN,

On reading the newspapers this morning, having arrived late yesterday evening, I was filled with shame, grief, and indignation, at the account of the blood spilt at Manchester. THIS, then, is the *answer* of the boroughmongers, to the *petitioning people?*—THIS is the *practical proof* of our standing in *no need of reform?*—these, the *practical blessings* of our glorious *boroughmonger domination?*—*this,* the *use* of a *standing army* in time of *peace?*—It seems our fathers were not such fools as some would make us believe, in opposing the establishment of a standing army, and sending King Williams's Dutch Guards out of the country. Yet, would to Heaven, they had been Dutchmen, or Switzers, or Hessians, or Hanoverians, or ANY THING RATHER THAN ENGLISHMEN, who have done SUCH deeds! What! kill men *unarmed! unresisting!* and, Gracious God! WOMEN too, *disfigured, maimed, cut down,* and *trampled upon* by DRAGOONS. Is this ENGLAND? This a CHRISTIAN LAND! A LAND OF FREEDOM! Can such things be? and pass by us, like a summer cloud, unheeded? Forbid it every drop of English blood, in every vein! that does not proclaim its owner bastard. Will the GENTLEMEN of ENGLAND support, or wink at such proceedings? they have a great stake in their country. They hold great estates, and they are bound in duty, and in honour to consider them as retaining fees on the part of their country for upholding its rights and liberties. Surely, they will at length awake! and find they have duties to perform! they never can stand tamely by, as lookers on, while bloody Neroes rip open their mother's womb! They must JOIN THE GENERAL VOICE, loudly demanding justice and redress; and HEAD PUBLIC MEETINGS throughout the United Kingdom, to put a stop in its commencement, to a REIGN OF TERROR AND OF BLOOD. To afford consolation, as far as it can be afforded, and *legal redress* to the *widows* and *orphans* and *mutilated victims* of this unparalleled and barbarous outrage. For this purpose, I propose that A MEETING should be called in WESTMINSTER, which the gentlemen of the Committee will arrange, and whose summons I will hold myself in readiness to attend. Whether the penalty of our meeting will be *death,* by military execution, I know not; but this I know, A MAN CAN DIE BUT ONCE; and NEVER BETTER, than in VINDICATING the LAWS and LIBERTIES of his COUNTRY.

Excuse this hasty address. I can scarcely tell what I have written. It may be a libel; or the Attorney-General may call it so—just as he pleases. When the seven bishops were tried for a libel, the army of James the Second, then encamped on Hounslow Heath, for supporting arbitrary power, gave three cheers on hearing of their acquittal; the king, startled at the noise, asked " what's that?" " Nothing, Sir!" was the answer, " but the soldiers shouting at the acquittal of the seven bishops." " Do ye call that nothing?" replied the misgiving tyrant; and shortly after abdicated the government. 'Tis true, James could not inflict the torture on his soldiers!—could not tear the living flesh from their bones with a cat of nine tails!—could not flay them alive!—Be this as it may, OUR DUTY IS to MEET! and " *England expects every man to do his duty!*"

I remain, Gentlemen,

Most truly and faithfully,

Your most obedient Servant,

Kirby Park, Aug. 22, 1819.   F. BURDETT.

LETTERS OF THE BLACK DWARF.

From the Black Dwarf in London, to the Yellow Bonze at Japan.

Murder most foul, as at the best it is!
But this most foul, dark, and unnatural!

I am, my friend, petrified with horror and disgust. I am awaked, as from a frightful dream, and I find myself surrounded with a sea of blood, in which are floating mangled carcases, and mutilated limbs. Did not indignation overpower horror, my blood would freeze at the carnage as my eyes drank in the horrible detail. Blood, innocent blood has been wantonly shed. The drought of the season has been allayed at Manchester by a shower of gore. The dogs have been fed with human blood; and the desolation of war has been exhibited in what was called a period of peace. Talk

Plate 1

Extract 3: from T. J. Wooler, *The Black Dwarf* 3 (34) (25 August 1819): 549–64

SIR FRANCIS BURDETT'S ADDRESS TO THE ELECTORS OF WESTMINSTER[40]

GENTLEMEN,

On reading the newspapers this morning, having arrived late yesterday evening, I was filled with shame, grief, and indignation, at the account of the blood spilt at Manchester. THIS, then, is the *answer* of the boroughmongers, to the *petitioning people*? – THIS is the *practical proof* of our standing in *no need of reform*? – these, the *practical blessings* of our glorious *borough-monger domination*? – this, the *use* of a *standing army* in time of *peace*? – It seems our fathers were not such fools as some would make us believe, in opposing the establishment of a standing army, and sending King William's Dutch Guards out of the country.[41] Yet, would to Heaven, they had been Dutchmen, or Switzers, or Hessians, or Hanoverians,[42] or ANY THING RATHER THAN ENGLISHMEN, who have done SUCH deeds! What! kill men *unarmed*! *unresisting*! and, Gracious God! WOMEN too, *disfigured*, *maimed*, *cut down*, and *trampled upon* by DRAGOONS. Is this ENGLAND? This a CHRISTIAN LAND! A LAND OF FREEDOM! Can such things be? and pass by us, like a summer cloud, unheeded? Forbid it every drop of English blood, in every vein! that does not proclaim its owner bastard. Will the GENTLEMEN of ENGLAND support, or wink at such proceedings? they have a great stake in their country. They hold great estates, and they are bound in duty, and in honour to consider them as retaining fees on the part of their country for upholding its rights and liberties. Surely, they will at length awake! and find they have duties to perform! they never can stand tamely by, as lookers on, while bloody Neroes rip open their mother's womb![43] They must JOIN THE GENERAL VOICE, loudly demanding justice and redress; and HEAD PUBLIC MEETINGS throughout the United Kingdom, to put a stop in its commencement, to a REIGN OF TERROR AND OF BLOOD. To afford consolation, as far as it can be afforded, and *legal redress* to the *widows* and *orphans* and *mutilated victims* of this unparalleled and barbarous outrage. For this purpose, I propose that A MEETING should be called in WESTMINSTER, which the gentlemen of the Committee will arrange, and whose summons I will hold myself in readiness to attend. Whether the penalty of our meeting will be *death*, by military execution, I know not; but this I know, A MAN CAN DIE BUT ONCE; and NEVER BETTER, than in VINDICATING the LAWS and LIBERTIES of his COUNTRY.

Excuse this hasty address. I can scarcely tell what I have written. It may be a libel; or the Attorney-General may call it so – just as he pleases. When the seven bishops were tried for a libel, the army of James the Second, then encamped on Hounslow Heath, for supporting arbitrary power, gave three cheers on hearing of their acquittal; the king, startled at the noise, asked, 'what's that?' 'Nothing, Sir!' was the answer, 'but the soldiers shouting at the acquittal of the seven bishops.' 'Do ye call that nothing?' replied the misgiving tyrant; and shortly after abdicated the government.[44] 'Tis true, James could not inflict the torture on his soldiers! – could not tear the living flesh from their bones with a cat of nine tails! – could not flay them alive! – Be this as it may, OUR DUTY IS to MEET! and *England expects every man to do his duty!*[45]

I remain, Gentlemen,

Most truly and faithfully,

Your most obedient Servant,

F. BURDETT.

LETTERS OF THE BLACK DWARF

From the Black Dwarf in London, to the Yellow Bonze at Japan

Murder most foul, as at the best it is!
But this most foul, dark, and unnatural![46]

I am, my friend, petrified with horror and disgust. I am awaked, as from a frightful dream, and I find myself surrounded with a sea of blood, in which are floating mangled carcases, and mutilated limbs. Did not indignation overpower horror, my blood would freeze at the carnage as my eyes drank in the horrible detail. Blood, innocent blood has been wantonly shed. The drought of the season has been allayed at Manchester by a shower of gore. The dogs have been fed with human blood; and the desolation of war has been exhibited in what was called a period of peace. Talk not to me of the horrors of Japan, or Morocco, or Algiers! What is it to me, whether the human victim be sacrificed to the great idol, Juggernaut,[47] or to the cruelty of an eastern despot, or even an English boroughmonger? I see the blood flowing down the streets, and I detest the abominable agent who has poured it living from the veins.

An immense assembly of men, women and children were congregated together, on the subject of their sufferings, and their wrongs. Shall I be believed, when I tell thee, that a ferocious company of armed men, rushed with sabres upon this assembly, and commenced the work of indiscriminate slaughter! Yet this is recorded in the annals of this country in letters of blood, which will never be erased from the page of its history. Ah, my friend, civilization is worse than barbarity: for it deceives our hopes, and blasts the expectations it has raised. Thou hast seen a British sailor, and admired the generous ardour of his soul. Thou hast seen a British soldier, and hung with rapture over the details of his heroism and his devotion. Let not thy respect for these characters be at all impeached, by what I now tell thee. It is not the soldier, nor the sailor that have been employed in the work of slaughter. Fiends have been dressed in the uniform of soldiers, to do what devils would have scorned to do. They *have trampled* on and SABRED WOMEN – Children have been bathed in their mother's blood – and the peaceable citizen has been butchered at noon day, when he deemed himself walking under the protection of the day, as in the beams of the smiling sun. But what is law, when power would trample it under foot? What is justice, when a boroughmonger can kill it with his frowns? I will some day particularize to thee, this monster, called here a boroughmonger. It far surpasses in voracity and rapacious guilt, anything thou hast heard, or read of, in ancient and modern history. But the thing has hitherto been deemed a coward. It has often drank blood in *secret*, and fed upon the *tears* and *sighs* of its victims, when it could only incarcerate them in its horrible dens. But the thing has become braver. It has been driven to the courage of despair; and being on the eve of capture, trial, and conviction it has rushed out of its cell at noon-day, and torn to pieces all that came within its grasp! It threatened extermination to all its enemies: but it has exhausted itself.... An eye-witness, after describing the peace and order of the meeting, adds – 'The Yeomanry cavalry made their charge with the most infuriate frenzy; – they cut down men, women, and children, indiscriminately, and appeared to have commenced a premeditated attack with the most insatiable thirst for blood and destruction. They merit a medallion on one side of which should be inscribed THE SLAUGHTERMEN OF MANCHESTER, and a reverse, bearing a description of their slaughter of defenceless men, women, and children, unprovoked and unnecessary.'

These '*Yeomanry Cavalry,*' are probably strangers to thee. But thou mayest remember my old friends, the *York Hussars*, well. The York Hussars were Yeomanry Cavalry, but they did not like the name. Perhaps they were endowed with a prophetic spirit, and anticipated how deeply it would be disgraced. They therefore changed the name; and though their commander, the great Lord Grantham, who attacked thy little friend, said they were embodied to *cut down reform*, I do not believe my Yorkshire friends, the Hussars, whether *shaved*, or *unshaved*, would have *sabred women* and *children*. I will give even Lord Grantham sufficient credit for humanity, to believe that he would not, when he saw an infant swaddled in its mother's arms, have ordered any of his troop to have lanced the bosom on which it reposed, and for the aliment of nature, have suffocated it with the stream of its parent's life. No, my friend, the Yorkshire Hussars are *men*, and I feel confident that they would not *sabre women*! The Manchester Yeomanry are another sort. I will tell thee what they have done; in the language of one who corresponds with the learned editor of the old Times, whom some men call *Joseph Surface*.[48] 'It is allowed by every one here, that much *unnecessary cruelty* was inflicted; and it is even affirmed that intoxication only could explain the wanton violence they committed. They *cut down* and *trampled under* their *horses hoofs*, the poor deluded creatures who had assembled without provocation, and without mercy. I *could* send you the *depositions* of *hundreds*, if it were *necessary*, that *not a stone was thrown*, not a stick was raised, and not an insult offered to the military before they commenced *their furious career* – that they trampled on those whom they could not disperse – that they *hunted them down like wild beasts*; and *cut at the living heaps* that were piled on each other, in running from their violence. The party of *Cavalry* that charged first was the *Manchester* and *Salford*, about 120 strong; the next was the *Cheshire Yeomanry Cavalry*, about 500 strong; and the last the fifteenth hussars.' These *heroes* must be remembered. It is the duty of the historian to be particular in such instances. I hope to send thee, if anybody will furnish me with it, a *list of all the Yeomanry Cavalry*, the *magistrates*, and *special constables*, who were conspicuous on that day. All the cases of suffering, the names of the individuals attacked and maimed, should be collected, and a pretty little book compiled, to keep in memory for ever the bloody transactions of the day. The *Yeomanry* were so furious for blood, that it is recorded of the *Cheshire Regiment*, that it 'broke through the line of constables, and *killed one of them*, the landlord of the Bull's Head'. His successor ought to alter the sign to that of the *asses head*; he need not seek far for an accurate portrait. That he is dead; and as he was killed by his associates in the *preservation* of order, there needs little to be said upon his fate.

It must be added, that the whole country is indignant at these measures, except the parties who figured as the actors in this tragedy. They, finding the whole nation arrayed against them, and that nobody is disposed to thank them for the torrent of blood that has been shed, have thanked *themselves*, at a meeting, where they turned everyone out who was disposed to think they ought to be thanked. This is a very good mode of ensuring *unanimity*! But there is something else to be done – they must be *punished*, as well as *thanked*; and they may as well *punish themselves*, to save others the trouble which they are very willing to take; as *thank themselves*, which is a trouble nobody else would take. The ministers seem quite at a stand upon the business. They are aware the Manchester Yeomanry, Constables, and Magistrates, intended to do the work of the boroughmongers, though they have done *more* than the boroughmongers wished them to do *at once*. They have slipped the bloodhounds too soon, and the bloodhounds were too *ferocious* than *wise*. The reformers were wanted to riot, or to be made to riot; but failing in their attempt, the blockheads employed to create riot, have themselves run riot in their rage. Any relation of the sufferers may prefer an indictment against any brave Yeomanry man who may be proved to have struck the blow; and put in the names of all the regiment as aiding and abetting the unlawful cutting and maiming, under an act first introduced by my departed friend, Lord Ellenborough, one of the most profound luminaries of the law.[49]

LETTER FROM MR. HUNT

New Bailey Prison, Manchester, Saturday, Aug. 21, 1819

DEAR SIR,

I do not know that I can send you any news, because, I suppose, you know, or at least hear more than I do; but as I know that you and all my friends in London will be happy to hear that I am well; pray inform them from me, that I never enjoyed better health in my life, and that I am in *tip top* spirits. What should make me otherwise? I sleep as sound as a bell, and I feel more pleasure in five minutes reflection, than the Bench of Lancashire Magistrates will obtain of consolation during the remainder of their lives. The blood of the poor murdered people sits heavy on their heads, and will haunt their guilty souls as long as they live. 'Let the gall'd jade wince, my withers are unwrung.'[50] I fear that it will never be forgiven, and that there will be but too strong a disposition to demand 'blood for blood.' Our enemies will not now, I hope, say any thing about assassination; they have taught the people how to assassinate by wholesale.

They have struck the first blow, and have taken the advantage of attacking a peaceable multitude, who studiously came to the meeting unarmed, by a large military force, the regulars keeping guard, while the Yeomanry Cavalry, butchered all that they could get at, and in their disorder, murdered alike friends and foes; I believe their friends suffered most; I have not heard of one Reformer suffering yet whom I know, or ever heard of. I never before saw such a multitude; I think there were three times as many as at Smithfield, and I never saw the people more disposed to be perfectly peaceable and good humoured. It seems there were various parties or Unions, each attended by flags, with mottos, something like those at Smithfield,[51] and each a band of music. As soon as they assembled they all struck up the national air of 'God save the King' and after that 'Rule Britannia.' But even these symptoms of loyalty, it seems, were not to be respected on this occasion. I was as much taken by surprise as any part of the people could have been, for I was particularly guarded and cautious to give the Magistrates no pretence for interrupting the Meeting. I arrived at Mr. Johnson's[52] on Monday, and I was never two miles from it but once during the whole week; although I had repeated and kind invitations, not only in Manchester but the neighbour-hood, and that was on Saturday previous to this bloody business. It was reported that the Magistrates had issued a warrant against me, for some supposed or real offence, in order to put it in execution by apprehending me at the Meeting on Monday – now mark this – That they should not have any pretence for interrupting the proceedings, I drove into Manchester, and waited upon the Magistrates who were sitting at the New Bailey; I informed them that as I had heard there was a warrant issued by them against me, I thought it was my duty at once to wait upon them to say, that I was, and should be, at all times ready to meet any charge they may have against me without giving them the least trouble. They politely answered 'they knew of no such thing, or any such intention.' Therefore I retired perfectly satisfied in my own mind that it was only an idle report. This fact cannot be too generally known, and as I have not seen it in any of the Newspapers, perhaps you will send the whole of this to the STATESMAN.[53]

Recollect that I received this answer *from two of the very Magistrates (one of them a Clergyman) who signed the warrant against me on Monday.* Be assured my good fellows, that they have not the shadow of a shade of pretence for charging me with *High Treason.* But they are in a dreadful scrape, and they will flounder further into the mire every struggle that they make.   I am, dear Sir,   H. HUNT.

TO CORRESPONDENTS

Subscription to obtain legal redress for the persons arrested and injured at Manchester. – It is with pleasure we remark that Major Cartwright[54] has been named the treasurer of a subscription for this purpose. Mr. Hobhouse[55] has sent him a subscription of one hundred pounds; and regrets that he was prevented from attending the meeting. Subscriptions are received at the offices of the BLACK DWARF, and WOOLER'S BRITISH GAZETTE;[56] at the Statesman's office; by Mr. Dolby, Wardour Street, Soho; and Mr. Carlile, 55, Fleet Street.

To the Editor of the Black Dwarf

Craven Street. Aug. 23. 1819

DEAR SIR,

Perceiving through the medium of your *Dwarf* that a number of reformists, have come to the resolution not to use exciseable articles, but viewing this determination to be adopted upon political grounds only, and probably by many with apparent great sacrifices from long confirmed habits, therefore if it can be pointed out to them how physically and morally destructive and pernicious the use of most of these articles are, they will be discarded cheerfully and promptly. I will therefore do myself the pleasure of giving you a few extracts from works written by one of our most able physicians, and who is out of the reach of all suspicion of being influenced by any motive, but that of the purest philanthropy,

I am, Dear Sir,

Your obedient servant,

R. W.

'Tobacco is a narcotic in common use. Persons in the habit of chewing, snuffing or smoking this Indian leaf, are not aware that a few grains of it taken into the stomach cause sudden death; nay, the smoke of it injected into the rectum, has frequently proved fatal; it acts powerfully on the nervous system, destroys the sensibility of the stomach, and it is observed that those who devour it in great quantity die of apoplexy, palsy, and dropsy.' *Vide, Trotter on the Nervous Temperament, page,* 148.[57]

'Every inordinate cup is unblessed, and the ingredient is a devil!'

SHAKESPEARE[58]

DRAM DRINKING. – 'The first step to health is to avoid the cause of disease; but there are some physicians who contend that it is hurtful for habitual drunkards to leave off the bottle at once. Were the habit of drinking a solitary practice, there might be some truth in this dictatorial precept, but as ardent spirit is a strong poison to both soul and body, and forms no part of that nourishment which can be converted into animal matter, I have never been able, after the most unwearied application in the exercise of my profession, to find a single fact so destructive of moral, and physical health. Whenever I have known habitual inebriety completely overcome, it has been where all species of licquors were given up in toto from the first.' – *Vide, Trotter, page,* 340.

'Malt licquors, and particularly porter, have their narcotic power much increased by noxious compounds which enter them, and the bitters which are necessary to their preservation by long use, injure the nerves of the stomach and add to the stupefactive quality. Malt licquor drinkers are known to be prone to apoplexy and palsy from this very cause; and purl drinkers in a still greater degree, a mixture peculiar to this country. This poisonous morning beverage was, till lately, confined to the metropolis and its vicinity, but has now like all other luxuries found its way into all provincial towns.' – *Trotter, M.D. on Drunkenness,* p. 50.

25

PUBLIC MEETING TO CONSIDER THE LATE PROCEEDINGS AT MANCHESTER

On Saturday last, a very numerous, and respectable meeting was held at the Crown and Anchor Tavern. The bill having announced that the chair would be taken at twelve precisely, the room was nearly filled before that hour, and long before the business commenced symptoms of impatience were generally manifested. About one o'clock the approach of the principal personages of the meeting was announced by the clapping of hands, and Major Cartwright, Mr. Wooler, Mr. Gale Jones, Mr. Waddington,[59] and several other distinguished reformers, made their appearance at the table. Mr. Wooler said, the importance of the occasion on which they had met was of so very urgent a nature, as to render it impossible to wait any longer for the expression of public opinion on the circumstances which had happened during the week, and which were now fully before the world. Every endeavour had been made to place some gentlemen in the chair, whose rank in society would give additional importance to the resolutions – if they wanted such importance, which they could not, except for the sake of formality. The general friend of his country, Major Cartwright, being incompetent to the laborious situation, from the infirmity of his health, had declined the honour intended him; and, therefore, with the concurrence of the meeting, he would propose that Mr. Waddington do take the chair.

Major CARTWRIGHT seconded the motion, and it was carried by acclamation.

Mr. WADDINGTON rose and said, it required more than common courage to be able to stand before the meeting after the venerable name of Cartwright was associated with the chair. But when the age of that distinguished patriot was recollected – when the important services he had rendered his country for almost half a century were borne in mind, he (Mr. W.) trusted he should not be deemed impertinent and presumptuous if, at this moment, when moments were so precious, he should come forward and accept the distinguished honour conferred upon him. He certainly would take the chair, and he assured the meeting he should govern his conduct by this useful motto, 'audi alteram partem.'[60] No man, or party of men, could have reason to expect that, in the enlightened age in which he lived, when the people, in their most numerous assemblies, conducted themselves with temperate deliberation and sober discussion, when literature was widely extended, and when general knowledge pervaded the great mass of the population of the country, a meeting of this kind should become necessary. Were he to dwell for a moment upon the memorable events at Manchester during the last week, with a view to rouse their feelings, he should only insult their understandings. Scenes such as these never disgraced the most turbulent times of foreign nations. Even in the worst period of the American revolution, at which he was present, he never heard of such outrages; in the history of any country on earth, he never read a page so sanguinary as that upon which they were met to dwell (*loud applauses*). He had seen freemen contending for liberty in other countries: he had seen the revolutions of the Peninsula, of France, and of Belgium,[61] but never until this moment did he hear, that the magistrates of a civilized nation – the conservators of the public peace, had called upon the military of the country to fire upon the unoffending freemen of the land; to destroy its harmless women, and butcher its helpless infants. With these observations, he trusted that he had properly introduced himself to their notice; conscious, however, that there were many gentlemen present of superior understanding, better qualified to fill the situation to which he had been chosen. It was for the inhabitants of Westminster, on this occasion, to do their duty in eloquent and firm language, ever recollecting that they were the sons of Sydney, Hampden, and Russell.[62] (*General applause.*)

Mr. Wooler then came forward to address the meeting.... If the course to be pursued was that of blood, it should be remembered that the enemies of reform were the authors of it. They it was who set the bad example, and men who acted so, were generally in the end the worst off – the persons who suffered most from their own ill example. If the meetings for reform were legal, of which there could be no doubt, they who assembled for such a purpose had a right to be protected by law. If the law had not sufficient force, they must look for protection elsewhere. To travel on the King's high road was a legal object. They whose business called upon them to do so were entitled to the protection of the law; if it was not strong enough to protect them from depredation, they had no recourse but to arm themselves. It was legal to do so. It was a duty thus to supply the defect of law. In the same manner, if persons assembled for legal and constitutional purposes, were not protected by those whose duty it was to prevent a violation of right; if they were to be illegally cut down and butchered, they had no other resource than to go armed to such meetings; they had a right to do so. If an illegal force was to be let loose upon a legal meeting, it was infinitely better to go there armed for the protection of the peace than thus to allow it to be trampled under foot. It was more legal, more honest, more constitutional, better in every point of view, that well-disposed men should go armed for their protection, than that a body such as that at Manchester should be let loose for indiscriminate massacre upon an assembly legally convened. He was not prepared to expect the frightful events that occurred there; but all the circumstances, both previous and subsequent to that tragedy, gave proof of deliberate preparation for bloodshed.... (*A cry from some person in the meeting, 'Blood for blood!'*) This invitation to revenge was met by a general hiss throughout the whole room.

Mr. Wooler proceeded. A voice in the crowd exclaimed 'blood for blood!' For that which was illegally shed at Manchester they desired no blood, no sacrifices but those which the law required, and ought to inflict for such murderous and unprovoked conduct. (*Loud applause.*) ... Nothing could satisfy him (Mr. Wooler) unless a special commission was immediately sent down to Manchester, and the delinquents brought to condign punishment, as was the case in Derby with respect to Brandreth.[63] ... It would be the opinion of the present age, and the theme of the future historian, that none but fiends could have devised, and none but devils executed such a plan (*great applause.*)

Mr. Wooler then proposed the following resolutions: –

It was resolved unanimously,

1. That in the opinion of this assembly the public meeting convened at Manchester, for Monday last, the 16th inst., to consider of the best and most effectual means of obtaining Parliamentary Reform, was perfectly legal, and constitutional.

2. That if the magistrates deemed such a meeting illegal, it was their duty to have demonstrated such illegality, and taken proper precautions against its being held.

3. That to proceed to disperse such a legal assembly by force of arms, can only be considered as a wanton massacre of our inoffending and peaceable countrymen; and that the barbarity with which a ferocious yeomanry executed the rash orders of a vindictive magistracy, sparing neither age nor sex, equals in guilt the blackest atrocities which stain the annals of the French Revolution.

4. That the flagrant conduct of the Magistrates at Manchester, on Monday, the 16th inst., imperiously demands, that, as in London, the right of choosing Sheriffs and Magistrates should be restored to the people as previous to the reign of Edward II.[64]

5. That the jesuistical circular of Lord Sidmouth,[65] so ably exposed by Mr. Jeremy Bentham;[66] the obscure and indefinite proclamation of the Regent; and the recent calumnies upon reform delivered from the sacred seat of justice, may have had a powerful effect in producing this lamentable outrage on the laws; and that it is much to be regretted that high birth and dignified situation should be lent to such an improper excitation of the angry passions of the enemies of reform.

6. That Henry Hunt, Esq. Chairman, Messrs. Johnson, Knight, Saxton,[67] and others arrested on this occasion, appear to have conducted themselves with exemplary and constitutional discretion, and have therefore commanded the respect and protection of every patriot in the United Kingdom.

7. That the exemplary behaviour of the regular troops employed on that occasion, forms a humane contrast to the conduct of the Yeomanry Cavalry,

and may be fairly construed into a pledge that the British regular force will not trample upon the rights, nor destroy the liberties of their fellow subjects.

8. That the electors of Westminster, the Borough of Southwark, the Livery of London, and the inhabitants of the empire at large be invited to meet and express the abhorrence and indignation which must be felt by all at the violation of the law by those especially appointed for its protection; and the wanton barbarity of wretches who have usurped the uniform to disgrace the name of soldiers.

9. That this meeting would have presented a petition to the Regent, praying him to bring the authors of these atrocities to justice; but that the interception of petitions to his Royal Highness by Lord Sidmouth, renders it hopeless to expect that any complaint of the people will reach his ear.

10. That a Committee be appointed to consider of the best and most effectual means of carrying the above Resolutions into effect....

The chairman put the resolution appointing Major Cartwright as treasurer, and observed, that his praises on the gallant veteran's conduct were wholly unnecessary. Every man who knew him loved him; even his very enemies, respected him. Trifling causes produced great changes. Hampden's refusal to pay 2s produced the most important results – the expulsion of the Stuarts and the acts of Habeas Corpus;[68] and he hoped sincerely, the treatment pursued towards Mr. Hunt, would be attended with the most beneficial consequences. Other countries had suffered severely, but no country had suffered more than England, and no people in the world suffered more than Englishmen from a grinding taxation. They should all recollect the old saying, 'Look at home,' when people talk of the prosperity of their condition.... Dr Watson now stepped forward, and announced that Mr. Blandford the Secretary of the Committee of Two Hundred, had just been arrested, for distributing a placard.[69]...

Votes of thanks were proposed to the chairman and Mr. Wooler, who briefly returned thanks; and the meeting broke up about four o'clock.

STANZAS OCCASIONED BY THE MANCHESTER MASSACRE!

Oh, weep not for those who are freed
From bondage so frightful as ours!
Let *tyranny* mourn for the deed,
And howl o'er the prey she devours!

The mask for a century worn,
Has fallen from her visage at last;
Of all its sham attributes shorn,
Her reign of delusion is past.

In native deformity now
Behold her, how shatter'd and weak!
With *murder* impress'd on her brow,
And *cowardice* blanching her cheek.

With guilt's gloomy terrors bow'd down,
She scowls on the smile of the slave!
She shrinks at the patriot's frown;
She *dies* in the grasp of the brave.

Then brief be our wail for the dead,
Whose blood has seal'd tyranny's doom;
And the tears that affliction will shed,
Let vengeance, bright flashes illume.

And shame on the passionless thing
Whose soul can *now* slumber within him!
To slavery let him cling,
For liberty scorns to win him.

Her manlier spirits arouse
At the summons so frightfully given!
And glory exults in their vows,
While virtue records them in Heaven.

**Extract 4: from T. J. Wooler, *The Black Dwarf* 3 (36)
(8 September 1819): 594–6**

A SCENE FROM THE NEW TRAGI-COMEDY ENTITLED THE
'UNDEBAUCHED ROYALISTS,' OR, THE REFORMERS ROUTED

Characters
Magistrates! or, Preservers of the Peace!!

Rev. Dr. Hay-down-derry[70]	Flinty
Rev. Samuel Scapegrace	Gooseacre
Shallowpate	Gobble
Lawless	Killaway
Shallowgall	

Scene. – *A superb apartment*. The whole of the Dramatis Personae are seated at a table, which is covered with a splendid desert and the choicest wines.

T. J. WOOLER

DR. HAY-DOWN-DERRY

A bumper toast! no day-light must I see,
I give you Church and King, with three times three!⁷¹
A glorious cause, assembles us this day,
Which bids us all without reserve, be gay:
The vile reforming people bite the dust,
Subdued by our decrees most wise and just.
What loyal subject can deny our merit,
Decry our zeal, intelligence, and spirit!
'Twas well we met to thank ourselves, 'tis true,
For this, no others would have dared to do.

SCAPEGRACE

Our R—t's gracious thanks are all we need,
To be assured we've done a glorious deed.
Nor let us at the people's satires fret,
Though headed by that libeller, B—rd—t.
Thank heaven, the town is now in perfect quiet;
We need not fear that H—t will breed a riot.
'Tis fit he feel the law's chastising rod,
Who scoffs at powers that are 'ordained of God!'
This paper underneath my door was thrust;
Proclaim it a foul libel each one must.

LAWLESS

No doubt – no doubt – yet spite of all our merits,
Methinks, my noble friends are *out of spirits*.
So with the leave of our most reverend host,
To warm your hearts, I will propose a toast:
May all Reformers the disasters share
Of those who suffered in the late affair!
With three times three – now read their scribbling wares,
We've made *our charge*, and now the dogs make *theirs*.

SCAPEGRACE (*reads*)

You magistrates of M., who ought to have been the *Preservers* of peace, have been the *Breakers* of it; and have shamelessly violated the laws you had sworn to maintain! A meeting of the distressed inhabitants of this place was called, in the form and manner prescribed by the laws of the country, with which you were well acquainted. Fifty thousand persons, in consequence,

31

quietly assembled to exercise the *right* of Seagirtonians,[72] to petition the legislature for redress of grievances. *All was calm*; and we were listening to our leader, who was enforcing the duty of preserving the peace, when your troops galloped up to us, and then halted. We received them with three cheers, considering them as friends, equally anxious as ourselves to promote order; and our several bands struck up the national airs of Rule, Rule great Seagirt, and God save the King. Alas, these friendly greetings availed us nothing. In a moment they dashed in among the unarmed and unsuspecting multitude, and cutting their way through them, took our leader, with several of our friends, prisoners, without the least resistance on their part or that of the meeting. A dreadful scene of terror and confusion ensued. Several persons were murdered, and hundreds of others badly wounded! Thus was our peaceable meeting dispersed by an armed force! Thus was war made, by your orders, upon defenceless men, women, and children! These are your exploits! They will never be forgotten! You did not prevent the crowd from assembling – you did not order them to disperse after they had assembled, but when quietly congregated together, in a legal way, you let in your executioners among them! Thus it is, you, ye magistrates, who have set the example of a brutal violence to a suffering and famished population. Dangerous proceedings! Impolitic step! – MAY IT NEVER BE IMITATED BY REFORMERS,

> Let the gall'd jade wince,
> Our withers are unwrung![73]

OMNES

A monstrous libel!

KILLAWAY

Horrible to hear,
For the base writer, nothing's too severe.
What independent, jacobinic fury!

LAWLESS

Hang him the wretch without a Judge or Jury!

SHALLOWPATE

A senseless dog as e'er Philippic penn'd.[74]

FLINTY

Upon a rack he ought to make his end. . . .

Extract 5: from T. J. Wooler, *The Black Dwarf* 3 (36)
(15 September 1819): 599–602

Monday being announced as the day on which Mr. Hunt was to return to town, a scene was presented to the inhabitants of the metropolis which we believe has not been equalled in the memory of the oldest, and is not likely to be forgotten by the youngest, person who witnessed it. The extreme fineness of the day contributed to increase the interest of the scene. Twelve o'clock was the hour first mentioned as that at which the procession would move forward from Islington; but long before that time, every avenue leading to it was thronged with crowds, who eagerly pressed forward, either to secure a good situation at the starting place, or to proceed beyond that, and meet Mr. Hunt at Highgate. Every species of vehicle, from the glass coach and landau, to the humble tax-cart or cumbrous coal-wagon, was seen crowded with passengers, moving towards the spot where it was supposed Mr. Hunt would alight from his own carriage, and enter that prepared by his friends. Except that there was a little confusion in the progress of the multitudes, one would have supposed that some terrible visitation of Providence had obliged the inhabitants of the city to desert their homes; for, we believe, never before did London disgorge in one day so many thousands of its population. At an early hour of the morning, two or three chariots and pairs, in which were Messrs. Watson, Preston, Thistlewood, Waddington, &c.,[75] passed through the city on their way to the appointed rendezvous at Islington. They were preceded by a landaulet, drawn by six bays; the three outriders wore Mr. Hunt's favours in their hats, and the horses were handsomely decorated with ribands of the same colour (red). There were besides these, two open carriages filled with Mr. Hunt's friends, amongst whom were several well-dressed females.... At length, at a few minutes before 3, and after being announced by several horsemen, who coursed at another's heels, Mr. Hunt's carriage approached. The road then became agitated, with unusual bustle.

The multitude on horseback, on foot, and in vehicles of various descriptions, who preceded and followed him, threw up such clouds of dust, that to breathe was difficult; and to see to any distance was for a time impossible. Mr. Hunt was accompanied in the post chaise by two females elegantly dressed. To the great disappointment of many on the line through which he passed towards Holloway turnpike, the glasses of the chaise were up, but it was unavoidable from the quantity of dust. The shouts which rent the air on his approach, might, we may safely assert, have been heard a mile on either side. Joy appeared on every face, and we verily believe, that if an individual had arrived for the purpose, and with the means of paying off the national debt, he could not have met a more enthusiastic reception. Before the chaise reached the turnpike, some of the crowd wished to unharness the horses and drag it along themselves; but this Mr. Hunt would not permit. He proceeded on a slow pace to the spot where his friends waited for him. There, having greeted Dr. Watson, Thistlewood, &c. and stopped for a few moments, he got into the landaulet, and the procession moved on in the following order: –

Some hundreds of footmen bearing large branches of oak, poplar, and various other trees.

A footman, bearing the emblem of union – a bundle of sticks stuck on a pitchfork, supported by groups of men on horseback, and on foot.

A horseman with a scroll inscribed on it, Magna Charta and the Bill of Rights.[76]

The Committee bearing white wands, and all wearing knots of red riband and laurel leaves in their hats.

A green silk flag, with gold letters and Irish harp; inscription, 'Universal, civil and religious liberty;' borne and supported by six Irishmen, and numerous other footmen.

A band of music.

Horsemen.

A white flag surmounted and bordered with crape: inscription in black, 'To the immortal memory of the Reformers massacred at Manchester, Aug. 16, 1819.'

Groups of horsemen and footmen.

A large tricoloured flag, red, white and green, with the words 'England, Scotland, and Ireland,' in gold letters.

Groups of men bearing white wands and red favours.

The old red flag, with the inscription 'Universal Suffrage.'

Two barouches, in which were some friends of Mr. Hunt.

Two carriages, in which were some gentlemen connected with the press.

A sky-blue flag, inscription, 'The palladium of liberty, a free press.'

Groups of footmen.

A carriage containing Messrs. Watson, Thistlewood and Preston, and other friends of Mr. Hunt.

A scarlet silk flag; inscription in gold letters, 'Hunt, the heroic Champion of Liberty.'

Groups of men on horseback and on foot.

A band of music.

Mr. HUNT, standing in a landaulet, drawn by six handsome bays, decorated with scarlet ribands.

Behind the carriage stood a man, bearing a large red flag, which waved over Mr. Hunt's head; inscription, 'Liberty or Death.'

Groups of horsemen and footmen.

A white silk flag; inscription, 'Trial by Jury.'
[Most of the flags had small pieces of black crape fastened at the ends, out of respect to the memory of the unfortunate persons who fell at Manchester.]

The procession was closed by a crowd of pedestrians, extending back as far as the eye could see. Standing, as we happened to be, in a good situation, the whole assemblage presented one of the most imposing spectacles we ever beheld. To a person in front, the approach of the procession seemed like that of a moving grove. The mixture of green boughs with the wands of the Committee, gave me no faint idea of the approach of Birnan wood to Dunsinane.[77]... The order and decorum observable in this immense multitude were truly pleasing, and evinced a firm determination on the part of those assembled to preserve order at all events.

SELECT BIBLIOGRAPHY

Belchem, John, *'Orator' Hunt: Henry Hunt and English Working-Class Radicalism* (Oxford: Clarendon Press, 1985). A study by a leading labour historian of the career of Henry Hunt. The book is particularly useful for its detailed exposition of the radical networks in operation in London and the provinces in the post-war years.

Epstein, James, *Radical Expression: Political Language, Ritual and Symbol in England, 1790–1830* (Oxford: Oxford University Press, 1994). A book which reflects the growing interest among critics and historians (see also Worrall) in radical culture, where issues of language and form rank alongside events and biographies.

Gilmartin, Kevin, *Print Politics* (Cambridge: Cambridge University Press, 1996). A thorough exploration of the discourse of radical journalism in the period, theoretically informed by post-structuralism and the ideas of Habermas. The illumination of contradictions within the radical position is particularly valuable.

Klancher, Jon P., *The Making of English Reading Audiences 1790–1832* (Madison: University of Wisconsin Press, 1987). Building on the earlier work of E. P. Thompson (see below), Klancher evinces different reading constituencies in the period: evangelical, commercial, radical and middle class. These categories are a helpful aid to understanding the explosion of periodical and newspaper production at a time of great concern about standards of taste and the relation between culture and politics.

Nattrass, Leonora, *William Cobbett: The Politics of Style* (Cambridge: Cambridge University Press, 1995). The most recent full-length study of Cobbett, useful for its demonstration that Cobbett appealed to diverse types of reader, not only the radical artisan.

Read, Donald, *Peterloo: The 'Massacre' and its Background* (Manchester: Manchester University Press, 1958). Still the standard work on Peterloo, this book provides a wealth of detail about radicalism in Manchester, and takes an even-handed approach to the vexed question of culpability.

Rickword, Edgell, *Radical Squibs and Loyal Ripostes: Satirical Pamphlets of the Regency Period, 1819–1821* (Bath: Adams and Dart, 1971). Though this book is rather rare, it contains an excellent selection of satirical visual responses to Peterloo, including mock-commemorative medallions which show soldiers slaughtering helpless protestors.

Royle, Edward and James Walvin, *English Radicals and Reformers 1760–1848* (Brighton: Harvester, 1982). A clear and concise narrative of radical history in the period, which places political reform within the context of other popular reform movements such as abolitionism and Catholic emancipation.

Scrivener, Michael, *Radical Shelley: The Philosophical Anarchism and Utopian Thought of Percy Bysshe Shelley* (Princeton: Princeton University Press, 1982). The section on the *Mask of Anarchy* shows convincingly the parallels between the imagery in Shelley's poem and responses to Peterloo in radical poems and satires.

Thompson, E. P., *The Making of the English Working Class* (1963; Harmondsworth: Penguin, 1977). This pioneering work is still the best introduction to the period, and it provides a host of insights and illuminating historical details.

Weiner, Joel, *Radicalism and Freethought in Nineteenth-century Britain: The Life of Richard Carlile* (London: Greenwood, 1983). A comprehensive biography of the leading radical publisher of the 1820s, which charts Carlile's shifting fortunes and ideological positions. The section on his prison years is particularly useful for showing the enormous pressures under which radical journalists worked.

Williams, Raymond, *Cobbett* (Oxford: Oxford University Press, 1983). Williams focuses on the idiosyncratic blend of iconoclasm and nostalgia in Cobbett's style and vision, a feature Williams regards as symptomatic of English radicalism at this time.

Worrall, David, *Radical Culture: Discourse, Resistance and Surveillance, 1790–1820* (Hemel Hempstead: Harvester Wheatsheaf, 1992). A study by a literary critic of the discourse and poetry of the London Spenceans, including the poets Allen Davenport and E. J. Blandford, and the black activist Robert Wedderburn.

2

POLITICAL ECONOMY

John Seed

It has appeared, that from the inevitable laws of our nature, some human beings must suffer from want. These are the unhappy persons who, in the great lottery of life, have drawn a blank.

(Malthus, *Essay on Population*, 1798)[1]

'Political economy', Adam Smith argued in *The Wealth of Nations* (1776),

considered as a branch of the science of a statesman or legislator, proposes two distinct objects: first, to provide a plentiful revenue or subsistence for the people, or more properly to enable them to provide such a revenue or subsistence for themselves; and secondly to supply the state or commonwealth with a revenue sufficient for the public services. It proposes to enrich both the people and the sovereign.[2]

Two initial points need to be stressed here. First, political economy was not simply the equivalent of modern 'economics'. It focused on the production of wealth, the organization of labour, international trade, public finance and taxation, and so on, but it was also concerned with political policy, with social values, with human nature. Smith's *Wealth of Nations*, the founding text of political economy, was as much philosophy, political theory, even sociology, as economics and it included substantial discussions of history, education and religion. Second, and following on from this, if its proponents made claims for political economy's scientific status, for its possession of truth, it also represented specific interests and specific moral and social values. As Smith's definition indicates, political economy was not simply an academic study. It played an *active* role in advising governments and in shaping all kinds of policies. *The Wealth of Nations* was uncompromising in its commitment to individualism, to free trade and to laissez-faire generally. It was a reforming intervention in late eighteenth-century public debate.

This section examines political economy's intervention in one of the central economic and political debates of this period: the question of the poor. In particular, the focus is on the influence of one particular book: *An Essay on the Principle of Population, as it Affects the Future Improvement of Society, with Remarks on the Speculations of Mr. Godwin, M. Condorcet, and Other Writers*. Published anonymously in 1798 by Joseph Johnson, the radical publisher of Tom Paine and Mary Wollstonecraft, it was to become one of the most influential works of political economy in the nineteenth century and its author, Thomas Robert Malthus (1766–1834), a controversial and sometimes vilified figure. His central argument, that poverty was an inevitable fact of life and the result of a perennial population surplus, was debated, disseminated and disputed in political tracts, parliamentary speeches, government reports, sermons, magazine articles, even in fiction.[3]

Why was the *Essay on Population* so influential? There was nothing radically new in its pages. The centrality of population to questions of wealth and poverty had been emphasized, as Malthus acknowledged, by a number of his predecessors, including Smith.[4] But the *Essay on Population* was timely. First, it provided a voice for wider dissatisfactions with the old poor laws in the 1790s. The traditional policy of providing relief to the local poor by raising a parish rate, dating back to the early seventeenth century, was under increasing pressure. Rising population, enclosures and a more calculating use of labour were creating a reservoir of unemployment in the countryside. The war with France from 1793 and a series of bad harvests, in 1794, 1795, 1798 and 1799, exacerbated the problem. Rising rural unemployment and rising food prices meant rising poor rates, discontented farm labourers and resentful ratepayers. Malthus was one of a number of voices critical of the excessive generosity of the poor laws and the dependence of the poor on the kindness of strangers.[5] Equally significant was the *Essay*'s provision of a simple and apparently effective demolition of radical arguments for political change, such as those propounded by Tom Paine. No reform of the electoral system or wholesale transformation of institutions would make any difference to the situation of the labouring poor. Nature caused poverty, not men. Malthus thus legitimized – with the simplest of equations – the increasing antagonism of men of property to the claims of the poor for both poor relief and political representation.

Extract 1, from the *Essay*'s first edition of 1798, proposes that poor relief cannot, in the long run, help the poor.[6] On the contrary, it contributed to their suffering by taking away the moral disciplines essential for independence. It encouraged the labouring poor to marry young and to breed without thought of the long-term consequences. It discouraged the working-class family from saving money to prepare for inevitable spells of unemployment, sickness and eventual old age. Retaining the traditional right to public support diverted ever-greater resources from the virtuous and hard-working members of the community (the ratepayers) to the weak, the irresponsible and the idle. Thus Malthus exonerated the propertied from guilt. Since generosity was, in the long term, economic suicide for England, hard-heartedness was a positive duty. The second part of this extract underlines the dark pessimism of Malthus. War and famine were nature's ways of preserving some kind of balance between population and food supply. Death patrolled the outer limits of the social order.

Extract 2 is by Sir Benjamin Thompson, Count von Rumford (1753–1814), an American who had supported the British Crown during the American War of Independence. An influential figure in intellectual circles in London from the mid-1790s and a founder of the Royal Institution in 1799, he dabbled in all kinds of social reforms. This extract, from a letter published in 1800, is representative of contemporary anxieties about the demoralizing effects of indiscriminate charity and the need to discipline the lower orders. It indicates the social attitudes which Malthus's *Essay* both responded to and reinforced.

In 1803 a much expanded and revised two-volume edition of the *Essay on Population*, also published by Joseph Johnson, appeared.[7] Malthus made some concessions to criticisms of the hopelessness of his vision of the future. Population increase could be slowed by moral restraint of various kinds – sexual abstinence, later marriage and so on. And education could have a long-term influence in persuading the poor to live within their means and limit the size of their families. Of course contraception was ruled out as too abhorrent even to discuss.[8] Overall, however, the main arguments of the first edition of the *Essay* remained in place. **Extract 3** is a notorious passage Malthus added to this 1803 edition – and removed from subsequent editions. Note, incidentally, that both Rumford and Malthus use the term 'clamorous importunity' to describe the poor. A traditional right has become a noisy pestering. It is reasonable to assume that Malthus, an Anglican cleric in a rural parish, was a keen reader of the *Annals of Agriculture* and had thus seen Rumford's letter.[9]

There were of course dissenters from these increasingly dominant views of the poor. William Blake in the 1790s saw the deepening hostility to the poor as fundamentally *political*. There was a conspiracy of priest and king to starve the people into submission to the established regime. In *The Four Zoas* (1797) Urizen provides instructions in how to govern the poor in terms that could almost have been drawn from Malthus, though the poem predates the *Essay* by at least a year:

Compell the poor to live upon a Crust of bread, by soft mild arts.
Smile when they frown, frown when they smile; & when a man looks pale
With labour & abstinence, say he looks healthy & happy;
And when his children sicken, let them die; there are enough
Born, even too many, & our Earth will be overrun
Without these arts. If you would make the poor live with temper,
With pomp give every crust of bread you give; with gracious cunning
Magnify small gifts; reduce the man to want a gift, & then give with pomp
Say he smiles if you hear him sigh. If pale, say he is ruddy.

Preach temperance: say he is overgorg'd & drowns his woe
In strong drink, tho' you know that bread and water are all
He can afford ...

('Night the Seventh' [a], ll. 117–28)

One of Malthus's most persistent critics was William Hazlitt (1778–1830). Son of a Unitarian minister, Hazlitt was a brilliant essayist and a consistent radical. He also had a sharp ear for hypocrisy. 'To hear Mr. Malthus talk', he shrewdly notes, 'one would suppose the rich were really a very hard-working, ill-used people, who are not suffered to enjoy the earnings of their honest industry in quiet by a set of troublesome, unsatisfied, luxurious, idle people called *the poor.*' These words come from *A Reply to the Essay on Population, by the Rev. T. R. Malthus. In a series of Letters*, published in 1807, which was an expansion of three letters published in William Cobbett's radical weekly *The Political Register.* **Extract 4** focuses on Malthus's passage about 'nature's mighty feast' and exposes its distortions of the real relations between the labouring poor and their employers. Hazlitt raises important questions about the relative rights of property and labour and the ways in which the political system favours the former. He returned to savage Malthus in a number of later essays.[10]

Malthus's influence, whatever opposition it provoked, made steady progress during the Napoleonic wars. It became the accepted wisdom in important periodicals, such as the *Edinburgh Review.* It became part of the language of parliamentary debate. Prominent churchmen thundered their acceptance of its doctrine as in harmony with Christian faith. Issues of 'surplus population' were given a new urgency during the long spell of severe depression, unemployment, spiralling poor rates and popular disturbances in rural districts after 1815.

Major (later Colonel) Robert Torrens (1780–1864) adopts an uncomplicated Malthusian programme in his 1817 'Paper on the Means of Reducing the Poor's Rates' (**extract 5**), though he is less gloomy than his master. Since surplus population is the essential cause of poverty, it must be removed. Education, through which the labouring poor will learn to restrain their sexual appetites and thus control the population, will succeed only in the very long run. The colonies provided a perfect short-term solution. Emigration provided an answer to the disposal of 'surplus population' and became an important issue during the 1820s, the subject of parliamentary debate and official enquiries.[11]

David Ricardo (1772–1823) was the greatest of the English political economists and his *The Principles of Political Economy and Taxation*, first published in 1817, a massively influential text. Though he disagreed with Malthus on some issues, he was profoundly influenced by the *Essay on Population.* His first parliamentary speech, in March 1819, was to oppose a bill relaxing the rules for granting poor relief, especially to unmarried mothers. This, Ricardo told the House, would exacerbate 'the tendency towards a redundant population':

if a provision were made for all the children of the poor, it would only increase the evil; for if parents felt assured that an asylum would be provided for their children, in which they would be treated with humanity and tenderness, there would then be no check to that increase of population which was so apt to take place among the labouring classes.[12]

Sound economic policy clearly required inhumanity and lack of tenderness to hungry children. **Extract 6** is a lucid exposition of classical political economy's theory of wages and its unblinking recognition that death also was one of the disciplines of the market.

The problems of unemployment, low wages and rising costs of poor relief in the countryside attracted a series of parliamentary reports in the decade after Waterloo. **Extract 8**, from an 1824 Select Committee Report into rural labour, presents an officially-sanctioned account of how poor relief was operating in some parts of rural England. The grim picture of an exploited workforce is, however, glossed by an interpretation drawn from political economy. Malthus's arguments thus shaped and legitimized government policy and the local behaviour of farmers and landowners.

One voice more than any other challenged the pretensions of political economy and its systematic distortions of reality – that of William Cobbett (1763–1835).[13] As Hazlitt put it:

He is a kind of *fourth estate* in the politics of the country. He is not only unquestionably the most powerful political writer of the present day, but one of the best writers in the language. He speaks and thinks plain, broad, downright English.[14]

Malthus was a particular target of Cobbett's prodigious indignation. In **extract 7** he ingeniously reverses (as Hazlitt had done) the Malthusian picture of a society being drained of its wealth by the idle poor. On the contrary, it is an idle and unproductive elite – the retinue of consumers who fill the pages of Jane Austen's novels – whose uncontrolled breeding is crippling the economy. Taxation appropriates wealth from those who produce it – the farm labourer, the skilled artisan, the farmer – and distributes it to those who produce nothing (except homilies on the undeserving poor).

In **extract 9** Cobbett responds to the 1824 Select Committee on the wages of agricultural labourers (**extract 8**) and again exposes the reality of the distribution of wealth in England in the 1820s. Far from being the beneficiaries of charity, the labouring poor are systematically exploited by the poor laws. They receive a combination of wages and poor relief which barely provides a subsistence, while a substantial part of the wealth they produce is extracted by taxation of various kinds. This is distributed in pensions, sinecures and interest payments on the national debt to idle consumers who have the brass neck to grumble about 'the clamorous importunity' of the poor. For Cobbett, whose weekly *Political Register* was a major focus for popular radicalism throughout this period, the solution, like the problem, is *political*: a reform of parliament to enfranchise the (male) working class and elect a government dedicated to reducing taxes and the parasitism of 'the Dead Weight'.

Cobbett's increasingly desperate warnings about the profound social bitterness which was tearing apart rural society in the 1820s were ignored. Unemployment and starvation wages provoked sporadic rioting, threatening letters, rick burning and a deepening hatred of the propertied. And the authorities reacted in turn with repression and further tightening of controls on labour. The Hammonds cite the case of an out-of-work shepherd in Kent with a wife and five children. They were granted nine shillings a week poor relief. However, the parish overseer would only pay the relief on a daily basis. The shepherd was forced to walk thirteen miles to get his eighteen pence and then thirteen miles home each day (except Sunday). He did this, six days each week for thirteen weeks – fifty-four journeys of twenty-six miles – until he physically collapsed.[15] By such means the parish authorities taught the unemployed what it meant to be surplus population.

Finally in the autumn of 1830 there was an explosion – the Swing riots – across twenty counties in southern England. For several months there were incendiary fires, broken threshing machines, large crowds of farm labourers moving from farm to farm demanding increased wages. Social authority in the countryside almost collapsed – though remarkably there was very little physical violence. Order of a kind was restored with more than two thousand arrests, hundreds of men transported or imprisoned and nineteen executed.[16]

Extract 10 reaffirms political economy and the workings of the market in the face of the Swing riots. Nassau Senior (1790–1864), professor of political economy at Oxford University, reiterates the arguments of Malthus and Ricardo and of the 1824 Select Committee. The desperate acts of the farm labourers were not the reactions of individual men driven beyond endurance by starvation wages and iron laws. The Swing riots were a consequence of the poor laws which had undermined the farm-worker's independence and weakened the salutary disciplines of the labour market. Senior's unbending commitment to political economy and the existing distribution of wealth left only two alternatives: either complete social and economic collapse; or the removal of the Poor Law and the exposure of labour to the rigours of the free market. Senior, in fact, was a central figure in the Poor Law Commission which drafted the 1824 report and finally got rid of the traditional system of poor relief. But the New Poor Law, with its refusal of outdoor relief and its harsh workhouses, was met by further violent opposition from agricultural labourers during the 1830s and 1840s.[17]

A final point. In the *Essay on Population*, Malthus adopted the pose of a seeker after scientific truth, even where it went against what he 'ardently wished' to be true.

His tone was one of cautious investigation and he clinched his argument by an impressive equation: food supply increased arithmetically (1, 2, 3, 4), but population increased geometrically (2, 4, 8, 16). As Hazlitt noted of Malthus's equation: 'mathematical terms carry with them an imposing air of accuracy and profundity.'[18] A similar tone and rhetoric is at work in other texts of political economy. Look for instance at the use of a technical metaphor at the end of the Torrens passage (**extract 5**). Here emigration, whether voluntary or compelled, ceases to be a painful human and social experience of uprooting, of leaving, perhaps for ever, familiar surroundings, neighbours and friends, even family. Instead it becomes a siphoning off of excess steam – a clean, painless and necessary technical operation. Similarly, observe how Ricardo claims for his arguments the status of 'laws' comparable to the law of gravity (**extract 6**). Part of the impact of Malthus, and of political economy as a whole in this period, was precisely its deployment of an austere English prose reinforced by scientific metaphors and the rhetorical use of quantification. Political and economic texts need to be read with critical attention to the uses of language, style and metaphor – the skills of the literary critic are needed here as surely as they are in the interpretation of poems or novels.

Hazlitt and Cobbett are careful readers of the text of political economy. They write from a powerful sense that the 'laws' of political economy are not laws at all but the moral and political *acts* of groups and individuals. While political economy uses Malthus's principle of population to *naturalize* poverty, Hazlitt and Cobbett insist on *politicizing* it. The reduction of the wages of labourers to the level of a minimum subsistence is not a 'natural' event like gravity, as the 'laws' of political economy propose. It is a human *act*. Individual farmers and individual landowners force wages down and reap bigger profits; governments extract taxation and distribute it – via pensions, funds, public offices and so on – to an unproductive social elite. Cobbett and Hazlitt rebel against the abstractions of political economy and against the dehumanizing of relations between people which it authorizes. Human labour is not a commodity to be bought and sold like an inhuman object. And if some people, as Malthus says, are born with a blank lottery ticket that signals they have no right even to live, this is a *political* decision. A lottery, after all, is organized.

Extract 1: from [Thomas Malthus], *An Essay on the Principle of Population, as it affects the future improvement of society, with remarks on the speculations of Mr. Godwin, M. Condorcet, and other writers* (London: Joseph Johnson, 1798), pp. 83–9 (from chapter 5), pp. 139–41 (from chapter 7)

The poor-laws of England tend to depress the general condition of the poor in these two ways. Their first obvious tendency is to increase population without increasing the food for its support. A poor man may marry with little or no prospect of being able to support a family in independence. They may be said therefore in some measure to create the poor which they maintain; and as the provisions of the country must, in consequence of the increased population, be distributed to every man in smaller proportions, it is evident that the labour of those who are not supported by parish assistance, will purchase a smaller quantity of provisions than before, and consequently, more of them must be driven to ask for support.

Secondly, the quantity of provisions consumed in workhouses upon a part of the society, that cannot in general be considered the most valuable part, diminishes the shares that would otherwise belong to more industrious, and more worthy members; and thus in the same manner forces more to become dependent. If the poor in the workhouses were to live better than they do now, this new distribution of the money of the society would tend more conspicuously to depress the condition of those out of the workhouses, by occasioning a rise in the price of provisions.

Fortunately for England, a spirit of independence still remains among the peasantry. The poor-laws are strongly calculated to eradicate this spirit. They have succeeded in part; but had they succeeded as completely as might have been expected, their tendency would not have been so long concealed.

Hard as it may appear in individual instances, dependent poverty ought to be held disgraceful. Such a stimulus seems to be absolutely necessary to promote the happiness of the great mass of mankind; and every general attempt to weaken this stimulus, however benevolent its apparent intention, will always defeat its own purpose. If men are induced to marry from a prospect of parish provision, with little or no chance of maintaining their families in independence, they are not only unjustly tempted to bring unhappiness and dependence upon themselves and children; but they are tempted, without knowing it, to injure all in the same class with themselves. A labourer who marries without being able to support a family, may in some respects be considered as an enemy to all his fellow-labourers.

I feel no doubt whatever, that the parish laws of England have contributed to raise the price of provisions, and to lower the real price of labour. They have therefore contributed to impoverish that class of people whose only possession is their labour. It is also difficult to suppose that they have not powerfully contributed to generate that carelessness, and want of frugality observable among the poor, so contrary to the disposition frequently to be remarked among petty tradesmen and small farmers. The labouring poor, to use a vulgar expression, seem always to live from hand to mouth. Their present wants employ their whole attention, and they seldom think of the future. Even when they have an opportunity of saving they seldom exercise it; but all that is beyond their present necessities goes, generally speaking, to the ale-house. The poor-laws of England may therefore be said to diminish both the power and the will to save, among the common people, and thus to weaken one of the strongest incentives to sobriety and industry, and consequently to happiness.

It is a general complaint among master manufacturers, that high wages ruin all their workmen; but it is difficult to conceive that these men would not save a part of their high wages for the future support of their families, instead of spending it in drunkenness and dissipation, if they did not rely on parish assistance for support in case of accidents. And that the poor employed in manufactures consider this assistance as a reason why they may spend all the wages they earn, and enjoy themselves while they can, appears to be evident from the number of families that, upon the failure of any great manufactory, immediately fall upon the parish; when perhaps the wages earned in this manufactory, while it flourished, were sufficiently above the price of common country labour, to have allowed them to save enough for their support, till they could find some other channel for their industry.

A man who might not be deterred from going to the ale-house, from the consideration that on his death, or sickness, he should leave his family upon the parish, might yet hesitate in thus dissipating his earnings, if he were assured that, in either of these cases, his family must starve, or be left to the support of casual bounty. In China, where the real as well as the nominal price of labour is very low, sons are yet obliged by law to support their aged and helpless parents. Whether such a law would be adviseable in this country, I will not pretend to determine. But it seems at any rate highly improper, by positive institutions, which render dependent poverty so general, to weaken that disgrace, which for the best and most humane reasons ought to attach to it. . . .

Famine seems to be the last, the most dreadful resource of nature. The power of the population is so superior to the power in the earth to produce subsistence for man, that premature death must in some shape or other visit the human race. The vices of mankind are active and able ministers of depopulation. They are the precursors in the great army of destruction; and often finish the dreadful work themselves. But should they fail in this war of extermination, sickly seasons, epidemics, pestilence and plague, advance in terrific array, and sweep off their thousands and ten thousands. Should success be still incomplete; gigantic inevitable famine stalks in the rear, and with one mighty blow, levels the population with the food of the world.

Must it not then be acknowledged by an attentive examiner of the histories of mankind, that in every age and in every State in which man has existed, or does now exist,

That the increase of population is necessarily limited by the means of subsistence.
That population does invariably increase when the means of subsistence increase.

45

And,

> That the superior power of population is repressed, and the actual population kept equal to the means of subsistence by misery and vice.

Extract 2: 'Letter of Count Rumford to Dr Majendie, Dec. 5, 1799', printed in Arthur Young, ed., *Annals of Agriculture and Other Useful Arts* 34 (1800): 339–41

The aged and infirm, and young children, cannot earn by their labour enough to defray the expenses of their subsistence; but those who are able to work must not be maintained in idleness, at the public expence, and must certainly not in times of general distress. All they can reasonably expect is, that they and their families be enabled to live for as small a sum of money, or for the same quantity of labour, in times of scarcity, as their subsistence usually costs them in time of plenty. Much more for them at any time would be unjust, and in a time of general alarm, would be productive of the most fatal evils. It would have a tendency to make them careless, idle, and profligate, and instead of being grateful for the assistance received, they would soon learn to consider it their right; and if it were discontinued, would demand it with clamorous importunity. But if the assistance afforded to the poor be so applied as to be felt by them as an honourable reward for their good conduct, and as an encouragement to persevere in their industrious habits, in that case, their morals will be rather improved, than injured by the benefits received.

In all cases where it is possible, I think that a school of industry, for children, should be constructed, with a public kitchen; and it is certainly necessary that measures should be taken for giving *constant employment* to the poor of all descriptions, that are able to work. The full amount of their earnings should always be given to them. This is proper, not only to encourage their industry, but also to keep alive in them a spirit of independence, without which they soon become disheartened and extremely helpless and miserable. Where the poor are paid for their labour, it is evidently just and proper that they should defray, as far at least as is in their power, the expences of their maintenance. It sometimes happens, though very rarely, that profitable employment cannot be found for the poor; they should nevertheless be put to work; and even be kept to labour constantly and diligently, under the direction of those who, in such circumstances, must provide for their subsistence. Were no profitable employment to be found for them, and were there no other way of preventing their being *idle*, some public work might be undertaken for the sole purpose of employing them.

But in the neighbourhood of Windsor the poor can hardly be in want of useful employment. His Majesty has taken care to prevent that evil. It is much to be wished that his opulent subjects in Great Britain and Ireland might be induced to follow his illustrious example.

As industry and economy are the preventives, and the only cure of indigence; and as want is one of the strongest inducements to labour, it is evident that much caution is necessary in supplying the wants of the poor, and destroying the effects of those incitements which Providence, in infinite wisdom, has contrived to rouse mankind from a state of indolence and torpid indifference, and stimulate them to that constant exertion of their bodily strength and mental faculties, which we know to be necessary to the health of the body and of the mind, and essential to happiness and virtue. It seldom requires much ingenuity to make the assistance that is given to the poor operate as an incitement to industry; for rewards are as powerful motives as punishments, and the truly benevolent will always prefer them. But it should never be forgotten, that all that which is given to the poor, or done for them, that does not encourage their industry, never can fail to have a contrary tendency; and consequently must do real harm to them, and to society.

Extract 3: from T. R. Malthus, *An Essay on the Principle of Population; or, a View of its Past and Present Effects on Human Happiness; with an Inquiry into our Prospects Respecting the Future Removal or Mitigation of the Evils which it Occasions*, second edition, 2 vols (London: Joseph Johnson, 1803), 2 (from book IV, chapter 6: 531–2)

Nothing would so effectually counteract the mischiefs occasioned by Mr. Paine's Rights of Man as a general knowledge of the real rights of man. What these rights are, it is not my business at present to explain; but there is one right which man has generally been thought to possess, which I am confident he neither does, nor can possess – a right to subsistence when his labour will not fairly purchase it. Our laws indeed say that he has this right, and bind the society to furnish employment and food to those who cannot get them in the regular market; but in so doing, they attempt to reverse the laws of nature; and it is in consequence to be expected, not only that they should fail in their object, but that the poor who were intended to be benefited, should suffer most cruelly from this inhuman deceit which is practised upon them.

A man who is born into a world already possessed, if he cannot get subsistence from his parents on whom he has a just demand, and if the society does not want his labour, has no claim of *right* to the smallest portion of food, and, in fact, has no business to be where he is. At nature's mighty feast there is no vacant cover for him.[19] She tells him to be gone, and will execute her own orders, if he do not work upon the compassion of some of her guests. If these guests get up and make room for him, other intruders immediately appear demanding the same favour. The report for a provision for all that come fills the hall with numerous claimants. The order and harmony of the feast is disturbed, the plenty that before reigned is changed into scarcity; and the happiness of the guests is destroyed by the spectacle of misery and dependence in every part of the hall, and by the clamorous importunity of those who are justly enraged at not finding the provision which they had been taught to expect. The guests learn too late their error, in counteracting those strict orders to all intruders, issued by the great mistress of the feast, who, wishing that all her guests should have plenty, and knowing that she could not provide for unlimited numbers, humanely refused to admit fresh comers when her table was already full.

Extract 4: from William Hazlitt, *A Reply to the Essay on Population, by the Rev. T. R. Malthus: In a series of Letters: To which are added, Extracts from the Essay, with Notes* [1807], reprinted in *The Complete Works of William Hazlitt*, ed. P. P. Howe, 21 vols (London: J. M. Dent and Sons, 1930–4), 1: 316–17, 318–19

This is a very brilliant description, and a pleasing allegory. Our author luxuriates in the dearth of nature: he cannot contain his triumph: he frolics with his subject in the gaiety of his heart, and his tongue grows wanton in praise of famine. But let us examine it not as a display of imagination, but as a piece of reasoning. In the first place, I cannot admit the assertion that 'at nature's mighty feast there is no vacant cover for the poor man'. There are plenty of vacant covers but that the guests at the head of the table have seized upon all those at the lower end, before the table was full. Or if there were no vacant cover, it would be no great matter, he only asks for the crumbs which fall from rich men's tables, and the bones which they throw to their dogs. 'She (nature) tells him to be gone, and will quickly execute her own orders, if he do not work on the compassion of some of the guests'. When I see a poor old man, who after a life of unceasing labour is obliged at last to beg his bread, driven from the door of a rich man by a surly porter, and half-a-dozen sleek well-fed dogs, kept for the pleasure of their master or mistress, jumping up from the fire-side, or bouncing out of their warm kennels upon him, I am, according to Mr Malthus, in the whole of this scene, to fancy nature presiding in person and executing her own orders against this unwelcome intruder, who as he is bent fairly double with hard labour, and can no longer get employment in the regular market, has no claim of right (as our author emphatically expresses it) to the smallest portion of food, and in fact has no business to be where he is. The preference which is often given to the inferior animals over the human species by the institutions and customs of society is bad enough. But Mr Malthus wishes to go farther. By the institutions of society a rich man is at liberty to give his superabundance either to the poor or to his dogs. Mr Malthus will not allow him this liberty, but says that by the laws of nature he is bound to give it to his dogs, because if we suffer the poor to work upon our compassion at all, this will only embolden their importunity, 'and the order and harmony that before reigned at nature's feast will be disturbed and changed into want and confusion'. This might probably be the consequence, if the rich, or the chief guests had provided the entertainment for themselves; or if nature, like a liberal hostess, had kindly provided it for them, at her own proper cost and expence, without any obligations to the poor.... But the question really is, not whether all those should be supplied who press forward into the hall without having contributed any thing to the plenty that abounds, but whether after the different guests have contributed largely, each of them having brought his share and more than his share, the proprietors of the mansion have the right to turn them all out again, and only leave a few scraps or coarse bits to be flung to them out of the windows, or handed to them out of the door....

[I]t is not the question whether the proprietor should starve himself in order that the labourer may live; but whether the proprietor has a right to live in extravagance and luxury, while the labourer is starving. As to his absolute right to the produce of the soil, that is to say, of the labour of others, we have seen that he has no such right either to the whole of the surplus produce, or to as much of it as he pleases. With respect then to the share of the produce which the labourer has a right to demand, 'it is not likely that he should exchange his labour, without receiving a sufficient quantity of food in return', to enable him to live, unless the right of the proprietor to exact the labour of others on what terms he chuses, is seconded by a kind of power, which has very little connection with the power of the earth to bring forth no more produce. As to the right of the rich, in a moral point of view, wantonly to starve the poor, it is I think best to say nothing about it. Social institutions, on which our author lays great stress as enlarging the power of subsistence and the right along with it, do not deny relief to the poor. For this very reason Mr Malthus wishes to shoulder them aside, in order to make room for certain regulations of his own, more agreeable to the laws of nature and the principle of population. A little farther on he says, 'As a previous step even to any considerable alteration in the present system, which would contract or stop the increase of the relief to be given, it appears to me that we are bound in justice and honour formally to disclaim the right of the poor to support'. It would be more modest in Mr Malthus to let them disclaim it for themselves. But it appears that the reason for contracting the relief afforded them by the present system, and denying the right altogether, is that there is no subsistence for an unlimited number. As to the point at which it may be prudent or proper for the rich to withhold assistance from the poor, I shall not enquire into it. But I shall dispute Mr Malthus's right to thrust the poor man out of existence because there is no room for him 'at nature's mighty feast', till he can give some better reason for it than that there is no room for an unlimited number! – The maintainance of the needy poor is a tax on the inequality of conditions and the luxury of the rich, which they could not enjoy but in consequence of that general depression of the lower classes which continually subjects them to difficulties and want. It is a douceur to keep them quiet, and prevent them from enforcing those more solid, and important claims, not interfering with the right of property, but a direct consequence of the right of personal freedom, and of their right to set their own price on their own exertions, which would raise them above the reach of want, and enable them to maintain their own poor. But they cannot do this without a general combination of the labouring part of the community; and if any thing of this kind were to be attempted, the legislature we know would instantly interfere to prevent it. I know indeed that the legislature assumes a right to prevent combinations of the poor to keep themselves above want, though they disclaim any right to meddle with monopolies of corn, or other combinations in the regular course of trade, by which the rich and thriving endeavour to grind the poor.[20] But though the men of property have thus retained the legislature on their side, Mr Malthus does not think this practical security sufficient: he thinks it absolutely necessary to recur to first principles; and that they may see how well qualified he is to act as chamber counsel in the business, he makes them a present of his Essay, written expressly for the purpose, and containing a new institute of the laws of nature, and a complete theory of population, in which it is clearly proved that the poor have no right to live any longer than the rich will let them. In this work which those to whom it is addressed should have bound in morocco, and constantly lying by them as a text-book to refer to in all cases of difficulty, it is shewn that there is no injustice in forcing the poorer classes to work almost for nothing, because they have no right to the produce of their labour, and no inhumanity in denying them assistance when they happen to be in want, because they ought not to be encouraged in idleness. Thus armed with 'metaphysical aid', and conscience-proof, the rich will I should think be able very successfully to resist the unjust claims of the poor – to a subsistence!

Neither the fundamental laws of property, then, nor the principle of population seem to imply the necessity of any great inequality of conditions. They do not even require the distinction of rich and poor, much less do they imply the right of the rich to starve the poor.

Extract 5: from Major Robert Torrens, 'A Paper on the Means of Reducing the Poor's Rates, and of affording effectual and permanent relief to the Labouring Classes' (1817), in *The Pamphleteer; Respectfully Dedicated to both Houses of Parliament* 10 (20) (1817): 518–19, 521

When all the good and well-situated lands of a country have already been appropriated and occupied, it is found impossible to increase capital and subsistence as rapidly as the powers of procreation may multiply the people; and there is no possibility of obviating poverty and misery except by regulating population.

... Now there seem to be only two ways of keeping down population to the level of capital and subsistence: and these are, a prudential or moral restraint for preventing the birth of superfluous numbers; and a well-regulated system of colonization for removing such numbers, should they be born. The first must necessarily depend upon the extension of knowledge, and the formation of prudential habits among the mass of the people. And when we contemplate the probable effects of the Schools of Bell and Lancaster,[21] as well as of our numerous banks for the accumulation of small savings, we may anticipate an incalculable improvement in the condition of the labouring classes, and look forward with confidence to the period when a prudential check on population shall apportion the supply of labour to the demand, and thereby banish poverty, with its consequences, discontent and turbulence, and disaffection, from the land.

But the benefit to be expected from our school and bank societies, though certain, is remote; and these excellent institutions are calculated to prevent the future recurrence of pauperism; not to remove that which actually exists. While, therefore, we adopt preventive measures with a reference to the future, and employ our utmost efforts to afford the people the means of moral instruction, and to present them with all possible inducement to the acquiring of prudential habits, it is necessary, if we would effect any immediate reduction in the enormous burthen of the poor's rate, and at the same time prevent a considerable portion of the surplus hands which the transition from war to peace has thrown upon the labour market, from perishing of famine, to resort to the second means of regulating the amount of our population, and adopt a more extended system of colonization. Happily the vast regions of Canada, the Cape of Good Hope, and New Holland, furnish us with an almost unlimited vent for our redundant population; and enable us, without difficulty, and without expence, to provide for every able-bodied pauper in the United Kingdom.

... For the immediate relief of actual distress there remains no remedy, except an extension of colonization. This would produce an instantaneous and almost magical effect. Transplanting to the colonies those who cannot find employment at home, would be followed at once by a reduction of the Poor's Rates, and by a mitigation of the distress which has overspread the country. While the glut of hands was thus removed from the labour market, and while those who remained received, in consequence, a rate of wages adequate to their support, want would cease to engender the desire of change; the ideas of relief and of revolution would lose their fatal connection in the minds of the multitude; and the spirit of discontent and disaffection, which rarely becomes formidable except when aggravated and perpetuated by the goad of famine, would no longer endanger our establishments. To an old and populous country, in which education and knowledge have not been sufficiently extended to give operation to a prudential and moral check upon the number of births, a well-regulated system of colonization acts as a safety-valve to the political machine, and allows the expanding vapour to escape, before it is heated to explosion.

Extract 6: from David Ricardo, *The Principles of Political Economy and Taxation* (London: John Murray, 1817), pp. 110–15[22]

Like all other contracts, wages should be left to the fair and free competition of the market, and should never be controlled by the interference of the legislature.

The clear and direct tendency of the poor laws is in direct opposition to these obvious principles: it is not, as the legislature benevolently intended, to amend the condition of the poor, but to deteriorate the condition of both rich and poor; instead of making the poor rich, they are calculated to make the rich poor; and whilst the present laws are in force, it is quite in the natural order of things that the fund for the maintenance of the poor should progressively increase till it has absorbed all the neat[23] revenue of the country, or at least so much of it as the state shall leave to us, after satisfying its own never-failing demands for the public expenditure.

This pernicious tendency of these laws is no longer a mystery, since it has been fully developed by the able hand of Mr Malthus; and every friend to the poor must ardently wish for their abolition. Unfortunately, however, they have been so long established, and the habits of the poor have been so formed upon their operation, that to eradicate them with safety from our political system requires the most cautious and skilful management. It is agreed by all who are most friendly to a repeal of these laws, that if it be desirable to prevent the most overwhelming distress to those for whose benefit they were erroneously enacted, their abolition should be effected by the most gradual steps.

It is a truth which admits not a doubt, that the comforts and well being of the poor cannot be permanently secured without some regard on their part, or some effort on the part of the legislature, to regulate the increase of their numbers, and to render less frequent among them early and improvident marriages. The operation of the system of poor laws has been directly contrary to this. They have rendered restraint superfluous, and have invited imprudence by offering it a portion of the wages of prudence and industry.

The nature of the evil points out the remedy. By gradually contracting the sphere of the poor laws; by impressing on the poor the value of independence, by teaching them that they must look not to systematic or casual charity, but to their own exertions for support, that prudence and forethought are neither unnecessary nor unprofitable virtues, we shall by degrees approach a sounder and more healthful state.

No scheme for the amendment of the poor laws merits the least attention, which has not their abolition for its ultimate object; and he is the best friend of the poor, and to the cause of humanity, who can point out how this end can be attained with the most security, and at the same time with the least violence. It is not by raising in any manner different from the present, the fund from which the poor are supported, that the evil can be mitigated. It would not only be no improvement, but it would be an aggravation of the distress which we wish to see removed, if the fund were increased in amount, or were levied according to some late proposals, as a general fund from the country at large. The present mode of its collection and application has served to mitigate its pernicious effects. Each parish raises a separate fund for the support of its own poor. Hence it becomes an object of more interest and more practicability to keep the rates low, than if one general fund were raised for the relief of the poor of the whole kingdom. A parish is much more interested in an economical collection of the rate, and a sparing distribution of relief, when the whole saving will be for its own benefit, than if hundreds of other parishes were to partake of it.

It is to this cause, that we must ascribe the fact of the poor laws not having yet absorbed all the net revenue of the country; it is to the rigour with which they are applied, that we are indebted for their not having become overwhelmingly oppressive. If by law every human being wanting support could be sure to obtain it, and obtain it in such a degree as to make life tolerably comfortable, theory would lead us to expect that all other taxes together would be light compared with the single one of poor rates. The principle of gravitation is not more certain than the tendency of such laws to change wealth and power into misery and weakness; to call away the exertions of labour from every object, except that of providing mere subsistence; to confound all intellectual distinction; to busy the mind continually in supplying the body's wants; until at last all classes should be infected with the plague of universal poverty. Happily these laws have been in operation during a period of progressive prosperity, when the funds for the maintenance of labour have regularly increased, and when an increase of population would be naturally called for. But if our progress should become more slow; if we should attain the stationary state, from which I trust we are yet far distant, then will the pernicious nature of these laws become more manifest and alarming; and then, too, will their removal be obstructed by many additional difficulties.[24]

Extract 7: from William Cobbett, *Rural Rides* (London: William Cobbett, 1830), pp. 133–4

8 August 1823

... This Dead Weight is, unquestionably, a thing, such as the world never saw before. Here are not only a tribe of pensioned naval and military officers, commissaries, quarter-masters, pursers, and God knows what besides; not only these, but their wives and children are to be pensioned, after the death of the heroes themselves. Nor does it signify, it seems, whether the hero were married, before he became part of the Dead Weight, or since. Upon the death of the man, the pension is to begin with the wife, and a pension for each child; so that, if there be a large family of children, the family, in many cases, *actually gains by the death of the father*! Was such a thing as this ever before heard of in the world? Any man that is going to die has nothing to do but to marry a girl to give her a pension for life to be paid out of the sweat of the people; and it was distinctly stated, during the Session of Parliament before the last, that the widows and children of insane officers were to have the same treatment as the rest! Here is the envy of surrounding nations and the admiration of the world! In addition, then, to twenty thousand parsons, more than twenty thousand stock-brokers and stock-jobbers perhaps;[25] forty or fifty thousand tax-gatherers; thousands upon thousands of military and naval officers in full pay; in addition to all these, here are the thousands upon thousands of pairs of this Dead Weight, all busily engaged in breeding ladies and gentlemen; and all, while Malthus is wanting to put a check upon the breeding of the labouring classes; all receiving a *premium for breeding*! Where is Malthus? Where is this check-population parson? Where are his friends, the Edinburgh Reviewers? Faith, I believe they have given him up. They begin to be ashamed of giving countenance to a man who wants to check the breeding of those who labour, while he says not a word about those two hundred thousand breeding pairs, whose off-spring are necessarily to be maintained at the public charge.

Extract 8: from the 'Report from the Select Committee on Labourers Wages', in *Parliamentary Papers*, 1824 (392), 6: 3–5

THE SELECT COMMITTEE appointed to inquire into the practice which prevails in some parts of the Country, of paying the Wages of Labour out of the Poor-Rates, and to consider whether any, and what Measures can be carried into execution, for the purpose of altering that practice, and to report their Observations thereupon to the House; – HAVE, pursuant to the Order of the House, examined into the Matter to them referred; and have agreed upon the following REPORT:

From the evidence, and other information collected by Your Committee, it appears that, in some districts of the country, able-bodied labourers are sent round to the farmers, and receive a part, and in some instances the whole of their subsistence from the parish, while working upon the land of individuals. This practice was, doubtless, introduced as a means of employing the surplus labourers of a parish; but by an abuse, which is almost inevitable, it has been converted into a means of obliging the parish to pay for labour, which ought to have been hired and paid for by private persons. This abuse frequently follows immediately the practice of sending the unemployed labourers upon the farms in the parish. The farmer, finding himself charged for a greater quantity of labour than he requires, naturally endeavours to economize, by discharging those labourers of whom he has the least need, and relying upon the supply furnished by the parish for work, hitherto performed entirely at his own cost. An instance has been quoted, of a farmer's team standing still, because the farmer had not received the number of roundsmen he expected.[26] Thus the evil of this practice augments itself; and the steady, hard-working labourer, employed by agreement with his master, is converted into the degraded and inefficient pensioner of the parish....

This practice is the natural result of another, which is far more common, namely, that of paying an allowance to labourers for the maintenance of their children. In some counties, as in Bedfordshire, this payment usually begins when the labourer has a single child, wages being kept so low, that it is utterly impossible for him to support a wife and a child without parish assistance.

The evils which follow from the system above described, may be thus enumerated:–

1st. – The employer does not obtain efficient labour from the labourer whom he hires. In parts of Norfolk, for instance, a labourer is quite certain of obtaining an allowance from the parish, sufficient to support his family; it consequently becomes a matter of indifference to him, whether he earns a small sum or a large one. It is obvious, indeed, that a disinclination to work must be the consequence of so vicious a system. He, whose subsistence is secure without work, and who cannot obtain more than a mere sufficiency by the hardest work, will naturally be an idle and careless labourer. Frequently the work done by four or five such labourers, does not amount to what might easily be performed by a single labourer working at task-work. Instances of this fact are to be found in the evidence, and in the statements of all persons conversant with the subject.

2dly. – Persons who have no need of farm-labour are obliged to contribute to the payment of work done for others. This must be the case wherever the labourers necessarily employed by the farmers receive from the parish any part of the wages which, if not so paid, would be paid by the farmers themselves.

3dly. – A surplus population is encouraged; men who received but a small pittance know that they have only to marry, and that pittance will be augmented in proportion to the number of their children. Hence the supply of labour is by no means regulated by the demand, and parishes are burthened with thirty, forty, and fifty labourers, for whom they can find no employment, and who serve to depress the situation of all their fellow-labourers in the same parish. An intelligent witness, who is much in the habit of employing labourers, states, that when complaining of their allowance, they frequently say to him, 'We will marry, and you must maintain us'.

4thly. – By far the worst consequence of the system is, the degradation of the character of the labouring class.

There are but two motives by which men are induced to work: the one, the hope of improving the condition of themselves and their families; the other, the fear of punishment. The one is the principle of free labour, the other the principle of slave labour. The one produces industry, frugality, sobriety, family affection, and puts the labouring class in a friendly relation with the rest of the community; the other cause, as certainly, idleness, imprudence, vice, dissension, and places the master and the labourer in a perpetual state of jealousy and mistrust. Unfortunately, it is the tendency of the system of which we speak, to supersede the former of these principles, and introduce the latter. Subsistence is secured to all; to the idle as well as the industrious; to the profligate as well as the sober; and, as far as human interests are concerned, all inducement to obtain a good character is taken away. The effects have corresponded with the cause. Able-bodied men are found slovenly at their work, and dissolute in their hours of relaxation; a father is negligent of his children; the children do not think it necessary to contribute to the support of their parents; the employers and the employed are engaged in perpetual quarrels, and the pauper, always relieved, is always discontented; crime advances with increasing boldness, and the parts of the country where this system prevails are, in spite of our gaols and our laws, filled with poachers and thieves.

The evil of this state of things has often induced individuals to desire further means of punishing labourers who refuse or neglect to work, and the Legislature has sometimes listened with favour to such proposals; but we are persuaded that any attempt to make the penalties of this kind more efficacious, would either be so repugnant to the national character as to be totally inoperative, or, if acted upon, would tend still further to degrade the labouring classes of the kingdom.

The effects of this system very clearly show the mistake of imagining that indiscriminate relief is the best method of providing for the happiness of the labouring classes. Employers, burdened with the support of a surplus population, endeavour to reduce the wages of labour to the lowest possible price. Hence, where the system to which we allude has gained ground, the labourers are found to live chiefly on bread, or even potatoes, scarcely ever tasting meat or beer, or being able even to buy milk; while in other parts of the country, where high wages are still prevalent, the food and whole manner of living of the labourers are on a greatly better scale. This difference is, doubtless, to be attributed to the excess of population in particular parts of the country; but that excess is in great part to be attributed to the mal-administration of the Poor-laws during the latter years of the late war.

Extract 9: from William Cobbett, 'To Lord John Russell, on the report of the Committee of the House of Commons to Inquire into the Practice of Paying the Wages of Labour out of the Poor-Rates', *Cobbett's Weekly Register* 51 (7) (14 August 1824): 387–96

We all knew the dismal facts before; but, here they are *confessed* by yourselves. It is necessary, that the world, that other nations, know the state in which we are; and these confessions of your own, of the big House itself, are, in this respect, of the greatest consequence. I propose to make some remarks upon this Report, and on the evidence attached to it. I propose to show how little, how very, very little, your Lordship and your colleagues of the Committee appear to know relative to the causes, the workings, or the effects of the evil you were inquiring about....

But, first of all, let me insist on my right to almost implicit confidence in what I may say with regard to this subject. For *seventeen years* I have been complaining of the calumnies heaped on the labourers by those who talked of the increase of the Poor-rates. In answer to MALTHUS, to STURGES BOURNE and the HAMPSHIRE PARSONS, to SCARLETT;[27] to all who reviled the poor as the robbers of the land, and who ascribe the increase in the amount of the Poor-rates to idleness in the labourers, to want of care, to dissolute habits, and the like; in answer to all these, I said, for years and years, 'it is not, in fact, an increase in Poor-rates; it is money raised under the name of Poor-rates, to be paid to the labourers *in the shape of wages*; and this, because it is the most effectual way of grinding down the labourer; a desire to do which has been created by the difficulties of the occupiers of the land, owing to the debt and taxes'. This was my answer to the whole of these revilers.

At last, at the end of about seventeen years, your Lordship and your Committee have found out, that it is not *Poor-rates* but that it is *miserable wages*, that the poor creatures get. And whose fault is this? What says your Report as to this question? What has been the cause of this standard of human misery? Your Report is not very distinct upon this head; but, there runs throughout this Report a sort of complaint against the *farmers*, as if they *gained* by this practice.

This is, perhaps (for I do not speak *positively*), as childish an idea, something as shallow as ever found its way into Parliamentary Report. The farmers the gainers by this oppression of the labourers! Why, the very thought seems to discover a want of capacity to know why a stool falls when its legs are knocked from under it. And yet this very idea, this worse than whimsical thought, appears to be looked upon as the brilliant star that gives light and character to the whole Report.

Let me strip the whole thing of its useless trappings, and place it naked before the reader. The Report says that this practice of paying wages out of Poor-rates, is used 'as a means of obliging the *parish* to pay for labour, which ought to be paid for by *private persons*'. – it says, that, by this practice, 'persons who have no need of farm-labour, are *obliged to contribute to the payment of work done for others*'. The meaning of which is this: that the farmers, by going to the poor-book for the wages, or part of the wages, of their labourers, make the gentlemen, the parsons, the traders, and all others, help to pay *for the work done for the farmers only.*

If this were so: if this were not a childish thought; if this had one single particle of common sense in it, what an admirable *cure* your Lordship and the Committee have provided! It is nothing short of this; that the Magistrates should 'point out to the farmers the *mischievous consequences* of placing their labourers upon the public fund!' Good God! '*Mischievous consequences?*' And, to *whom*, pray? Not to the *farmers*; for, your dislike of the practice, consists, in part, of the *gain* which arises to the farmers at the expense of the rest of the parish. Who, then, feels the '*mischievous consequences*'? The rest of the parish, to be sure; but not the farmers. To suppose, then, that the farmers will give up the practice, merely upon being told, that it is injurious to other persons, and that it tends to degrade the labourers; to suppose such a thing, really seems to be little short of a proof of downright childishness.

However, what sort of mind must that be, which can entertain this idea of *gain* to the *farmers* from such a cause? Is it not clear, that, upon an average, the farmers cannot be *gainers* (any more than other people) by this oppression of the labourers? If, by means of paying wages out of the poor-rates, the farmer (farmer JOBSON, for instance) gets his labour done for *a hundred pounds a-year*, instead of *two hundred pounds a-year*: if Jobson do this, is not his farm worth *a hundred a-year more*? And will not Jobson's *landlord* take care to have that additional hundred a-year? What, then, does Jobson *get* by the paying of wages out of Poor-rates? When a man goes to take a farm, he calculates *the amount of labour* amongst other things; and, if Jobson find, that the labour is made cheap by this resort to the poor-book, he will give so much more for the farm. It is nonsense to talk of men's *dispositions*, in a case like this: the landlord will, of course, let his farm to the highest bidder; and, if Jobson will not give a rent in due consideration of the payment of labour out of the Poor-rates, some other farmer will. It is a matter of *open market*; a matter of *fair competition*. Suppose that, in the parish of Ryegate, things were so situated as to cause JOBSON's labour (for a year) to be done, by means of Poor-rate payments, for *fifty pounds a-year*. Then suppose that, in the parish of Betchworth, adjoining the other, HODGE, who has precisely such a farm as JOBSON, is compelled to pay *a hundred and fifty pounds a-year for his labour.*[28] Does your lordship and your Committee of the Collective suppose, that HODGE and JOBSON would give *the same amount of rent*? No: you will hardly suppose this; and yet, this is what you must suppose, and must prove too, unless you give up as whimsical, as nonsensical, as childish in the extreme, the idea, that the *farmers* are the *gainers* by this oppressive practice.

If there were a particular class who gained by this practice, it would be *the landlords*. But, even this is taking a much too confined view of the matter. The gain is divided amongst all those who do not labour: it is a system of pure oppression, arising out of the taxes: all gain, in some sort; all who eat taxes; all gain from the labourer. The intermediate class do not suffer so much. When pressed, they press those below them: and, at last, when the pressure reaches the labourer, he is all but squeezed out of existence. Nothing can be more childish than to suppose, that those who own, or who occupy, the land, gain (unless they be tax-eaters) by this oppression of the labourers. Is it not clear, that, in whatever proportion the farm-labour is paid for by the community at large, *in that same proportion* farm produce must be *lower in price*? If a law were passed to cause the whole of the farm-labour to be paid by others than the farmers, is it not clear that farm produce would *sell for a great deal less* in consequence of this? A farmer would then be no better off than he is now. He would gain nothing by the change. His out-goings would be diminished; but, his prices (or in-comings) must diminish in the same proportion; or, he would soon find that competition would destroy him.

Thus, then, my LORD JOHN, away goes this pretty dream! The *cause* of this curious mode of oppressing the labourers is not to be found in the *disposition* nor in the *interest* of the farmers. It is to be found in that enormous load of taxes, which presses the several classes down upon each other: it is to be found in the Debt, in the Dead-weight, in the enormous amount of sinecures and pensions and grants: it is to be found in all these, and in that standing army in time of peace, which is now costing more than our army ought to cost in time of war. In short, the cause of this horrid effect is to be found in *Acts of Parliament*, to some one or other of which, or to some collections of them, every evil, now complained of, can be directly traced.

... It would have been surprising, indeed, to me, if a Report coming from such a quarter had forborne entirely from harping upon the string of '*surplus population*'. This monstrous idea is not so current as it was: people seem to be a little ashamed of repeating the ridiculous outcry. Still, you must have a little touch of it. One of the consequences, you say, of thus half starving the labouring people, is, to '*encourage* a surplus population'. Strange idea! That an increase of the population should be caused by keeping them in a state of half starvation! Now, you tell us, that, by this practice, the single man is made to work for *three shillings* a week; and a man and his wife for *four and sixpence*. This is fine *encouragement* to marry, to be sure! But, upon what ground do you assert that this practice encourages an increase of the people? You say: 'Men who receive but a small pittance, know that they have *only to marry*, and that pittance will be augmented *in proportion to the number of their children*'. What, then, getting but little from the parish, and wanting to get more, they marry in order to have a parcel of children! What, then, is your notion upon this matter, my Lord John? Your lordship, to the misfortune of the fair sex, is a bachelor, I believe; if you had been a married man, you would have known that children EAT. You would, indeed, my Lord John. They have all of them got mouths, not only to eat with, but to make a devilish noise with, if the eating do not come in proper time and quantity. So, that these labourers of yours, who marry in order to augment their own meal, must be fellows destitute of all calculation; and yet you tell us, that an intelligent witness, Mr. JOHN DAWES, assures you that the labourers say, 'we will marry, and then you must maintain us'. I do not believe this witness; and I am surprised why you should have believed him, in preference to two other of your witnesses. The Reverend PHILIP HUNT, and HENRY DRUMMOND, ESQ. The former tells you that '*very few labourers marry voluntarily*'. And the latter tells you this: 'I believe nothing is *more erroneous*, than the assertion, that Poor-laws tend to improvident marriages: I never knew an instance of a girl being married till she was *with child*; never ever knew of a marriage taking place *through a calculation for future support*'. Strange, indeed, my Lord John, that your report should be directly in the teeth of this evidence! Especially the evidence of Mr.

DRUMMOND, who, besides being an active Justice of the Peace, is well known to have taken uncommon pains in order to promote the well-being of the labouring classes. However, it is against nature to suppose, that a system which necessarily reduces people to a state of half starvation, should tend to the increase of that people.

This idea of a redundant population, can serve no other purpose than that of taking from the shoulders of the Government the charge of having produced such a state of misery.

Extract 10: from Nassau William Senior, *Three Lectures on the rate of wages, delivered before the University of Oxford in Easter Term, 1830, with a Preface on the Causes and Remedies of the Present Disturbances*, second edition (London: John Murray, 1830), pp. vi–xii, xiii–xiv

The principal cause of the calamities that we are witnessing, has been the disturbance which the poor-laws, as at present administered in the south of England, have created in the most important of all political relations, the relation between the employer and the labourer.

The slave (using that word in its strict sense) cannot choose his owner, his employment, or his residence; his whole services are the property of another, and their value, however high, gives him no additional claim. On the other hand, he is entitled to subsistence for himself and his family: clothing, lodging, food, medical attendance – everything, in short, which is necessary to keep him in health and strength is provided for him, from the same motives, and with the same liberality, that they are provided for the other domestic animals of his master. He is *bound* to labour, and has a *right* to be maintained. This, notwithstanding the various degrees of mitigation which have been introduced by custom or by law, is, in substance, the condition of slaves, wherever slavery exists. . . .

The freeman (using that term in its full meaning) is the master of his exertions, and of his residence. He may refuse to quit the spot, or to change the employment, in which his labour has become unprofitable. As he may refuse to labour at all, he may ask for his services whatever remuneration he thinks fit; but as no one is bound to purchase those services, and as no one is obliged to afford him food, clothing, or any of the necessaries of life, he is forced, if he would subsist, to follow the trade, and dwell in the place, and exert the diligence which will make his services worth purchasing; and he is forced to offer them for sale, by the same necessity which forces the capitalist to offer him wages in exchange for them. And the bargain is settled, like all other free bargains, by the respective market values of the things exchanged. As marriage has no tendency to increase the value of his labour, it has no tendency to increase his remuneration. He defers it, therefore, till the savings made while he was single afford a fund to meet the expenses of a family; and population is kept down by the only check that is consistent with moral or physical welfare – the prudential check.

To this state of things there is a near approach among the labouring classes in the most advanced districts of the continent of Europe, in the lowlands of Scotland, and even throughout the British empire, among the best educated of those classes who derive their chief subsistence from their exertions, including professional persons, domestic servants, skilled artisans, and that portion of the shopkeepers whose profits are, in fact, the wages of their labour.

The poor-laws, as administered in the southern districts of England, are an attempt to unite the irreconcilable advantages of freedom and servitude. The labourer is to be a free agent, but without the hazards of free agency; to be free from the coercion, but to enjoy the assured subsistence of the slave. He is expected to be diligent, though he has no fear of want; provident, though his pay rises as his family increases; attached to a master who employs him in pursuance of a vestry resolution;[29] and grateful for the allowance which the magistrates order him as a right.

In the natural state of the relation between the capitalist and the labourer, when the amount of wages to be paid, and of work to be done, are the subjects of a free and open bargain; when the labourer obtains, and knows that he is to obtain, just what his services are worth to his employer, he must feel any fall in the price of his labour to be an evil, but is not likely to complain of it as an injustice. Greater exertion and severer economy are his first resources in distress; and what they cannot supply, he receives with gratitude from the benevolent. The connexion between him and his master has the kindliness of a voluntary association, in which each party is conscious of benefit, and each feels that his own welfare depends, to a certain extent, on the welfare of the other. But the instant wages cease to be a bargain – the instant the labourer is paid, not according to his *value*, but his *wants*, he ceases to be a freeman. He acquires the indolence, the improvidence, the rapacity, and the malignity, but not the subordination of the slave. He is told that he has a *right* to wages, but that he is *bound* to work. Who is to decide how hard he ought to work, or how hard he does work? Who is to decide what amount of wages he has a *right* to? As yet, the decision has been made by the overseers and the magistrates. But they are interested parties. The labourer has thought fit to correct that decision. For the present he thinks he has a *right* to 2s. 3d. a day in winter and 2s. 6d. in summer. And our only hope seems to be, that the promise of such wages will bribe him into quiet. But who can doubt that he will measure his rights by his wishes, or that his wishes will extend with the prospect of their gratification? The present tide may not complete the inundation, but it will be a dreadful error if we mistake the ebb for a permanent receding of the waters. A breach has been made in the sea-wall, and with every succeeding irruption they will spread higher and spread more widely. What we are suffering is nothing to what we have to expect. Next year, perhaps, the labourer will think it *unjust* that he should have less than 4s. a day in winter and 5s. in summer; – and woe to the tyrants who deny him his *right*!

It is true, that such a right could not be permanently enforced; – it is true, that if the labourer burns the corn-ricks in which his subsistence for the current year is stored – if he consumes in idleness or in riot the time and the exertions on which next year's harvest depends – if he wastes in extravagant wages, or drives to foreign countries, the capital that is to assist and render productive his labour, *he* will be the greatest sufferer in the common ruin. Those who have property may escape with a portion of it to some country in which *their rights* will be protected; but the labourer must remain to enjoy his own works – to feel that the real rewards for plunder and devastation are want and disease....

Have sufficient means been taken even to expose the absurdity of what appears so obvious to the populace – that the landlords ought to reduce their rents and the clergy their tithes, and then the farmer would give better wages? If the farmer had his land for nothing, still it would not be his interest to give any man more wages for a day's work than his day's work was worth. He could better *afford* it, no doubt, to be paid as a *tax*; but why should the farmer pay that tax more than the physician or the shopkeeper? If the farmer is to employ, at this advanced rate of wages, only whom he chooses, the distress will be increased, since he will employ only that smaller number whose labour is worth their increased pay. If he is to employ a certain proportion of the labourers, however numerous, in his parish, he is, in fact, to pay rent and tithes as before, with this difference only, that they are paid to paupers, instead of to the landlord and the parson; and that the payment is not fixed but an indefinite sum, and a sum which must every year increase in an accelerated ratio, as the increase of population rushes to fill up this new vacuum, till rent, tithes, profit, and capital, are all eaten up, and pauperism produces what may be called its natural effects – for they are the effects which, if unchecked, it must ultimately produce – famine, pestilence, and civil war.

That this country can preserve its prosperity, or even its social existence, if the state of feeling which I have described becomes universal among the lower classes, I think no one will be bold enough to maintain. That it is extensively prevalent, and that, under the present administration of the poor-laws, it will, at no remote period, become universal in the southern districts, appears to me to be equally clear. But who, in the present state of those districts, will venture to carry into execution a real and effective alteration of the poor-laws? Remove, by emigration, the pauperism that now oppresses those districts, and such an alteration, though it may remain difficult, will cease to be impractical.

SELECT BIBLIOGRAPHY

Modern editions of Malthus

An Essay on the Principle of Population and *A Summary View of the Principle of Population*, ed. A. Flew (Harmondsworth: Penguin, 1970). Reprints, with minor amendments, the first 1798 edition of the *Essay*. This is the essential edition for anyone interested in placing the text within political debates of the 1790s.

An Essay on the Principle of Population, ed. D. Winch (Cambridge: Cambridge University Press, 1992). Reprints the much revised and expanded 1803 edition and includes Malthus's additions and corrections for the editions of 1806, 1807, 1817 and 1826. It is also richly annotated with useful additional material.

The Works of Thomas Robert Malthus, ed. E. A. Wrigley and D. Souden, 8 vols (London: Pickering and Chatto, 1986).

General studies

Copley, Stephen and Kathryn Sutherland, eds, *Adam Smith's 'Wealth of Nations': New Interdisciplinary Essays* (Manchester: Manchester University Press, 1995). A stimulating collection of Essays on political economy, several of them by literary scholars.

Hammond, J. L. and B. Hammond, *The Village Labourer* (London: Longman and Green, 1911). A pioneering work of critical social history. Essential reading. There are numerous modern editions.

Himmelfarb, Gertrude, *The Idea of Poverty: England in the Early Industrial Age* (London: Faber and Faber, 1984). A useful, sometimes provocative and always readable survey. Usually takes a contrary position to the Hammonds and Thompson. Chapters 1 to 5 are directly relevant.

Hobsbawm, Eric and George Rudé, *Captain Swing* (Harmondsworth: Penguin, 1973). The opening four chapters provide a brilliant overview of English rural society in this period.

James, Patricia, *Population Malthus: His Life and Times* (London: Routledge and Kegan Paul, 1979). The standard biography.

Polanyi, Karl, *The Great Transformation: The Political and Economic Origins of Our Time*, second edition (Boston: Beacon Press, 1957). An original and imaginative historical polemic against political economy, using this period of English social history as a case study.

Poynter, J. R., *Society and Pauperism: English Ideas on Poor Relief 1795–1834* (London: Routledge and Kegan Paul, 1969). A useful introductory survey of the topic.

Thompson, E. P., *The Making of the English Working Class*, second edition (Harmondsworth: Penguin, 1968). Probably the single most influential study of this period, deeply hostile to political economy in all its forms. Chapters 6, 7 and 16 are especially relevant.

Winch, Donald, *Malthus* (Oxford: Oxford University Press, 1987). Crisp, lucid and to the point.

3

ATHEISM

Martin Priestman

A comprehensive attempt to illustrate the complexities of religious debate in this period would take up far more than a single section of this book. Instead, this section aims to highlight a dimension of that debate which was then perceived as genuinely new: the possibility of atheism – the outright, declared disbelief in the existence of God. I say 'possibility' because defenders of religion had long argued that sincerely-held atheism was logically inconceivable, and the word 'atheist' itself was generally used more as an accusation than a straightforward description of an intellectual position.[1] Thus, while many arguments against at least the orthodox Christian view of God had been set in place during the rationalist 'Enlightenment' of the eighteenth century, it was not until 1782 that the first printed British declaration of atheism was made by William Hammon in a pamphlet called *Answer to Dr Priestley's Letters to a Philosophical Unbeliever*, to be followed only in 1796 by Samuel Francis's *Watson Refuted*, one of many pamphlets engendered in the controversy surrounding Thomas Paine's *The Age of Reason* (1793–5) which will be discussed below.[2]

At the time, readers would be well aware that such declarations of atheism deliberately went well beyond the more acceptable positions of scepticism and deism. Scepticism, associated pre-eminently with the philosopher David Hume, held that there was no rational basis for accepting either Christianity or the existence of God, but left open (often somewhat ironically) the possibility that faith could substitute for reason.[3] Deism, or 'natural religion', was the belief in a broadly benign creator of the universe, about whose attributes, beyond this initial power of design, it was futile to speculate. Within this position it was possible for deists to range from the acceptance of established Christianity as an important basis for morality, to a defiant repudiation of any doctrines which went beyond the simple affirmation of a universal creator. Examples of the former tendency included – or were thought to include – many of the most influential philosophers and scientists of the seventeenth- and eighteenth-century rationalist Enlightenment: Francis Bacon, John Locke, Isaac Newton and Lord Shaftesbury.[4] Many representatives of the latter tendency – such as John Toland and Thomas Woolston – were prosecuted for their outspokenness, since throughout the eighteenth century and well into the nineteenth, 'blasphemy against the Almighty, by denying his being or providence; or by contumelious reproach of our saviour Jesus Christ' was legally punishable: as late as 1763, Peter Annet was not only imprisoned but pilloried at the age of 70 for querying the divine inspiration of the opening books of the Old Testament.[5]

In this experience of legal suppression, the more outspoken deists had much in common with the non-Anglican Christian Dissenters – from whose ranks indeed many of them sprang, and many of whom had in turn incorporated some deist arguments in what became known as 'Rational Dissent'.[6] For the Dissenters, the struggle for toleration of their differing views had long been bound up with a concern for other liberties, such as more representation in Parliament and limits to the powers of a monarchy seen as parasitic on the taxes of the (often Dissenting) middle class. Deist and Dissenting voices were thus often hard to disentangle in the radical rhetoric of universal human rights which rose to a climax in the wake of the 1789 French Revolution. Hence two of the period's leading political radicals were Thomas Paine (1737–1809), a militant deist from a Dissenting Quaker background, and Joseph Priestley (1733–1804), a Dissenting Unitarian minister who devoted considerable energy to refuting the anti-Christian arguments of Paine's *The Age of Reason* while at the same time campaigning for many of the political goals outlined in his *The Rights of Man* (1791–2).

The newly outspoken atheism, then, was by no means the only religiously radical or dangerously freethinking position available at the time (indeed, Hammon's self-declaration was a direct response to Priestley's deliberately provocative call for an open debate on religion, regardless of the blasphemy laws). None the less, atheism was clearly perceived as a step into newly dangerous territory, especially after the French Revolution's brief establishment of the worship of pure 'Reason' in Notre Dame Cathedral in 1793.[7] It was widely understood that much of the momentum towards the Revolution had been built up earlier in the eighteenth century by the freethinking intellectuals known as *philosophes*. While some of these – such as Jean-Jacques Rousseau – were deistic believers in natural religion, many others – such as Claude-Adrien Helvétius and Baron D'Holbach – were atheistic materialists.[8] Owing much to the Greek philosopher Epicurus and the Latin poet Lucretius, their type of materialism maintained that the universe consisted entirely of matter, which lasted for ever though in ever-changing combinations, and was intrinsically active and hence required no external force to set it in motion. To many British Christians – even initially radical ones such as Samuel Taylor Coleridge – the Revolution's espousal of such views simply underlined the intrinsic godlessness of the French; and though there had long been much more British sympathy for Rousseau's deism, the imposition in 1794 of a Rousseauist cult of 'The Supreme Being' by the bloodstained Robespierre led to a new distrust of deism too, as tarred with much the same brush.[9]

This distrust was confirmed by the British Government's comprehensive and much-repeated attempts to suppress *The Age of Reason*, which Paine published while in a Paris jail under sentence of imminent execution, as a challenge to the full-blown atheism into which he saw the Revolution as slipping. None the less, pirated editions of its bluntly disrespectful critique of established Christianity made many anti-religious arguments newly available to a common readership and largely began the 'atheizing' of working-class radicalism.

Another area of intellectual enquiry developing rapidly in the early nineteenth century made some position on the origin and operation of the universe particularly hard to sidestep: the physical sciences. For some writers, certainly, science simply reinforced the truths of Christianity: William Paley's *Natural Theology* (1802) argued that every new discovery confirmed the 'argument from design'; and after a youth of less orthodox opinions, the great physicist Humphry Davy defended a Christian interpretation of the universe in his last book *Consolations in Travel* (1830). For the atheist Painite publisher Richard Carlile in 1821, on the other hand, the new scientific developments had finally proved the case for materialism, and it was now the duty of scientists to stand up and declare their atheism.

At the very start of the new century, however, a survivor of the radical 1780s and 1790s such as Erasmus Darwin (1731–1802) could still use deist language as a flag of convenience for largely materialist scientific arguments. **Extract 1**, from his last poem, *The Temple of Nature* (1803), demonstrates the well-practised eighteenth-century technique by which a rejection of divine agency at any serious level is given a deistic coating by occasional allusions to a philosophically necessary 'first cause'. Darwin's derivation of the present universe from an initial cosmic explosion, and of human and all other forms of life from a combination of 'spontaneous generation' and evolutionary adaptation, was extraordinarily radical for its time, the latter theory being not just an anticipation but a source of his grandson Charles Darwin's evolutionism. A doctor and practising scientist, Darwin was a leading member of the Birmingham-based 'Lunar Society' along with Priestley, Josiah Wedgwood (1730–95) and James Watt (1736–1819), and simultaneously a key influence on many of the major Romantic poets: in 1797 Coleridge called him 'the first *literary* character in Europe, and the most original-minded man'.[10] Though widely seen, by the closing stage of his previously acclaimed career, as a dangerous old-style infidel and radical, Darwin shows here his unique ability to make cutting-edge science more, rather than less, succinct and accessible by versifying it. Part of his prose 'Additional Note on Spontaneous Vitality' is also included to demonstrate more fully the science behind the – actually false – argument that life can repeatedly generate itself, as a feasible starting-point for the evolutionary hypothesis.

The political philosopher William Godwin's essay 'Of Religion', written in 1818 but unpublished until 1993 (**extract 2**), indicates in a different way the difficulties of a known radical and long-suspected atheist in being completely open about his religious disbelief. Though the rationalist anarchism of his *An Enquiry into Political Justice* (1793) was a constant reference-point for the Wordsworth/Coleridge generation's political and religious agonizings, Godwin's well-developed instinct for survival led him to leave the clearest expressions of his atheism unpublished until after his death. While unequivocal in its account of his personal 'conversion from Christianity' and from the notion of an afterlife which even Paine had attempted to retain, 'Of Religion' also suggests another tendency long ingrained within intellectual scepticism: the fear of releasing the 'elite' truth of atheism among the masses who might be unable to handle it. As a solution, Godwin proposes a cult of nature, imagination and the creative arts which retains elements of deist feeling and tallies closely with the programme of contemporary Romantic poets such as Wordsworth.

Godwin's son-in-law Percy Bysshe Shelley (1792–1822) is perhaps the best known of a new generation of outspoken atheists who refused to shelter behind deist terminology. His pamphlet 'The Necessity of Atheism' (1811), for which he and his friend T. J. Hogg were expelled from Oxford, rests mainly on the argument that belief is not voluntary but like other passions depends on certain 'excitements', all of which are lacking in the case of the existence of God (**extract 3**). There is no direct proof of it to the senses; it is harder to believe in a creator than the eternity of matter; and the testimony of others cannot persuade us when the other 'excitements' are lacking. Shelley's later and more fully argued *A Refutation of Deism*, published in 1814 (**extract 4**), is structured as a Platonic dialogue in which the Painite arguments of the deist 'Theosophus' are undermined by the orthodox Christian 'Eusebes', who uses a battery of sceptical and materialist arguments from such writers as Hume and D'Holbach to show that there is no viable halfway point between an irrational acceptance of Christian revelation and the full-blown atheism which Theosophus himself has described as a 'dark and terrible doctrine'. In refusing to allow either protagonist to show any emotional preference for atheism, Shelley deliberately presents his readers with a stark choice. If the deist middle ground is no longer philosophically tenable, can its previous occupants cope with the impoverished emotional associations of atheism, or will they need to come 'in from the cold' to the unchallengeable certainties of faith?

In 1812 Shelley's 'Letter to Lord Ellenborough' attacked the prosecution of Daniel Isaac Eaton for publishing part of Paine's *Age of Reason*. It was in large part through repeated illegal publications of Paine's book that the deist/atheist debate kept itself on the road and in the public eye. Its most dogged publisher was Richard Carlile, who also cheerfully pirated Shelley's less respectable works (such as his 1813 poem *Queen Mab*). Though he published Paine and other anti-Christian texts in a periodical called *The Deist* (1819), Carlile soon saw that title as inadequate to what was really becoming a campaign for popular atheism. By the time of his *Address to Men of Science* (1821), from which **extract 5** is taken, all deist compromise is rejected in favour of a thoroughgoing atheism which will, Carlile argues, remain a highly exposed and vulnerable position unless and until the 'men of science' collectively speak up for the truths they are politically cowed into suppressing. Carlile's *Address* explicitly links science and religion with political struggle, not least in the place and time from which it is literally 'addressed': 'Dorchester Gaol, May 1821. Eighteenth Month of the Author's Imprisonment and the Fourth Month of the Imprisonment of his Wife.' Having chosen six years' imprisonment rather than pay a massive fine intended to destroy his business, Carlile loudly proclaims his and his first wife Jane's readiness to sustain such punishments for the sake of the truths their press will continue to publish: 'I will give every Man of Science an opportunity of publishing his sentiments without any direct danger to himself: I will fill the gap of persecution for him.'[11]

One major response to this invitation is represented (**extract 6**) by the utilitarian tract *An Analysis of the Influence of Natural Religion on the Temporal Happiness of Mankind* (1822), acknowledged as a formative influence by John Stuart Mill in his *Autobiography* (1873).[12] While the authorial pseudonym 'Philip Beauchamp' acknowledges the continuing danger of public declarations of atheism, the pamphlet's real author would appear to be the classical scholar George Grote, acting in close collaboration with the ageing father of utilitarianism, Jeremy Bentham. Despite the earlier worries of Godwin (himself an influence on utilitarianism) that too rapid a disillusionment of the masses might lead to a breakdown of public order, the *Analysis* insists precisely on the social *non*-utility of even the most deistically 'natural' religion. Bred to expect rational rewards and punishments only in an unreal future state, and to disbelieve the 'experimental' evidence of their own senses, the common people will only be released into true and rational morality precisely by the destruction of such shibboleths. What is perhaps most striking in the passage excerpted is the repetitive, legalistic terminology, so effectively parodied in the figure of Mr Gradgrind in Charles Dickens's *Hard Times* (1854).[13] It is worth remembering, however, that such apparently dogmatic insistence on 'facts' was founded initially on a passionate commitment to a radical re-education of the masses in favour of their own certifiable experience.

On Bentham's death in 1832, one obituarist approved of him as a fellow 'philosophical infidel' but felt that his writings had 'nothing of electrical excitement in them, as in the writings of Thomas Paine'.[14] This was Eliza Sharples, writing as 'The Lady of the Rotunda' in her periodical *The Isis*, described by G. D. H. Cole as 'the first journal produced by a woman in support of sex equality and political and religious freedom'.[15] The leading articles reproduced Sharples's speeches at the Rotunda, a Blackfriars lecture theatre leased by the then-imprisoned Richard Carlile, whose common-law wife she became in 1833. **Extract 7**, reprinted here from the first of these articles, conveys something of the 'electrical excitement'

Sharples aims at as she helps to 'direct the coming storm' in the agitation leading up to the 1832 Reform Bill: she demands to be accepted by the men in the audience as a 'general', and by the women as a guide towards an equality denied them by religion. While similar linkages between proto-feminism, social egalitarianism and religious freethought had previously been made by such 1790s radicals as Mary Wollstonecraft and Mary Hays, neither had been an out-and-out atheist: though Wollstonecraft's husband Godwin wrote approvingly of her lack of reference to God at her death, her writings bespeak an idiosyncratic brand of deism, and Hays's denunciations of 'superstition' in *Memoirs of Emma Courtney* (1796) and elsewhere have to be read in the light of her principled unitarianism.[16] In her frankly atheist feminism, Sharples acknowledged as her chief inspiration Frances Wright (1795–1852), whose 1829 lectures on subjects ranging from Epicurus to the abolition of slavery drew large crowds in America and were reproduced in *Isis*.[17]

In the first third of the nineteenth century, then, atheism was present in or intersected with many other discourses – political, scientific, educational and sexual, as well as philosophical and religious. While some of its strands continued through the century – in utilitarianism, Owenite socialism[18] and various attempts to organize congregations on a quasi-sectarian basis – the prevalent image of a Victorian age of settled religious faith only occasionally disturbed by isolated cases of 'honest doubt' is not completely inaccurate. Repeated prosecutions under the blasphemy laws were partly responsible for this, but so were the undoubted organizational successes of Evangelicalism, Methodism and other revivalist move-ments, compared to which the notion of a sect devoted to proving the non-validity of sects was hard to sustain. If working-class and socialist organizations offered an important alternative home for atheist views, too much potential support would have been alienated if these had appeared very high on the agenda. Perhaps, finally, the stark choice presented by Shelley's *Refutation of Deism* was prophetic: with the rationalist undermining of the eighteenth-century compromise of 'natural religion' complete, for many the only choice left was between irrationalist religious fundamentalism and an atheism too 'dark and terrible' to contemplate.

Extract 1: from Erasmus Darwin, *The Temple of Nature* (1803)[19]

GOD THE FIRST CAUSE! – in this terrene abode   223
Young Nature lisps, she is the child of GOD.[20]
From embryon births her changeful forms improve,
Grow, as they live, and strengthen as they move.

Ere Time began, from flaming Chaos hurl'd
Rose the bright spheres, which form the circling world;
Earths from each sun with quick explosions burst,
And second planets issued from the first.   230

71

Then, whilst the sea at their coeval birth,
Surge over surge, involved the shoreless earth;
Nurs'd by warm sun-beams in primeval caves
Organic Life began beneath the waves.[21]

First HEAT from chemic dissolution springs,
And gives to matter its eccentric wings;
With strong REPULSION parts the exploding mass,
Melts into lymph, or kindles into gas.
ATTRACTION next, as earth or air subsides,
The ponderous atoms from the light divides,   240
Approaching parts with quick embrace combines,
Swells into spheres, and lengthens into lines.
Last, as fine goads the gluten-threads excite,
Cords grapple cords, and webs with webs unite;
And quick CONTRACTION with ethereal flame
Lights into life the fibre-woven frame. –
Hence without parent by spontaneous birth
Rise the first specks of animated earth;[22]
From Nature's womb the plant or insect swims,
And buds or breathes, with microscopic limbs. . . .   250

Organic Life beneath the shoreless waves   295
Was born and nurs'd in Ocean's pearly caves;[23]
First forms minute, unseen by spheric glass,
Move on the mud, or pierce the watery mass;
These, as successive generations bloom,
New powers acquire, and larger limbs assume;   300
Whence countless groups of vegetation spring,
And breathing realms of fin, and feet, and wing.

Thus the tall Oak, the giant of the wood,
Which bears Britannia's thunders on the flood;
The whale, unmeasured monster of the main,
The lordly lion, monarch of the plain,
The eagle soaring in the realms of air,
Whose eye undazzled drinks the solar glare,
Imperious man, who rules the bestial crowd,
Of language, reason, and reflection proud,   310
With brow erect who scorns this earthy sod,
And styles himself the image of his God;
Arose from rudiments of form and sense,
An embryon point, or microscopic ens![24]   314

72

From Additional Note 1, *Spontaneous Vitality of
Microscopic Animals* (glossing especially the above lines
247–8: 'Hence without parent by spontaneous birth/ Rise
the first specks of animated earth')

From the misconception of the ignorant or superstitious it has been thought somewhat profane to speak in favour of spontaneous vital production, as if it contradicted holy writ; which says, that God created animals and vegetables. They do not recollect that God created all things which exist, and that these have been from the beginning in a perpetual state of improvement; which appears from the globe itself, as well as from the animals and vegetables, which possess it. And lastly, that there is more dignity in our idea of the supreme author of all things, when we conceive him to be the cause of causes, than the cause simply of the events, which we see, if there can be any difference in infinity of power!

Another prejudice which has prevailed against the spontaneous production of vitality, seems to have arisen from the misrepresentation of this doctrine, as if the larger animals had been thus produced; as Ovid supposes after the deluge of Deucalion, that lions were seen rising out of the mud of the Nile, and struggling to disentangle their hinder parts.[25] It was not considered, that animals and vegetables have been perpetually improving by reproduction; and that spontaneous vitality was only to be looked for in the simplest organic beings, as in the smallest microscopic animalcules;[26] which perpetually, perhaps hourly, enlarge themselves by reproduction, like the roots of tulips from seed, or the buds of seedling trees, which die annually, leaving others by solitary reproduction rather more perfect than themselves for many successive years, till at length they acquire sexual organs or flowers.

A third prejudice against the existence of spontaneous vital productions has been the supposed want of analogy;[27] this has also arisen from the expectation, that the larger or more complicated animals should be thus produced; which have acquired their present perfection by successive generations during an uncounted series of ages. Add to this, that the want of analogy opposes the credibility of all new discoveries, as of the magnetic needle, and coated electric jar, and Galvanic pile; which should therefore certainly be well weighed and nicely investigated before distinct credence is given them; but then the want of analogy must at length yield to repeated ocular demonstration. . . .

. . . [M]icroscopic animals are believed to possess a power of generating others like themselves by solitary reproduction without sex; and these gradually enlarging and improving for innumerable successive generations.

Mr Ellis in Phil. Transact. V.LlX. gives drawings of six kinds of animalcula infusoria,[28] which increase by dividing across the middle into two distinct animals. Thus in paste composed of flour and water, which has been suffered to become acescent, the animalcules called eels, vibrio anguillula, are seen in great abundance; their motions are rapid and strong; they are viviparous, and produce at intervals a numerous progeny: animals similar to these are also found in vinegar: Naturalist's Miscellany by Shaw and Nodder, Vol. II.[29] These e[e]ls were probably at first as minute as other microscopic animalcules; but by frequent, perhaps hourly reproduction, have gradually become the large animals above described, possessing wonderful strength and activity.

To suppose the eggs of the former microscopic animals to float in the atmosphere, and pass through the sealed glass phial, is so contrary to apparent nature, as to be totally incredible! and as the latter are viviparous, it is equally absurd to suppose, that their parents float universally in the atmosphere to lay their young in paste or vinegar! ...

There is therefore no absurdity in believing that the most simple animals and vegetables may be produced by the congress of the parts of decomposing organic matter, without what can properly be termed generation, as the genus did not previously exist; which accounts for the endless varieties, as well as for the immense numbers of microscopic animals.

Extract 2: from William Godwin, 'Of Religion' (1818), in Mark Philp, ed., *Political and Philosophical Writings of William Godwin*, vol. 7, *Religious Writings* (London: William Pickering, 1993), pp. 63–73[30]

I am an unbeliever. I am thoroughly satisfied that no book in existence contains a record and history of the revelation of the will of an invisible being, the master of us all, to his creatures.

So much has been said by the clergy in successive ages, of the indirect and slender grounds upon which the party of infidelity has been embraced, that I desire my unbelief may stand for what it is worth.

I do not wish to speak for myself on the subject of my moral character. If my integrity and the irreproachableness of my life can be sustained by no other evidence than my own, let them not be sustained. I suppose few persons can have less reason, founded on their deviation from moral rectitude, for apprehending evil to themselves on the supposition of a future state.

Setting aside therefore the idea of any sinister motives I can have for embracing the party of infidelity, let it next be enquired, whether I have bestowed on this question a sufficiently patient and strict examination.

I was bred after the strictest and severest forms of Christian religion.[31] By many I was regarded in my infancy as a saint, and as set apart for the public service of God from my mother's womb.

When I arrived, at seventeen years of age and after, to the exercise of my understanding, the original impressions of my mind became modified by an earnest passion for the discovery of truth. A thousand times, during the period of my collegiate life, I repeated to myself, 'I will follow truth, whithersoever she shall lead me.' I saw into how many sects and varieties of opinion mankind were divided, and how laborious and difficult an undertaking it must be, to discover, among all these wanderings and complexities, which was the path most untainted with error. But my passion for truth was pure; and I viewed with contempt and aversion the idea that I should ultimately become the dupe of a mistaken faith.

Notwithstanding however all my intrepidity and good resolutions, there were two things that shackled me in the exercise of my understanding. First, my personal situation. What would my friends say to me, if the progress of my enquiries should be terminated in unbelief? What a gauntlet of reproach and calumny would await me? What also would become of my prospects and destination in life? To what class of mankind and what profession should I belong? Add to this, I had by no means that confidence in my own infallibility, to think that my enquiries must necessarily terminate in unerring truth. Secondly, I had the dreadful denunciations of the gospel hanging over me; directed against those, who having all the advantages of Christian light and evidence, yet concluded in unbelief. 'The heart of man,' I had read, 'is deceitful above all things, and desperately wicked.'[32] I was deeply impressed with the complexity of human motive, and the impossibility that a man should know, that evidence alone governed him in his conclusions.

These were appalling considerations. Yet I worked on as well as I could. Whatever were my demerits in other respects, I was persevering and indefatigable in research. I would sooner have died, than wittingly have suffered myself to be biased by sinister and indirect motives in favour of what was not truth.

Under the operation of all these causes, I think I may say that I remained a Christian, till the year 1781. In the year following I reverted to Christianity under the mitigated form of Socinianism;[33] for the impressions of my early youth had laid too deep a hold upon me to be suddenly shaken off.

In 1783 I took my final leave of the clerical profession,[34] and thus was delivered from one of those trains of motives, which unconsciously, yet unavoidably, biased me in my conclusions. It however cost me five years more, before I finally settled into that creed on the subject of revelation, which alone is worthy of the enlightened man in all ages and all countries. Long after all considerations of reputation and my condition of life ceased to restrain me in my inference, the terrible consequences as to a future state, of a final error in this momentous point, hung over and alarmed me. . . .

Indeed it is idle to suppose, that the Christian doctrine of a future state can upon general grounds be of much value. On which side lies its practical use? In the fear of future punishment? As far as that moulds the human character, we must be the veriest slaves that imagination can conceive. We have a tyrant perpetually controling us with his lash, with this additional horror, that he is acquainted with all our most secret motions, and sits like Jeremy Bentham, perched on the top of his Panopticon to spy into our weaknesses.[35] In this sense there is much force in the question proposed by Nathaniel, the Israelite, Can there any good thing come out of Nazareth?[36] Does the utility then of the doctrine of a future state lie in the hope of reward? But we have no idea of this reward; and all the conception that is suggested to us, is of tranquil existence and an inactive eternity. Either ways, the principle of virtue as it exists in a well formed mind, is immediately converted into a refined and long-sighted selfishness. . . .

Yet, notwithstanding all this, the removal of this fabulous and imaginary restraint upon human excesses may be dangerous to vulgar minds.[37] The morality of persons of this class hangs by a very slender thread. It was first learned as a set of rules imposed on them by parents and masters. They have never had their minds penetrated with the intrinsic excellence and beauty of temperance and benevolence, and are principally guided by considerations drawn from the opinions others will form respecting them, and from the denunciations of the criminal law. To such persons it may be truly dangerous to take away a motive, which perhaps never had any real influence upon them, but which stood there speciously upon record, and was spoken of by all men with respect. It is like taking away the extended ribband which divided the garden of the Thuillerries in the time of the French Revolution, upon the removal of which the whole mob rushed in impetuously, like the billows in a tempest.[38] The morality of such persons is sustained by so fragile considerations, that the introduction of any variety may be mischievous. Before, they were not governed by the sanctions of religion, and thought of them scarcely at all; but take away those sanctions, and you set their minds to work, and compel them to enquire, What have we lost, and what have we gained by the change?

I am therefore disposed to timidity and caution as to the sudden promulgation of principles of infidelity to persons without education, or not accustomed to habits of firm and manly reflection. But what then? Is the truth never to be told? Is one generation of men after another to be trained in the dreams of superstition without remedy and without end? Oh, no! The danger is only in the change. No man is the worse for not being a Christian; but some men may be the worse for being now Christians, and shortly after having the veil removed from their eyes. A blind man restored to sight will not immediately be able to conduct himself, and if some precaution be not used, a tragical accident may befal him. I should say the same thing here therefore as in the question of political improvement. Address yourself first to the men of reflection; do not inflame the passions of the vulgar; I plainly see that the number of the first of these classes is continually increasing; and it will need only a steady and watchful prudence, to enable us insensibly to expand the benefit to all without mischief. . . .

What then is the religion that remains to a race of men, who should see the whole system of things in the same light that I do? In the first place, they will be what I have already called lovers of nature. But we may go somewhat beyond this. To me a gallery of admirable paintings is the genuine Temple of God, understanding by the term God what I have just attempted to delineate. Let me be surrounded with the landscapes of Claude and the figures of Michael Angelo, and I am then in the proper theatre of admiration and worship.[39] This gallery is next in order to nature itself; with this advantage over such nature as I can come at, that I must travel to the ends of the earth before I can behold real landscapes such as Claude sets before me, and real figures, so sublime, so grand, so in the loftiest style of poetical conception, as Michael Angelo carved. To bring this still nearer to our idea of a temple, let concerts of music be from time to time performed in this gallery; let me witness in it the execution of the finest compositions of Handel.[40] In that case I shall be sure to see assembled, in addition to the works of art that adorn the walls, a number of human beings seated in decent order, dressed with more than their normal attention to neatness and propriety, and with their countenances composed to serenity and happiness.

Extract 3: Percy Bysshe Shelley, 'The Necessity of Atheism' (Worthing: E. W. Phillips, 1811)[41]

Quod clarâ et perspicuâ demonstratione careat pro vero habere mens omnino nequis humana.

BACON de Augment. Scient.[42]

ADVERTISEMENT

As a love of truth is the only motive which actuates the Author of this little tract, he earnestly entreats that those of his readers who may discover any deficiency in his reasoning, or may be in possession of proofs which his mind could never obtain, would offer them, together with their objections to the Public, as briefly, as methodically, as plainly, as he has taken the liberty of doing. Thro' deficiency of proof,
AN ATHEIST.

A close examination of the validity of the proofs adduced to support any proposition, has ever been allowed to be the only sure way of attaining truth, upon the advantages of which it is unnecessary to descant; our knowledge of the existence of a Deity is a subject of such importance, that it cannot be too minutely investigated; in consequence of this conviction, we proceed briefly and impartially to examine the proofs which have been adduced. It is necessary first to consider the nature of Belief.

When a proposition is offered to the mind, it perceives the agreement or disagreement of the ideas of which it is composed. A perception of their agreement is termed belief, many obstacles frequently prevent this perception from being immediate, these the mind attempts to remove in order that the perception may be distinct. The mind is active in the investigation, in order to perfect the state of perception, which is passive; the investigation being confused with the perception has induced many falsely to imagine that the mind is active in belief, that belief is an act of volition, in consequence of which it may be regulated by the mind; pursuing, continuing this mistake they have attached a degree of criminality to disbelief of which in its nature it is incapable; it is equally so of merit.

The strength of belief like that of every other passion is in proportion to the degrees of excitement.

The degrees of excitement are three.

The senses are the sources of all knowledge to the mind, consequently their evidence claims the strongest assent.

The decision of the mind founded upon our own experience derived from these sources claims the next degree.

The experience of others which addresses itself to the former one, occupies the lowest degree. –

Consequently no testimony can be admitted which is contrary to reason, reason is founded on the evidence of our senses.

Every proof may be referred to one of these three divisions; we are naturally led to consider what arguments we receive from each of them to convince us of the existence of a Deity.

1st. The evidence of the senses. – If the Deity should appear to us, if he should convince our senses of his existence; this revelation would necessarily command belief; – Those to whom the Deity has thus appeared, have the strongest possible conviction of his existence.

Reason claims the 2nd place, it is urged that man knows that whatever is, must either have had a beginning or existed from all eternity, he also knows that whatever is not eternal must have had a cause. – Where this is applied to the existence of the universe, it is necessary to prove that it was created, until that is clearly demonstrated, we may reasonably suppose that it has endured from all eternity. – In a case where two propositions are diametrically opposite, the mind believes that which is less incomprehensible, it is easier to suppose that the universe has existed from all eternity, than to conceive a being capable of creating it; if the mind sinks beneath the weight of one, is it an alleviation to increase the intolerability of the burden? – The other argument which is founded upon a man's knowledge of his own existence stands thus. – A man knows not only he now is, but that there was a time when he did not exist, consequently there must have been a cause. – But what does this prove? we can only infer from effects causes exactly adequate to those effects, – But there certainly is a generative power which is effected by particular instruments; we cannot prove that it is inherent in those instruments, nor is the contrary hypothesis capable of demonstration; we admit that the generative power is incomprehensible, but to suppose that the same effect is produced by an eternal, omniscient, Almighty Being, leaves the cause in the same obscurity, but renders it more incomprehensible.

The 3rd. and last degree of assent is claimed by Testimony – it is required that it should not be contrary to reason. The testimony that the Deity convinces the senses of men of his existence can only be admitted by us if our mind considers it less probable that these men should have been deceived, than that the Deity should have appeared to them – our reason can never admit the testimony of men, who not only declare that they were eye-witnesses of miracles but that the deity was irrational, for he commanded that he should be believed, he proposed the highest rewards for faith, eternal punishments for disbelief – we can only command voluntary actions, belief is not an act of volition, the mind is even passive, from this it is evident that we have not sufficient testimony, or rather that testimony is insufficient to prove the being of a God, we have before shewn that it cannot be deduced from reason, – they who have been convinced by the evidence of the senses, they only can believe it.

From this it is evident that having no proofs from any of the three sources of conviction: the mind cannot believe the existence of a God, it is also evident that as belief is a passion of the mind, no degree of criminality can be attached to disbelief, they only are reprehensible who willingly neglect to remove the false medium thro' which their mind views the subject.

It is almost unnecessary to observe, that the general knowledge of the deficiency of such proof, cannot be prejudicial to society: Truth has always been found to promote the best interests of mankind. – Every reflecting mind must allow that there is no proof of the existence of a Deity. Q.E.D.

Extract 4: from Percy Bysshe Shelley, *A Refutation of Deism: In a Dialogue* (London: Schulze and Dean, 1814)[43]

What then is this harmony, this order which you maintain to have required for its establishment, what it needs not for its maintenance, the agency of a supernatural intelligence?[44] Inasmuch as the order visible in the Universe requires one cause, so does the disorder whose operation is not less clearly apparent, demand another. Order and disorder are no more than modifications of our own perceptions of the relations which subsist between ourselves and external objects, and if we are justified in inferring the operation of a benevolent power from the advantages attendant on the former, the evils of the latter bear equal testimony to the activity of a malignant principle, no less pertinacious in inducing evil out of good, than the other is unremitting in procuring good from evil.

If we permit our imagination to traverse the obscure regions of possibility, we may doubtless imagine, according to the complexion of our minds, that disorder may have a relative tendency to unmingled good, or order be relatively replete with exquisite and subtle evil. To neither of these conclusions, which are equally presumptuous and unfounded, will it become the philosopher to assent.

Order and disorder are expressions denoting our perceptions of what is injurious or beneficial to ourselves, or to the beings in whose welfare we are compelled to sympathize by the similarity of their conformation to our own.[45]

A beautiful antelope panting under the fangs of a tiger, a defenceless ox groaning beneath the butcher's axe, is a spectacle which instantly awakens compassion in a virtuous and unvitiated breast. Many there are, however, sufficiently hardened to the rebukes of justice and the precepts of humanity, as to regard the deliberate butchery of thousands of their species as a theme of exultation and a source of honour, and to consider any failure in these remorseless enterprises as a defect in the system of things. The criteria of order and disorder are as various as those beings from whose opinions and feelings they result.

Populous cities are destroyed by earthquakes and desolated by pestilence. Ambition is everywhere devoting its millions to incalculable calamity. Superstition, in a thousand shapes, is employed in brutalizing and degrading the human species, and fitting it to endure without a murmur the oppression of its innumerable tyrants. All this is abstractedly neither good nor evil because good and evil are words employed to designate that peculiar state of our own perceptions, resulting from the encounter of any object calculated to produce pleasure or pain. Exclude the idea of relation, and the words good and evil are deprived of import.

Earthquakes are injurious to the cities which they destroy, beneficial to those whose commerce was injured by their prosperity, and indifferent to others which are too remote to be affected by their influence. Famine is good to the corn-merchant, evil to the poor, and indifferent to those whose fortunes can at all times command a superfluity. Ambition is evil to the restless bosom it inhabits, to the innumerable victims who are dragged by its ruthless thirst for infamy, to expire in every variety of anguish, to the inhabitants of the country it depopulates, and to the human race whose improvement it retards; it is indifferent with regard to the system of the Universe, and is good only to the vultures and the jackalls that track the conqueror's career, and to the worms who feast in security on the desolation of his progress. It is manifest that we cannot reason with respect to the universal system from that which only exists in relation to our own perceptions....

Thus, from the principles of that reason to which you so rashly appealed as the ultimate arbiter of our dispute, have I shewn that the popular arguments in favor of the being of a God are totally destitute of colour. I have shown the absurdity of attributing intelligence to the cause of those effects which we perceive in the Universe, and the fallacy which lurks in the argument from design. I have shewn that order is no more than a peculiar manner of contemplating the operation of necessary agents, that mind is the effect, not the cause of motion, that power is the attribute, not the origin of Being. I have proved that we can have no evidence of the existence of a God from the principles of reason....

Now, O Theosophus, I call upon you to decide between Atheism and Christianity; to declare whether you will pursue your principles to the destruction of the bonds of civilized society, or wear the easy yoke of that Religion which proclaims 'peace upon earth, good-will to all men.'

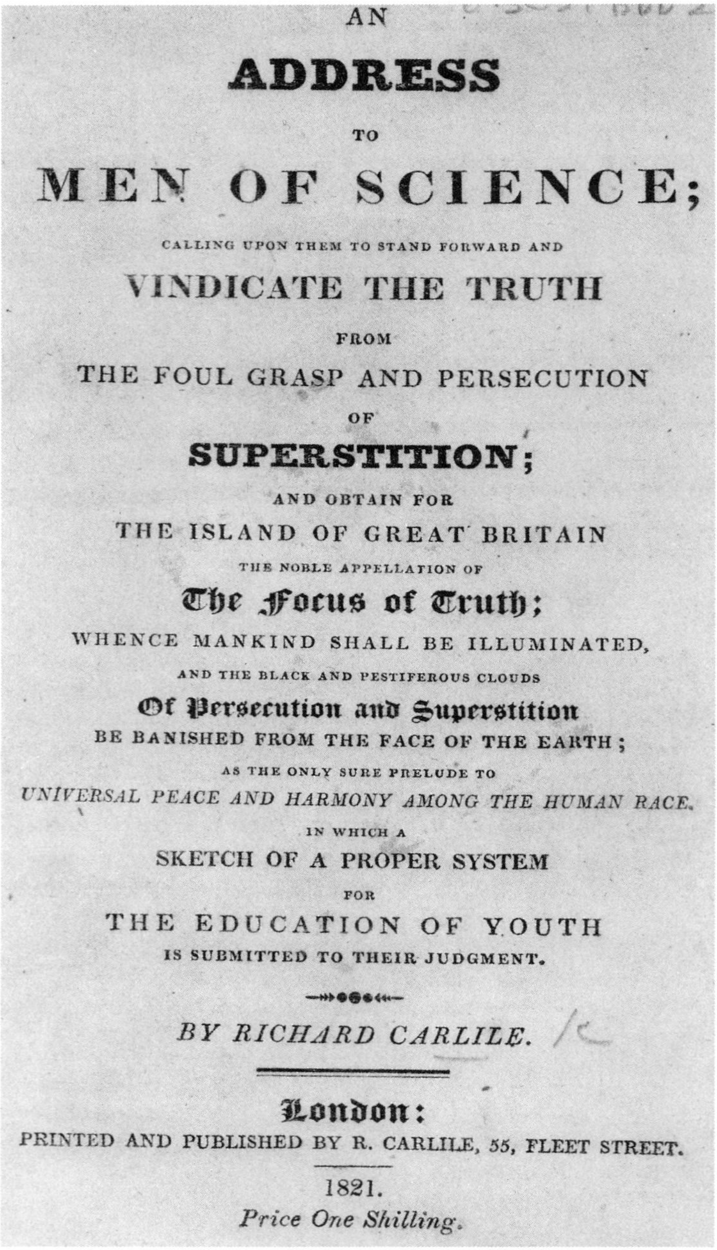

AN

ADDRESS

TO

MEN OF SCIENCE;

CALLING UPON THEM TO STAND FORWARD AND

VINDICATE THE TRUTH

FROM

THE FOUL GRASP AND PERSECUTION

OF

SUPERSTITION;

AND OBTAIN FOR

THE ISLAND OF GREAT BRITAIN

THE NOBLE APPELLATION OF

The Focus of Truth;

WHENCE MANKIND SHALL BE ILLUMINATED,

AND THE BLACK AND PESTIFEROUS CLOUDS

Of Persecution and Superstition

BE BANISHED FROM THE FACE OF THE EARTH;

AS THE ONLY SURE PRELUDE TO

UNIVERSAL PEACE AND HARMONY AMONG THE HUMAN RACE.

IN WHICH A

SKETCH OF A PROPER SYSTEM

FOR

THE EDUCATION OF YOUTH

IS SUBMITTED TO THEIR JUDGMENT.

—»»●●●««—

BY RICHARD CARLILE.

London:

PRINTED AND PUBLISHED BY R. CARLILE, 55, FLEET STREET.

1821.

Price One Shilling.

Plate 2

Extract 5: from Richard Carlile, *An Address to Men of Science; Calling upon them to Stand Forward and Vindicate the Truth from the Foul Grasp and Persecution of Superstition; and Obtain for the Island of Great Britain the Noble Appellation of The Focus of Truth; whence Mankind shall be Illuminated, and the Black and Pestiferous Clouds of Persecution and Superstition be Banished from the Face of the Earth; as the only sure Prelude to Universal Peace and Harmony among the Human Race. In which a Sketch of a Proper System for the Education of Youth is Submitted to their Judgment* (London: R. Carlile, 1821)[46]

Instead of viewing ourselves as the particular and partial objects of the care of a great Deity, or of receiving those dogmas of the priest which teach us that every thing has been made for the convenience and use of man, and that man has been made in the express image of the Deity, we should consider ourselves but as atoms of organized matter, whose pleasure or whose pain, whose existence in a state of organization, or whose non-existence in that state, is a matter of no importance in the laws and operations of Nature; we should view ourselves with the same feelings, as we view the leaf which rises in the spring, and falls in the autumn, and then serves no further purpose but to fertilize the earth for a fresh production; we should view ourselves but as the blossoms of May, which exhibit but a momentary splendour and beauty, and often within that moment are cut off prematurely by a blast. We are of no more importance in the scale of Nature than those myriads of animalcules whose natural life is but for the space of an hour, or but a moment. We come and pass like a cloud – like a shower – those of us who possess a brilliancy superior to others, are but as the rainbow, the objects of a momentary admiration, and a momentary recollection. Man has been most aptly compared to the seasons of the year, in our own climate, the spring, is his infancy; the summer, the time of his ardent manhood; the autumn, his decline of life; and the winter, his old age and death – he passes, and another series comes. He is produced by, and produces his like, and so passes away one generation after another, from, and to, all eternity. How ridiculous, then, is the idea about divine revelations, about prophesies, and about miracles, to procure proselytes to such notions! To what generation do they apply, or if they apply to all future generations, why were not the same revelations, prophesies, and miracles, necessary to all the past generations? What avail the dogmas of the priest about an end to the world, about a resurrection, about a day of judgment, about a Heaven and Hell, or about rewards and punishments after this life, when we assert that matter is imperishable and indestructible – that it always was what it now is, and that it will always continue the same. Answer this, ye Priests. Come forward, ye Men of Science, and support these plain truths, which are as familiar to your minds as the simplest demonstration in mathematics is to the experienced and accomplished mathematician. Future rewards and punishments are cried up as a necessary doctrine wherewith to impress the minds of men, and to restrain them from vice: but how much more impressive and comprehensible would be the plain and simple truth, that, in this life, virtue produces happiness, and vice nothing but certain misery.

Away then with the ridiculous idea, and the priestly dogma of immortality. Away with the contemptible notion that our bones, our muscles, and our flesh shall be gathered together after they are rotted and evaporated for a resurrection to eternal life. Away with the idea that we have a sensible soul which lives distinct from and after the dissolution of the body. It is all a bugbear, all a priestly imposture. The Chemist can analyse the body of man, and send it into its primitive gaseous state in a few minutes. His crucible and fire, or his galvanic battery, will cause it to evaporate so as not to leave a particle of substance or solid matter, and this chemical process is but an anticipation, or a hastening, of the workings of Nature; for the whole universe might be aptly termed a great chemical apparatus, in which a chemical analysis, and a chemical composition is continually and constantly going on. The same might be said of every organized body, however large, or however minute; its motions produce a constant chemical analysis and composition, a continual change; so that the smallest particle of matter is guided by the same laws, and performs the same duties, as the great whole. Here is an harmony indeed! Man alone seems to form an exception by his vicious conduct and demoralizing character. By assuming to himself a character or a consequence to which he is not entitled, and by making a pretension to the possession of supernatural powers, he plays such fantastic tricks as to disturb every thing within his influence, and carries on a perpetual war with Nature and her laws.

After those few observations upon the properties of matter either organized or inert (to which I know every Chemist in the country, whose science has conquered the bigotry of his education, will give his assent) I would call upon them all and every one to stand forward and teach mankind those important, those plain truths, which are so clear and so familiar to their own minds. It is the Man of Science who is alone capable of making war upon the Priest, so as to silence him effectually. It is the duty of the Man of Science to make war upon all error and imposture, or why does he study? Why does he analyze the habits, the customs, the manners and the ideas of mankind but to separate truth from falsehood, but to give force to the former, and to extinguish the latter? Why does he search into Nature and her laws, but to benefit himself and his fellow man by his discoveries, by the explosion of erroneous ideas, and by the establishment of correct principles? Science must be no longer studied altogether as an amusement or a pastime, which has been too much the case hitherto; it must be brought forward to combat the superstitions, the vices, and the too long established depravities among mankind, whence all their present and past miseries have emanated, and unless the former can be destroyed, the latter will still ensue, as a regular cause and effect.

It is evident that Men of Science have hitherto too much crouched to the established tyrannies of Kingcraft and Priestcraft. Speaking generally they have adopted some of the aristocratical distinctions of the day, and have supported the frauds upon mankind, which it was their peculiar duty to expose. This has given room to the advocates of superstition, to put forward as an authority for their dogmas, the names of Bacon, of Newton, of Locke, and many others.[47] They say that it is no disgrace even to err with such men, and thus, for the want of a more decided and determined character in the advocates of Science and Philosophy, the enemy has built a strong hold within our lines, and taken an important advantage of our irresolution. I will not believe that Bacon, or Newton, or Locke, in the latter part of their life, had any other ideas of the Christian religion, or any other religion, than I have. In their days, the faggots had barely been extinguished, nor was the fuel which supplied them exhausted. They might therefore deem it prudent to equivocate as a matter of safety. Besides, the two former were in the employ of a court, and consequently under the trammels of Kingcraft, which ever has, and ever will find its interest in the support of Superstition and Priestcraft....

In support of my assertion, that Men of Science have hitherto crouched too much to the established impostures of the day, I have merely to remark, that I am not aware of any one instance in which any Chemist of this country has made a public attack upon them, or called them in question in any public manner. Another proof of my assertion might be found in the Medical and Surgical professions. From the best information, I have learnt, that, with a very few exceptions, the whole body of those gentlemen in the Metropolis, have discarded from their minds all the superstitious dogmas which Priestcraft hath invented, and that they have adopted those principles which have a visible foundation in Nature, and beyond what is visible and comprehensible, their credence does not extend. Yet, when that spirited young man, Mr. Lawrence, having obtained a professor's gown in the College of Surgeons, shew[ed] a disposition in his public lectures to discountenance and attack those established impostures and superstitions of Priestcraft, the whole profession displayed that same cowardly and dastardly conduct, which hath stamped with infamy the present generation of Neapolitans, and suffered the professor's gown to be stripped from this ornament of his profession and his country, and every employment to be taken from him, without even a public remonstrance, or scarcely an audible murmur![48]

Extract 6: from George Grote and Jeremy Bentham ('Philip Beauchamp'), *An Analysis of the Influence of Natural Religion on the Temporal Happiness of Mankind* (London: R. Carlile, 1822)[49]

You believe that the Deity interferes occasionally to modify the train of events in the present life. Your belief is avowedly unconformable to experience, for the very essence of the divine interposition is to be extrinsic and irreconcileable to the course of nature. But mark the farther consequences: You dethrone and cancel the authority of experience in every instance whatever; and you thus place yourself out of condition to prove any one fact, or to disprove any other.

What steps do you take to prove that a man has committed murder? You produce a witness who saw him level his pistol at the head of the deceased, heard the report, and beheld the man drop. But this testimony d[e]rives all its persuasive force from the warrant and countersign of experience. Without this it is perfectly useless. Unless I know by previous experience that eye witnesses most commonly speak the truth – that a pistol ball takes the direction in which it is levelled and not the opposite – I should never be convinced, by the attestation of these particular facts, of that ulterior circumstance which you wish me to infer. To complete the proof, two things are requisite; the previous lessons of experience, and the applicability of these lessons to the present case. But no such application can take place unless the course of nature remains the same as it was before. A gratuitous assumption must therefore be made, that the course of nature continues inviolate and uniform. But to assume this in every particular case, is to assume the universal inviolability of the laws of nature. . . .

Expectations from the divine attribute of *pliability* have been and still continue universal. At least this is the foundation of the frequent prayers which are put up to Heaven for different species of relief – built, not upon the benevolence of God, for the[n] his assistance would be extended alike to all the needy, whether silent or clamorous; but upon his yielding and accessible temper, which though indifferent if not addressed, becomes the warm and compliant partizan of every petitioner.

Now these expectations, supposing them well founded and firmly entertained, cannot fail to introduce complete inactivity among the human race. Why should a man employ the slow and toilsome methods to which experience chains him down, when the pleasure which he seeks may be purchased by the simple act of prayer? Why should he plough, and sow, and walk his annual round of anxiety, when by mere expression of a request, an omnipotent ally may be induced to place the mature produce, instantly within his grasp? No, it is replied – God will not assist him unless he employs all his own exertions: he will not favour the lazy.[50] In this defence however it is implied, either that the individual is not to rely upon God at all, in which case there is no motive to offer up the prayer, or that he is to feel a reliance, and yet act as if he felt none whatever. It is implied, therefore, that the conduct of the individual is to be exactly the same as if he did not anticipate any super-human interference. By this defence, you do indeed exculpate the belief in supernatural agency from the charge of producing pernicious effects – because you reduce it to a mere non-entity, and make it produce no effects at all.

If therefore the request is offered up with any hope of being realised, it infallibly proves pernicious, by relaxing the efforts of the petitioner to provide for himself. Should he believe that God will, when he himself has done his utmost, make up the deficiency and crown his views with success, the effect will be to make him undertake any enterprizes whatever, without regarding the adequacy of his means. Provided he employs actively all the resources in his power, he becomes entitled to have the balance made up from the divine treasury. 'God never sends a child' (says the proverb) 'but he sends food for it to eat.'[51] What is the natural inference from this doctrine, except that a man may securely marry without any earthly means of providing for his family, inasmuch as God will be sure to send him some?[52] ...

I have thus analysed the several species of extra-experimental belief which religion begets in the mind, consisting in the persuasion of the existence, creative function, and agency both here and in a future life, of a supernatural Being. I have endeavoured to demonstrate from the very nature of this belief, that it cannot fail to disqualify the intellect for the pursuit of temporal happiness, more or less in proportion to the extent in which it is entertained. For as all our pleasure and all our exemption from want and pain, is the result of human provision – as these provisions are only so many applications of acquired knowledge, that is, of belief conformable to experience – it follows, that the whole fabric of human happiness depends upon the intimate and inviolable union between belief and experience. Whatever has the effect of disjoining the two, is decidedly of a nature to undermine and explode all the apparatus essential to human enjoyment – and if this result is not actually produced, it is only because the train laid is not sufficiently extensive, and is confined to the out-works instead of reaching the heart of the fortress. So far as any result at all is brought about, it is an advance towards the accomplishment of this work of destruction. And as every separate case, in which extra-experimental belief finds reception in the mind, paves the way for others, any one disjunction of belief from experience, has a tendency to produce their entire and universal discordance.

THE ISIS.

A London Weekly Publication,

EDITED BY

THE LADY OF THE ROTUNDA.

No. I. Vol. I.] SATURDAY, FEBRUARY 11, 1832. [PRICE SIXPENCE.

THE FIRST DISCOURSE
OF
THE LADY AT THE ROTUNDA.

Delivered on Sunday Evening, January 29, 1832, and repeated several evenings in the course of that week.

THE task which I purpose to perform, I am told, has no precedent in this country; so I have great need of your indulgent attention and most gentle criticism.

A woman stands before you, who has been educated and practised in all the severity of religious discipline, awakened to the principles of reason but as yesterday, seeking on these boards a moral and a sweet revenge, for the outrage that has been here committed on the Majesty of that Reason and on the Dignity of Truth, inasmuch as the barbaric administration of alleged law, that never had the consent of the people; of law, that has been made for the purpose, by the administerers of law, has arrested the voices and imprisoned the persons of the two brave and talented men, who first made this building a Temple of Reason and of Truth, and who first essayed to teach the people of this country the practical importance and incalculable value of free and public oral discussion. This, sirs, is my purpose; I appear before you, to plead the cause of those injured men, to endeavour to reason before you, as they reasoned before you, to follow their example, even if the sequel be a following them to a prison.

I have left a home, in a distant county, where comfort and even affluence surrounded me, a happy home, and the bosom of an affectionate and a happy family; I have left such a home, under the excitement which religious persecution has roused, to make this first and singular appearance before you, for a purpose, I trust, that is second to none.

So much, by way of an introduction, where no introduction has been otherwise made. I come at once to the preliminaries of my present discourse.

Would you have from me a profession of faith?— You shall have it.

Faith, in its relation to superstition, I have none. But of faith, in the relation of the word to whatever is lovely, whatever is good, and whatever is true, whatever is morally binding and honourable, I flatter myself that I am rich, and of large possessions. At least, sirs, I submit this my faith to your most severe critical judgments.

Vol. I.

But then, we are told, that they who have no faith, in relation to superstition, are scoffers and scorners.

Though I hold that truth cannot be scoffed, nor scorned, nor jested upon, where it is known, or other than by ignorance; that the sun of our heaven is too majestic to be ridiculed or laughed on; that nothing but ignorance, false conceit, or dishonesty, fears either a scoff, a scorn, a jest, a ridicule, or a laugh; still, I will not scoff at any thing or any person, I will not scorn, I will not rail; I will return good for evil in all things; I will not jest. From me, there shall here be found no ridicule, not even a laugh. I only ask permission to be allowed to smile on you, as I hope you will smile on me, when the proper occasion calls it forth; and if that smile relate to any errors or false conceits of others, the smile on my part shall be for you, who are not under the delusion; they who are ignorant and deluded, shall have, with my expressed passion and serious labour for their instruction, my solemn pity, while they remain in ignorance.

This shall not be the seat of the scorner while it is in my hands, but the theatre of Reason, of Truth, and of free Discussion; of an encouragement to every well-expressed desire for mutual instruction. I trust that I have been educated to the possession of such a proper share of becoming humility and gentleness as to be ever in the disposition to give no offence, and none to think.

Enough of myself, let us now discourse of principles.

I purpose to speak, in my continued discourses, if this shall find favour with you, of superstition and of reason, of tyranny and of liberty, of morals and of politics.

Of politics! politics from a woman! some will exclaim. YES, I will set before my sex the example of asserting an equality for them with their present lords and masters, and strive to teach all, yes, *all*, that the undue submission, which constitutes slavery, is honourable to none; while the mutual submission, which leads to mutual good, is to all alike dignified and honourable.

Superstition, I shall define to be the invention of the human imagination, where demonstration is not to be had, and where a system of alleged causes, falling back into a general first cause, is made of the fanciful idea of a personification of supposed principles.

Superstition may also be defined more briefly to be a picture, without its like in nature, traced by an erroneous action of the human brain.

All fiction is a superstition. Idolatry may be defined as the worship of the picture, or fiction, or personifica-

B

Plate 3

Extract 7: from Eliza Sharples ('The Lady of the Rotunda'), *The Isis* (London: David France, 1832)[53]

THE FIRST DISCOURSE OF THE LADY AT THE ROTUNDA

*Delivered on Sunday Evening, January 29, 1832, and
repeated several evenings in the course of that week*

The task which I purpose to perform, I am told, has no precedent in this country; so I have great need of your indulgent attention and most gentle criticism.

A woman stands before you, who has been educated and practised in all the severity of religious discipline, awakened to the principles of reason but as yesterday, seeking on these boards a moral and a sweet revenge, for the outrage that has been here committed on the Majesty of that Reason and on the Dignity of Truth, inasmuch as the barbaric administration of alleged law, that never had the consent of the people; of law, that has been made for the purpose, by the administerers of law, has arrested the voices and imprisoned the persons of the two brave and talented men, who first made this building a Temple of Reason and of Truth, and who first essayed to teach the people of this country the practical importance and incalculable value of free and public oral discussion.[54] This, sirs, is my purpose; I appear before you, to plead the cause of those injured men, to endeavour to reason before you, as they reasoned before you, to follow their example, even if the sequel be a following them to a prison.

I have left a home, in a distant county, where comfort and even affluence surrounded me, a happy home, and the bosom of an affectionate and a happy family; I have left such a home, under the excitement which religious persecution has roused, to make this first and singular appearance before you, for a purpose, I trust, that is second to none. . . .

Enough of myself, let us now discourse of principles.

I purpose to speak, in my continued discourses, if this shall find favour with you, of superstition and of reason, of tyranny and of liberty, of morals and of politics.

Of politics! politics from a woman! some will exclaim. YES, I will set before my sex the example of asserting an equality for them with their present lords and masters, and strive to teach all, yes, *all*, that the undue submission, which constitutes slavery, is honourable to none; while the mutual submission, which leads to mutual good, is to all alike dignified and honourable.

Superstition, I shall define to be the invention of the human imagination, where demonstration is not to be had, and where a system of alleged causes, falling back into a general first cause, is made of the fanciful idea of a personification of supposed principles.

Superstition may also be defined more briefly to be a picture, without its like in nature, traced by an erroneous action of the human brain.

All fiction is a superstition. Idolatry may be defined as the worship of the picture, or fiction, or personification; while contemplation of the principles has been defined as the religion of nature. Superstition, then, is an idea, or train of ideas, that is not known to be truth, that is not demonstrated, and that while so deficient, can never be made beneficial to the whole of mankind.

Truth never wears out. It is fortunate that we see superstition does wear out, that, in some minds, it becomes quite eradicated, as I hope it is or will be in yours and mine.

I have been full of superstition, but, I trust, that I have ceased to be so; that I have gained some truth, and enough to become so pleased with it, as to proceed fearlessly in the pursuit of more. And thus it is that I stand here, a novelty among women, to call mankind from the ways and evils of error and of superstition to the paths and pleasures of truth. I can assure ye that there are no other thorns in this path, to molest the pursuit, than such as offended ignorance or dishonesty may strew there; and if your kind protection shall be the besom to sweep away those thorns from before my feet, I will follow with a basket and strew the path with flowers, with the aroma of Araby, and with the bloom of perpetual spring.[55]

It would not be in vain, if man were superstitious enough to seek to make a paradise of the earth, instead of making his never-to-be-reached paradise of the conceits of his own brain. Help me, sirs, in this mighty undertaking, and some of us may see that we have made the world the better for living in it. Let this be the study of all, and all may be happy. Be this our peculiar study, and let us, at least, strive to be happy. . . .

Sirs, I shall seek to gather power around me in this establishment; and which of you will not accept me for your general, your leader, your guide? I will be worthy of the cause on which I ask you to embark. I have told you that I have left a happy home and comparative affluence, to launch the frail bark of my intellect, my soul, my genius, my spirit, on the ocean of politics; and I am fired with the daring to buffet its waves, and with the resolve to ride on the whirlwind, and to assist in the direction of the coming storm. I would that it should not be a storm; that all necessary should be accomplished with gentleness, with suasion, with kindness, with yielding, where yielding is required and proper, with resistance only where wrong is opposed; but, if human welfare requires more than this, let more come on.[56]

And to you, ladies, sisters, with your leave, I would say, I appeal, and ask in what way are you prepared to assist me? Will you gather round me, and give me that countenance in virtuous society which we all seek and need, and without which life to us is wretchedness? Will you not be offended at this step of mine, original to my understanding, but, I think, not unworthy of us, nor unbecoming in me? Are you prepared to advance, as you see I have already advanced? Breathes the spirit of liberty in you, or are you content to be slaves, because your lords may wish it? What say you, sisters? Will you advance, and seek that equality in human society which nature has qualified us for, but which tyranny, the tyranny of our lords and masters, has suppressed? I have need of your assistance, as, I am sure, you have need of mine. I think we have souls, which no scripture has yet granted; that we are worthy of salvation, which no religion has yet promised us; that we are as men in mind and purpose; that we may make ourselves 'helps meet for them,'[57] on the condition that they shall not seek our degradation, that they shall not be our tyrants, but that we shall be free to all the advantages, all the privileges, all the pleasures of human life.

SELECT BIBLIOGRAPHY

Berman, David, *A History of Atheism in Britain from Hobbes to Russell* (1988; London and New York: Routledge, 1990). A very useful guide to the nuances of argument involved, but sticks firmly to 'atheism' as such, with little to say on the broader freethinking tradition of deists such as Paine.

Cole, G. D. H., *Richard Carlile, 1790–1834* (London: Victor Gollancz, 1943). Brief but solid biography of Carlile and his circle.

Gay, Peter, *The Enlightenment: An Interpretation: The Rise of Modern Paganism* (1966; London: Weidenfeld and Nicolson, 1967). A comprehensive study of the eighteenth-century European Enlightenment, with the strands of deism, scepticism and atheism well traced.

Haakonssen, Knud, ed., *Enlightenment and Religion: Rational Dissent in Eighteenth-Century Britain* (Cambridge: Cambridge University Press, 1996). Takes issue with Gay's assumption of a single, progressive direction to Enlightenment thinking. A collection of excellent essays on the intertwined paths of religious dissent, politics and freethought in the eighteenth century.

Herrick, Jim, *Against the Faith: Some Deists, Sceptics and Atheists* (London: Glover and Blair, 1985). A useful consideration of representatives of the three traditions named in its title.

McCalman, Iain, *Radical Underworld: Prophets, Revolutionaries and Pornographers in London, 1795–1838* (Cambridge: Cambridge University Press, 1988). Invaluable account of religious, political and atheist cross-currents in the period, including figures such as Robert Wedderburn and George Cannon who might have featured here had there been room.

McNeil, Maureen, *Under the Banner of Science: Erasmus Darwin and His Age* (Manchester: Manchester University Press, 1987). A thorough and thought-provoking account of links between science, industry, politics and freethought in Darwin's circle.

Robertson, J. M., *A History of Freethought in the Nineteenth Century* (London: Watts and Co., 1929). Truly magisterial study of every aspect of the subject, in Britain and world-wide: still a crucial source despite its venerable age.

Royle, Edward, ed., *The Infidel Tradition from Paine to Bradlaugh* (London and Basingstoke: Macmillan, 1976). An illuminating selection of passages covering the most crucial branches of atheist debate and agitation in the nineteenth century.

Shelley, Mary, *Frankenstein, or The Modern Prometheus: The 1818 Text*, ed. Marilyn Butler (Oxford: Oxford University Press, 1994). Very useful for Introduction, notes and appendices filling out the materialist discourses in the context of which the novel was written, particularly those of William Lawrence and Erasmus Darwin.

Shelley, Percy Bysshe, *Shelley's Prose, or The Trumpet of a Prophecy*, ed. David Lee Clark (1954; London: Fourth Estate, 1988). An invaluable edition for its annotations and introductory material, which lucidly clarify Shelley's debts to various atheist traditions.

—— *Prose Works*, vol. 1, ed. E. B. Murray (Oxford: Clarendon Press, 1996). The standard scholarly edition.

Walter, Nicolas, *Blasphemy Ancient and Modern* (London: Rationalist Press Association, 1990). Brief, racily written account of the struggle for freedom of expression on religious matters in Britain, concentrating on the post-Paine period.

4

EMPIRE AND RACE

Kate Teltscher

At the start of the nineteenth century, Britain saw itself in possession of a vast territorial empire. Although the American colonies had been lost, the rest of the empire continued to grow. The largest naval force in Europe, Britain extended its power world-wide during the French Revolutionary and Napoleonic wars of 1793–1815. It controlled the most extensive and profitable of slave-worked plantation systems and, until 1807, dominated the West African slave trade. This new imperial role generated a series of debates about Britain's relation to the colonized and enslaved which will be traced through this section. The texts selected here represent three of the central concerns of the period: slavery, race and the relationship between Britain and India.

The issue which aroused greatest public interest was slavery. Abolitionist activity, which began with the establishment of the Society for the Purpose of Effecting the Abolition of the Slave Trade in 1787, had been suspended during the years of anti-Jacobin panic, but was revived in 1804 and culminated in the abolition of the slave trade in 1807. The passage of this bill was celebrated as Christianity's greatest triumph by the abolitionist campaigner, Thomas Clarkson (1760–1846), and the Act came as a timely boost to national self-esteem in the struggle against Napoleon.[1] Anti-slavery sentiment found occasion for public expression three years later in the outcry over the exhibition of the African Saartjie Baartman, the so-called 'Hottentot Venus' (see **extract 1**). The newspaper extracts and broadsheet ballad included here reveal the mixture of prurient interest and humanitarian concern that turned Baartman into a *cause célèbre*. Scantily clad to reveal the physical characteristic that so fascinated contemporaries – the steatopygia or protruding buttocks – Baartman enacted a theatrical tableau of slavery, in response to the commands of a stick-wielding 'master'. Letters to the press demanded to know if Baartman was enslaved to her manager Hendrick Caesar, and suggested a legal investigation. The Court of King's Bench arranged for Baartman to be questioned through two interpreters, and provision for her welfare was guaranteed by the abolitionist African Institution. On examination, Baartman asserted that she had travelled with Caesar from the Cape without compulsion, and that she had a half share in the profits. Baartman went on to stage her act in Paris until her death in 1815, at the age of 25. An autopsy was carried out on her body by the renowned comparative anatomist Georges Cuvier (1769–1832), and her preserved buttocks and genitalia were, extraordinarily, still on display at the Musée de l'homme in Paris in the 1980s.[2]

Of the some 10,000 blacks in Britain in this period, most lived as servants, attracting little attention. But two black radicals, William Davidson (1786–1820) and Robert Wedderburn (c. 1761–c. 1835), became active in the post-war reform movement and were closely watched by the authorities. Davidson was hanged in 1820 for his involvement in the Cato Street Conspiracy, and Wedderburn was jailed for his activities. Wedderburn was the son of a Scottish plantation owner in Jamaica and one of his slaves; according to Wedderburn, his father sold his pregnant mother back to her previous owner on condition that the child (Wedderburn) was born free. He joined the Navy to travel to Britain where he worked as a journeyman tailor. It was as a licensed Dissenting minister that he became a Spencean, a member of the largely working-class group of former Jacobins who followed Thomas Spence's doctrine of revolutionary agrarian communism. Wedderburn played an active part in the organization, leading debates and publishing periodicals. *The Axe Laid to the Root or A Fatal Blow to Oppressors, Being an Address to the Planters and Negroes of the Island of Jamaica* (1817) applied the teachings of Spence to the West Indian situation (see **extract 2**). Wedderburn writes with the authority of personal experience, addressing members of his family, both slaves and slave-holders. Inflected by the rhythms of preaching, his prose resounds with biblical rhetoric. As Iain McCalman has argued, the Jamaican setting functions as an analogue of domestic political repression, and in his advocacy of armed slave rebellion, Wedderburn also proposes working-class revolution in Britain.[3]

The demand for immediate slave freedom is echoed by the Quaker emancipationist, Elizabeth Heyrick (1769–1831), in her anonymous pamphlet of 1824, *Immediate, not Gradual Abolition, or an Inquiry into the Shortest, Safest, and most Effectual Means of Getting Rid of West Indian Slavery* (see **extract 3**). As the title suggests, Heyrick contested the gradual approach to slave emancipation advocated by male abolitionists. After 1807 there was a lull in anti-slavery activity until the 1820s. One trigger for renewed agitation was the death in prison of John Smith, a missionary found guilty of inciting slave rebellion in Demerara in 1824. Heyrick was among the first to respond to the Demerara uprising, urging a boycott of slave-grown produce, a tactic first deployed by abolitionists (particularly women) in the 1790s. Addressed to a female middle-class readership, Heyrick's pamphlets were central to the politicization of this class of women who, by the late 1820s, dominated the anti-slavery movement. Ladies' Anti-Slavery Associations were active in organizing the campaign to flood parliament with petitions which eventually resulted in the passage of the 1833 Emancipation Bill.

To what extent did the abolition of slavery alter the prevailing image of blacks?

Nancy Stepan has argued that 'the Negro was legally freed by the Emancipation Act of 1833, but in the British mind he was still mentally, morally and physically a slave'.[4] Stepan accounts for this apparent paradox by tracing the development of racial science in early nineteenth-century Britain. Comparative anatomy, pioneered by Cuvier in France (who conducted the autopsy on Baartman), and by the surgeon William Lawrence (1783–1867) in Britain, was influenced by the recent science of phrenology. Phrenology held that different human faculties were located in specific regions of the brain and were reflected in the external shape of the skull. For comparative anatomists, racial variations in the form of the skull were linked to differences in intellectual and moral capacity. In a series of lectures delivered to the Royal College of Surgeons (published in 1819) Lawrence divided the human species into five varieties: Caucasian, Mongolian, Ethiopian, American and Malay. Each was analysed according to skull formation, body structure, stature, language, susceptibility to disease and finally moral and intellectual qualities (see **extract 4**). Lawrence asserts that the brain structure of the Negro is similar to that of the monkey and is therefore of more limited intellectual capacity than the Caucasian brain. In aiming to apply the principles of zoological investigation to humankind, Lawrence was subject to accusations of materialism: that in dismissing the biblical account of life, he had reduced humans to mere animal body.[5] Marilyn Butler has recently argued that Lawrence's views on human life were an important source for Mary Shelley's *Frankenstein*.[6] The controversy generated by *Lectures on Physiology, Zoology, and the Natural History of Man* caused Lawrence to withdraw the book which then circulated in pirated editions.

While comparative anatomists explained the supposed moral degeneracy of non-white races by skull shape, Evangelicals blamed the absence of true faith. The members of the Clapham Sect, a group of influential and wealthy Evangelical Anglicans including William Wilberforce (1759–1833), Zachary Macaulay (1768–1838) and Charles Grant (1746–1823), championed the abolitionist cause in parliament and urged that missionary activity should be allowed in India. The East India Company had long blocked missions as potentially disruptive, but the members of the Clapham Sect, persisting in their advocacy of Evangelism, achieved their aim in 1813. Their campaign focused on the degradation of Indian society and religion, on the tyranny exercised by the brahman priesthood over Hindus.[7] Of the practices they condemned, the most sensational was *sati*, the rite of widow-burning. The British government in Calcutta first laid down a policy on *sati* in 1813; the rite was legal if voluntary and performed in accordance with British interpretation of Hindu scriptures. The administration was concerned that interference in religious matters might antagonize the Hindu community. Over the following years, the scriptural status of *sati* was debated by orthodox Calcutta brahmans and the Hindu reformer, Rammohun Roy (*c.* 1772–1833), who advocated the prohibition of the rite. It was in 1829 that William Bentinck, a Governor-General of Evangelical persuasion, outlawed *sati*.[8] The discussion over the appropriate British response to *sati* informs Robert Southey's Indian epic of 1810, *The Curse of Kehama* (see **extract 5**). Southey (1774–1843) opens his poem with an account of the funeral of Arvalan, murdered son of the tyrannical raja Kehama. Arvalan's two wives and their female slaves are burnt alive on his funeral pyre. This extravagant display of despotic power is authenticated by lengthy notes drawn from travel literature, histories, missionary accounts and a translation of Hindu law. *Kehama*, an important influence on Shelley, is strikingly ambivalent in its response to Hindu culture; at once echoing Evangelical condemnation of Hindu degeneracy and revelling in the freedom of oriental mythology.[9]

James Mill (1773–1836), by contrast, suffered from no such confusion of response. His *History of British India*, published in 1817 (see **extract 6**), is a comprehensive indictment of Indian civilization and character, written largely as a refutation of more sympathetic orientalist accounts, notably the work of William Jones (1746–94). Although Mill had no first-hand experience of India or knowledge of Indian languages (indeed, in his preface he laid claim to a scholarly disinterestedness *because* he never visited India), he subjected Indian society to rigorous utilitarian scrutiny. Like the Evangelicals, Mill ascribed the debased state of Indian society to political and religious tyranny, but the solution for Mill lay in the reform of government, laws and taxation. The *History* brought Mill (and his son, John Stuart Mill) important positions in the executive government of the East India Company, and from the 1830s the book was a set text at Haileybury, the training college for Company recruits. Thus institutionalized, the *History* enjoyed a position of near unassailable authority throughout the nineteenth century.

The final text in the section is included by way of counterbalance to such thundering condemnations of Indian character and culture. *The Travels of Mirza Abu Taleb Khan in Asia, Africa, and Europe, during the years 1799, 1800, 1801, 1802, and 1803, written by himself in the Persian Language* was first published in 1810, with a second edition following in 1814, and translations into French and German. Abu Talib Ibn Muhammad Khan Isfahani (1752–*c.* 1806) was employed by the East India Company in various capacities, fiscal and military, including the suppression of a rebel raja for the Resident of Lucknow. When his expectations of preferment failed, Abu Talib accompanied a British officer to Europe where he remained for several years. A copy of the Persian journal of his travels, which circulated among friends on his return, was presented to a Captain in the Bengal Artillery, and it finally reached Charles Stewart, Professor of Oriental Languages at Haileybury College, who prepared a translation of the work. The journal's lengthy passage from manuscript form to printed text is scrupulously traced in the translator's preface, which also notes that a copy of the Persian manuscript was deposited at Longman and Co. for inspection. This concern with authentication is intended to counter the suspicion that the book belonged to the fashionable genre of 'fictitious travels, ascribed to natives of the East'.[10] That the journal was certified as genuine was important to the Company because Abu Talib was generally well disposed towards the British. During his stay in London, where he was known as 'the Persian Prince', he was lionized by high society; there were audiences at court, visits to members of the aristocracy and returned East India Company grandees, tours of the British Museum and the Royal Society, portrait sittings and attendance at a masquerade.[11] But after the glittering account of his social triumphs there is a chapter (see **extract 7**) written at the request of his friend Lady Spenser, which details the defects and vices of the English character. Mediated through the translation of a Haileybury professor and followed by a much shorter account of English virtues, this is clearly a form of legitimized dissent; but the chapter does offer us the rare opportunity of listening to the voice of an Indian subject answering back.

Extract 1: from Daniel Lysons (comp.), *Collectanea: Or a Collection of Advertisements and Paragraphs from the Newspapers relating to Various Subjects* (British Library: C.103.k.11) I: ff. 101–3[12]

From Morning Post, *20 September 1810*

THE HOTTENTOT VENUS[13] – Just arrived (and may be seen between the hours of One and Five o'clock in the evening, at No 225, Piccadilly), from the Banks of the River Gamtoos, on the Borders of Kaffraria, in the interior of South Africa, a most correct and perfect Specimen of that race of people. From this extraordinary phenomena of nature, the Public will have an opportunity of judging how far she exceeds any description given by historians of that tribe of the human species. She is habited in the dress of her country, with all the rude ornaments usually worn by those people. She has been seen by the principal Litterati in this Metropolis who were all greatly astonished, as well as highly gratified, with the sight of so wonderful a specimen of the human race. She has been brought to this country at a considerable expence, by Hendrick Cesar, and their stay will be but of short duration – To commence on Monday next, the 24 inst. – Admittance 2s. each.

From Morning Chronicle, *12 October 1810*

TO THE EDITOR OF THE MORNING CHRONICLE

SIR, As a friend to liberty, in every situation of life, I cannot help calling your attention to a subject, which I am sure need only be noticed by you to insure your immediate observation and comment. You stand so deservedly high in the public opinion as a staunch friend of humanity and a sincere promoter of the abolition of the slave trade, that you will perhaps anticipate the cause I am now pleading, and to which I wish to call public attention. I allude to that wretched object advertised and publicly shewn for money – the 'Hottentot Venus'. This Sir, is a wretched creature – an inhabitant of the interior of Africa, who has been brought here as a subject for the curiosity of this country, for 2s. a-head. This poor female is made to walk, to *dance*, to shew herself, not for her own advantage, but for the profit of her master, who, when she appeared tired, holds up a *stick to her, like the wild beast keepers*, to intimidate her into obedience. I think, Sir, I have read somewhere (but you will know this better than me), that the air of the British Constitution is too pure to permit slavery to exist where its influence extends. If that be the case, why is this poor creature to live in the very heart of the metropolis, for I am sure you will easily discriminate between those beings who are sufficiently degraded to shew themselves for their *own* immediate profit, and where they act from their own free will; and this poor slave, who is obliged to shew herself, *to dance*, to be the object of the lowest ribaldry, by which her keeper is the only gainer. I am no advocate of these sights, on the contrary, I think it base in the extreme, that any human being should be thus exposed. It is contrary to every principle of morality and good order, but this exhibition connects the same offence to public decency, with that most horrid of all situations, *Slavery.*

> Your obedient servant,
> AN ENGLISHMAN.

From Morning Post, 29 October 1810

London, Saturday, Oct 27, 1810

Mr EDITOR – Considerable interest has been excited by the situation of an unfortunate being who has been for some weeks publicly shewn in Piccadilly, like a *prize ox* or a *rattle snake*, and from some letters that have appeared in a daily Paper, it seems to be more insinuated that she has been brought by artifice or force from her own country for this abominable purpose, and is at this moment in a state of slavery *in England*. Two of the letters are signed by a foreigner, purporting to be her keeper, which are of a kind so equivocating, the *writer* of them so evidently *avoids* satisfying the doubts of the Public as to the real situation of this poor creature, that they must conclude their suspicions to be well founded.

Now, Sir, feeling the honour of my country wounded, while *even a suspicion* of so atrocious a kind can be harboured, I intreat your kindness in publishing these remarks in the hope that they may meet the eye of some Member of the African Institution,[14] who would doubtless endeavour to investigate the matter, if indeed, the Magistracy do not feel themselves called upon to do so. If the case be as it has been suspected, a signal punishment should be inflicted on the guilty.

> I am Sir, Yours,
> WHITE MAN.

Broadsheet ballad

The storie of the Hottentot Ladie and her lawfull Knight, who essaied to release her out of captivitie, and what my lordes the judges did therin.

Oh have you been in London towne,
    Its rareities to see:
There is, 'mongst ladies of renowne,
    A most renowned she.
In Piccadillie streete so faire,
    A mansion she has got;
In golden letters written there,
    'THE VENUS HOTTENTOT'.

But you may ask, and well, I ween,
    For why she tarries there;
And what, in her is to be seen,
    Than other folks, more rare.
A rump she has, (though strange it be),
    Large as a cauldron pot,
And this is why men go to see
    This lovely HOTTENTOT.

Now this was shewn for many a day,
    And eke for many a night;
Till sober folks began to say,
    That all could not be right.
Some said, this was with her goodwill;
    Some said, that it was not,
And asked why they did use so ill
    This ladie HOTTENTOT.

At last a doughty Knight stood forth,
    Sir Vikar was his name;
A knight of singular good worth,
    Of fair and courtely fame.
With him the laws of chivalrie
    Were not so much forgot;
But he would try most gallantly
    To serve the HOTTENTOT.

He would not *fight*, but *plead* the cause
    Of this most injured she:
And so, appealed to all the laws,
    To set the ladie free.

A mighty 'Habeas corpus'
  He hoped to have got,
Including rump and all, and thus
  Release the HOTTENTOT.

Thus driving on with might and main
  This Gallant Knight did say,
He wish'd to send her home again,
  To Afric far away.
On that full pure and holy plan,
  To soothe her rugged lot;
He swore, in troth, no other man
  Should *keep* his HOTTENTOT.

He went unto the Judges grave,
  Whose mercies never fail;
And there, in gallant stile, and brave,
  Set forth the ladie's tale.
He said, a man of cruel heart,
  (Whose name is forgot,)
Did shew, for pay, the hinder part
  Of this fair HOTTENTOT.

That in this land of libertie
  Where freedom groweth still,
No one can shew another's tail
  Against the owner's will.
And wished my lordes to send some one,
  To know whether or not
This rare exhibiting was done
  To please the HOTTENTOT.

The judges did not hesitate
  This piteous tale to hear,
Conceiving her *full-bottom'd* state,
  Claim'd *their* especial care;
And told the knight that he might do
  As he thought best, and what;
E'en visit privately, and view
  His ladie HOTTENTOT.

Thus straight two gentlemen they set,
  (One English and one Dutch)
To learn if she did money get;

And, if she did, how much.
Who, having finished their intent,
   And visited the spot,
Did say 'twas done with full consent
   Of the fair HOTTENTOT.

When speaking free from all alarm,
   The whole she does deride;
And says she thinks there is no great harm
   In shewing her b—kside.
Thus ended this sad tale of woe,
   Which raised well, I wot,
The fame, and the revenues too,
   Of SARTJEE HOTTENTOT.

And now good people all may go
   To see this wondrous sight;
Both high born men, and also low,
   And eke the good Sir Knight.
Not only this her state to mind,
   Most anxious what she got;
But looking to her latter end,
   Delights the HOTTENTOT.

Extract 2: from Robert Wedderburn, *The Axe Laid to the Root* 1 (1817): 11–15

To all who love to hear of the increase of liberty, are these few lines directed

The slaves of Jamaica, are ready now to demand a day of their masters, in addition to the day and a half that was allowed before, being taught by the methodists that it is a crime to labour on the sabbath day; and it is the opinion of many, that they will have it.

This information is by my brother's wife, who is held as a slave by a clergyman of the church of England; whether she obtained this information from the conversation which passed at her master's table, or whether it is her own observation, on what she had heard among her fellow slaves, I will not avow; but this information is confirmed by a letter from a book-keeper to his mother, who informed me, that it is the opinion of her son, that the island of Jamaica will be in the hands of the blacks within twenty years. Prepare for flight, ye planters, for the fate of St. Domingo[15] awaits you. Get ready your blood hounds, the allies which you employed against the Maroons.[16]

101

Recollect the fermentation will be universal. Their weapons are their bill-hooks; their store of provision is every w[h]ere in abundance; you know they can live upon sugar canes, and a vast variety of herbs and fruits, – yea, even upon the buds of trees. You cannot cut off their supplies. They will be victorious in their flight, slaying all before them; they want no turnpike roads: they will not stand to engage organised troops, like the silly Irish rebels.[17] Their method of fighting is to be found in the scriptures, which they are now learning to read. They will slay man, woman, and child, and not spare the virgin, whose interest is connected with slavery, whether black, white, or tawny. O ye planters, you know this has been done; the cause which produced former bloodshed still remains, – of necessity similar effects must take place. The holy alliance of Europe, cannot prevent it, they have enough to do at home, being compelled to keep a standing army in the time of peace, to enforce the civil law.

My heart glows with revenge, and cannot forgive. Repent ye christians, for flogging my aged grandmother before my face, when she was accused of witchcraft by a silly European. O Boswell, ought not your colour and countrymen to be visited with wrath, for flogging my mother before my face, at the time when she was far advanced in pregnancy.[18] What was her crime? did not you give her leave to visit her aged mother; (she did not acquaint her mistress at her departure,) this was her fault. But it originates in your crime in holding her as a slave – could not you wait till she returned, but travel 15 miles to punish her on that visit. You set a pattern to your slaves to treat your wife with contempt, by taking your negro wenches to your adultrous bed, in preference to your wedded wife.

It being a general practice in the island, is no excuse for you, – who was a scholar and professed to be a christian – how can I forgive you? Oh! my father, what do you deserve at my hands? Your crimes will be visited upon your legitimate offspring: for the sins of a wicked father will be visited upon his children, who continues in the practice of their father's crimes. Ought I not to encourage your slaves, O my brother, to demand their freedom even at the danger of your life, if it could not be obtained without. Do not tell me you hold them by legal right. No law can be just which deprives another of his liberty, except for criminal offences: such law-makers according to the rules of equity, are felons of the deepest dye; for they attempt to justify wickedness. The time is fast approaching, when such rulers must act righteously, or be drawn from their seats; for truth and justice must prevail – combined armies cannot stop their progress – religious superstition, the support of tyrants, gives way.

The priesthood who took the lead, are compelled to sculk in the rear, and take shelter under Bell's system of education, to impress on the minds of youth their nonsensical creed; dreading the purity of the Lancasterian mode.[19] But you my countrymen, can act without education; the equality of your present station in slavery, is your strength. You all feel the injury – you are all capable of making resistance. Your oppressors know – they dread you – they can foresee their downfal when you determine to obtain your liberty, and possess your natural right – that is freedom. Beware, and offend not your God, like the jews of old, in choosing a king; agrandise no man by forms of law. He who preserves your liberty, will of necessity receive universal praise, like Washington, to endless generations, without the aid of hireling priests to celebrate his fame.[20]

Check if possible by law and practice, that avarice in man, which is never satisfied. If you suffer any among you to become emensly rich, he will want homage, and a title; yea, he will dispose of your lives, liberty, and property; and to support his divine right, he will establish a priesthood – he will call in foreign usurpers to assist him to oppress you. Under the protection of foreign bayonets, he will threaten to erect a gallows at every door. France is reduced to this state of humiliation. A black king is capable of wickedness, as well as a white one.

WEDDERBURN

Extract 3: from Elizabeth Heyrick, *Immediate, not Gradual Abolition, or an Inquiry into the Shortest, Safest, and most Effectual Means of Getting Rid of West Indian Slavery* (London: J. Hatchard and Son, 1824), pp. 3–5

It is now seventeen years since the *Slave Trade* was abolished by the Government of this country – but *Slavery* is still perpetuated in our West India colonies, and the horrors of the Slave Trade are aggravated, rather than mitigated. By making it felony for British subjects to be concerned in that inhuman traffic, England has only transferred her share of it to other countries. She has, indeed, by negociation and remonstrance, endeavoured to persuade them to follow her example – but has she succeeded? – How should she, whilst there is so little consistency in her conduct? Who will listen to her pathetic declamations on the injustice and cruelty of the Slave Trade – whilst she rivets the chains upon her own slaves, and subjects them to all the injustice and cruelty which she so eloquently deplores when her own interest is no longer at stake? Before we can have any rational hope of prevailing on our guilty neighbours to abandon this atrocious commerce – to relinquish the gain of oppression – the wealth obtained by rapine and violence, – by the deep groans, the bitter anguish of our unoffending fellow-creatures, we must purge ourselves from these pollutions; – we must break the iron yoke from off the neck of *our own slaves*, and let the wretched captives in our own islands go free. Then, and not till then, we shall speak to the surrounding nations with the *all-commanding eloquence of sincerity and truth*; and our persuasions will be backed by the *irresistible argument of consistent example*. But to invite others to be just and merciful, whilst we grasp in our own hands the rod of oppression – to solicit others to relinquish the wages of iniquity, whilst we are putting them into our own pockets – what is it but cant and hypocrisy? Do such preachers of justice and mercy ever make converts? On the contrary, do they not render themselves ridiculous and contemptible?

But let us, *individually*, bring this great question closely home to our own bosoms. We that hear, and read, and approve, and applaud the powerful appeals, the irrefragable arguments against the Slave Trade, and against slavery – are we *ourselves* sincere, or hypocritical? Are *we* the true friends of justice, or do we only cant about it? – To which party do *we* really belong? – to the friends of emancipation, or of perpetual slavery? Every individual belongs to one party or the other; not speculatively, or professionally merely, but practically. The perpetuation of slavery in our West India colonies, is not an abstract question, to be settled between the Government and the Planters – it is a question in which we are *all* implicated; – we are all guilty (with shame and compunction let us admit the opprobrious truth) of supporting and perpetuating slavery. The West Indian planter and the people of this country, stand in the same moral relation to each other as the thief and the receiver of stolen goods. The planter refuses to set his wretched captive at liberty; treats him as a beast of burden; compels his reluctant unremunerated labour under the lash of the cart-whip – why? – because WE furnish the stimulant to all this injustice, rapacity, and cruelty, by PURCHASING ITS PRODUCE. Heretofore, it may have been thoughtlessly and unconsciously – but now this palliative is removed; the veil of ignorance is rent aside; the whole nation must now divide itself into the *active supporters*, and the *active opposers* of slavery; – there is no longer any ground for a neutral party to stand upon.

The state of slavery, in our West Indian islands, is now become notorious; – *the secret is out*; – the justice and humanity, the *veracity* also, of slave owners, is exactly ascertained; – the credit due to their assertions, that their slaves are better fed, better clothed – are more comfortable, more *happy* than our English peasantry – is now universally understood. The tricks and impostures practised by the colonial assemblies, to hoodwink the people, to humbug the Government, and to bamboozle the *saints* (as the friends of emancipation are scornfully termed), have all been detected; and the cry of the nation has been raised, from one end to the other, against this complicated system of knavery and imposture – of intolerable oppression, of relentless and savage barbarity.

But is all this knowledge to end in exclamations, in petitions, in remonstrances? – Is there nothing to be *done*, as well as said? Are there no tests to prove our sincerity? – no sacrifices to be offered in confirmation of our zeal? Yes, there is *one* – (but it is in itself so small and insignificant, that it seems almost burlesque to dignify it with the name of sacrifice) – it is ABSTINENCE FROM THE USE OF WEST INDIAN PRODUC-TIONS; *sugar* especially, in the cultivation of which slave labour is chiefly occupied. Small, however, and insignificant as the sacrifice may appear, it would at once give the death blow to West Indian slavery. When there was no longer a market for the productions of *slave labour*, then, and *not till then*, will the slaves be emancipated.

Many had recourse to this expedient about thirty years ago, when the public attention was so generally roused to the enormities of the Slave Trade. But when the trade was abolished by the British legislature, it was too readily concluded that the abolition of slavery, in the British dominions, would have been an inevitable consequence; this species of abstinence was therefore unhappily discontinued.

'But (it will be objected) if there be no market for West Indian produce, the West Indian proprietors will be ruined; and the slaves, instead of being benefited, will perish by famine.' Not so – the West Indian proprietors understand their own interest better. The market, though shut to the productions of *slave labour*, would still be open to the productions of *free labour*; and the planters are not such devoted worshippers of slavery, as to make a voluntary sacrifice of their own interests upon her altar; – they will not doom the soil to perpetual barrenness, rather than suffer it to be cultivated by free men. It has been abundantly proved that voluntary labour is more productive, more advantageous to the employer, than compulsory labour. The experiments of the venerable and philanthropic Joshua Steele, have established the fact beyond all doubt.[21] But the planter shuts his eyes to such facts, though clear and evident as the sun at noon day. None are so blind as those who *will* not see. The conviction then must be *forced* upon these infatuated men. It is often asserted, that slavery is too deeply rooted an evil to be eradicated by the exertions of any principle less potent and active than *self-interest*: if so, the resolution to abstain from West Indian produce, would bring this potent and active principle into the fullest operation – would *compel* the planter to set his slaves at liberty.

But were such a measure to be ultimately injurious to the interest of the planter, that consideration ought not to weigh a feather in the scale against emancipation. The slave has a *right* to his liberty; a right which it is a crime to withhold, let the consequences to the planters be what they may. If I have been deprived of my rightful inheritance, and the usurper, because he has long kept possession, asserts his *right* to the property of which he has defrauded me; are my just claims to it at all weakened by the boldness of his pretensions, or by the plea that restitution would impoverish and involve him in ruin? And to what inheritance, or birth-right, can any mortal have pretensions so just (until forfeited by crime) as to liberty? What injustice and rapacity can be compared to that which defrauds a man of his best earthly inheritance, tears him from his dearest connexions, and condemns him and his posterity to the degradation and misery of interminable slavery?

Extract 4: from William Lawrence, *Lectures on Physiology, Zoology, and the Natural History of Man* (London: J. Callow, 1819), pp. 476–86

The distinction of colour between white and black races is not more striking, than the pre-eminence of the former in moral feelings and in mental endowments. The latter, it is true, exhibit generally a great acuteness of the external senses, which in some instances is heightened by exercise to a degree nearly incredible. Yet they indulge, almost universally, in disgusting debauchery and sensuality, and display gross selfishness, indifference to the pains and pleasures of others, insensibility to beauty of form, order, and harmony, and an almost entire want of what we comprehend altogether under the expression of elevated sentiments, manly virtues, and moral feeling. The hideous savages of Van Diemen's Land,[22] of New Holland,[23] New Guinea, and some neighbouring islands, the Negroes of Congo and some other parts, exhibit the most disgusting moral as well as physical portrait of man.

PERON describes the wretched beings whom he found on the shores of Van Diemen's Island, and of the neighbouring island, Maria, as examples of the rudest barbarism; 'without chiefs, properly so called, without laws or anything like regular government, without arts of any kind, with no idea of agriculture, of the use of metals, or the services to be derived from animals; without clothes, or fixed abode, and with no other shelter than a mere shed of bark to keep off the cold south winds; with no arms but a club and spear'.[24]

Although these and the neighbouring New Hollanders are placed in a fine climate and productive soil, they derive no other sustenance from the earth than a few fern-roots and bulbs of orchises; and are often driven by the failure of their principal resource, fish, to the most revolting food, as frogs, lizards, serpents, spiders, the larvæ of insects, and particularly a kind of large caterpillar found in groups on the branches of the eucalyptus resinfera. They are sometimes obliged to appease the cravings of hunger by the bark of trees, and by a paste made of pounding together ants, their larvæ and fern-roots.

Their remorseless cruelty, their unfeeling barbarity to women and children, their immoderate revenge for the most trivial affronts, their want of natural affection, are hardly redeemed by the slightest traits of goodness. When we add that they are quite insensible to distinctions of right and wrong, destitute of religion, without any idea of a Supreme Being, and with the feeblest notion, if there be any at all of a future state, the revolting picture is complete in all its features. What an afflicting contrast does the melancholy truth of this description form to the eloquent but delusive declamations of ROUSSEAU on the prerogatives of natural man and his advantages over his civilised brethren![25]

The same general character, with some softening, and some modifications, is applicable to most of the native Americans, of the Africans, and of the Mongolian nations of Asia; to the Malays, and the greater part of the inhabitants of the numerous islands scattered in the ocean between Asia and America. In the most authentic descriptions we every where find proofs of astonishing insensibility to the pains and joys of others, even their nearest relations; inflexible cruelty, selfishness and disposition to cheat; a want of all sympathetic impulses and feelings; the most brutal apathy and indolence, unless roused by the pressure of actual physical want, or stimulated by the desire of revenge and the thirst of blood. Their barbarous treatment of women, the indiscriminate and unrelenting destruction of their warfare, the infernal torments inflicted on their captives, and the horrible practice of cannibalism, fill the friend of humanity with pity, indignation, and horror.

With the deep shades of this dismal picture some brighter spots are mingled, which it is a pleasing task to select and particularise.

The inferiority of the dark to the white races is much more general and strongly marked in the powers of knowledge and reflection, the intellectual faculties, using that expression in its most comprehensive sense, than in moral feelings and dispositions. Many of the former, although little civilized display an openness of heart, a friendly and generous disposition, the greatest hospitality, and an observance of the point of honour according to their own notions, from which nations more advanced in knowledge might often take a lesson with advantage.

Many of the Negroes possess a natural goodness of heart and warmth of affection: even the slave-dealers are acquainted with their differences in character, and fix their prices, not merely according to their bodily powers, but in proportion to the docility and good dispositions of their commodity, judging of these by the quarter from which they are procured.

Although the Americans appeared so stupid to the Spaniards, that they were with some difficulty convinced of their being men and capable of becoming Christians (for which purpose a papal bull was necessary); and although this deficiency of intellect is still attested by the more candid and impartial reports of modern travellers; the empires of Mexico and Peru show that some tribes at least were capable of higher destinies, and of considerable advancement in civilization. They were united under a regular government, they practised agriculture, and the other necessary arts of life; and were not entirely destitute of those which have some title to the name of elegant. . . .

In the savage tribes of North America we often meet with lofty sentiments of independence, ardent courage, and devoted friendship, which would sustain a comparison with the most splendid similar examples in the more highly gifted races. Honourable and punctual fulfilment of treaties and compacts, patient endurance of toil, hunger, cold, and all kinds of hardships and privations, inflexible fortitude, and unshaken perseverance in avenging insults or injuries according to their own peculiar customs and feelings, shew that they are not destitute of the more valuable moral qualities.

The Mongolian people differ very much in their docility and moral character. While the empires of China and Japan prove that this race is susceptible of civilization, and of great advancement in the useful and even elegant arts of life, and exhibit the singular phenomenon of political and social institutions between two and three thousand years older than the Christian era, the fact of their having continued nearly stationary for so many centuries, marks an inferiority of nature, and a limited capacity, in comparison to that of the white races.

When the Mongolian tribes of central Asia have united under one leader, war and desolation have been the objects of the association. Unrelenting slaughter, without distinction of condition, age or sex, and universal destruction, have marked the progress of their conquests, unattended with any changes or institutions capable of benefiting the human race, unmingled with any acts of generosity, any kindness to the vanquished, or the slightest symptoms of regard to the rights and liberties of mankind. The progress of ATTILA, ZINGIS, and TAMERLANE, like the deluge, the tornado, and the hurricane, involved everything in one sweeping ruin.[26]

In all the points which have been just considered, the white races present a complete contrast to the dark-coloured inhabitants of the globe. While the latter cover more than half the earth's surface, plunged into a state of barbarism in which the higher attributes of human nature seldom make their appearance, strangers to all the conveniences and pleasures of advanced social life, and deeming themselves happy in escaping the immediate perils of famine; the former, at least in this quarter of the world, either never have been in so low a condition, or, by means of their higher endowments, have so quickly raised themselves from it, that we have no record of their existence as mere hunting or fishing tribes. In the oldest documents and traditions, which deserve any confidence, these nobler people are seen at least in the pastoral state, and in the exercise of agriculture; the practice of which is so ancient, that the remotest and the darkest accounts have not preserved the name of the discoverer, or the date of its introduction. No European people, therefore, has been in a condition comparable to that of the present dark-coloured races, within the reach of any history or tradition.

The invention of arts and sciences in the East, and their surprising progress in Europe, are due to the white men. The comparatively rational system of Heathenism contained in the Grecian mythology, with its elegant fables and allegories; and the three religions, which exhibit the only worthy views of the Divinity, that is, Judaism, Christianity, and Mohamedanism, all derive their birth from the same quarter.

The Caucasian variety claims also the Persian ZOROASTER,[27] and if I mistake not, the founders of the religion of BRAMAH,[28] who in the peninsula of India had signalized themselves by great advances in art and sciences in the very remotest antiquity.

In the white races, we meet, in full perfection, with true bravery, love of liberty, and other passions and virtues of great souls; here only do these noble feelings exist in full intensity, while they are, at the same time, directed by superior knowledge and reflection to the accomplishment of the grandest purposes. They alone have been as generous and mild towards the weak and the vanquished, as terrible to their enemies; and have treated females with kindness, attention and deference. Here alone are compassion and benevolence fully developed; the feeling for the pains and distresses of others, and the active attempt to relieve them; which, first exerted on our nearest connexions, is extended to our countrymen in general, and embraces, ultimately, in its wishes and exertions, the interests of all mankind.

The white nations alone have enjoyed free governments; that is not the lawless dominion of mere force, as in many barbarous tribes, but institutions recognising the equality of all in political rights, giving protection to the weak against the powerful, securing to all equal freedom of opinion and conscience, and administered according to laws framed with the consent of all. The spirit of liberty, the unconquerable energy of independence, the generous glow of patriotism, have been known chiefly to those nobler organisations, in which the cerebral hemispheres have received their full development. The republics of Greece and Rome, of Italy in the middle ages, of Switzerland and Holland, the limited monarchy of England, and the United States of America, have shewn us what the human race can effect, when animated by these sacred feelings; without which nothing has been achieved truly great or permanently interesting. This is the charm that attaches us to the history, the laws, the institutions, the literature of the free states of antiquity, and that enables us to study again and again with fresh pleasure the lives and actions of their illustrious citizens.

Even the more absolute forms of government have been conducted among the white races, with a respect to human nature, with a regard to law and private rights, quite unknown to the pure despotisms, which seem to be the natural destiny of our dark brethren. The monstrous faith of millions made for one has never been doubted or questioned in all the extensive regions occupied by human races with the anterior and superior parts of the cranium flattened and compressed.

That these diversities are the offspring of natural differences, and not produced by external causes, is proved by their universality, whether in respect to time, place, or external influence.

Extract 5: from Robert Southey, *The Curse of Kehama*, 2 vols (1810; London: Longman, Hurst, Rees, Orme and Brown, 1818), 1: ll. 83–200

O sight of grief! the wives of Arvalan,
Young Azla, young Nealliny, are seen!
    Their widow-robes of white,
    With gold and jewels bright,
    Each like an Eastern queen.
Woe! woe! around their palankeen,[29]
    As on a bridal day,
With symphony, and dance, and song,   90
Their kindred and their friends come on.
The dance of sacrifice! the funeral song!
And next the victim slaves in long array,
    Richly bedight to grace the fatal day,
    Move onward to their death;
    The clarions' stirring breath
Lifts their thin robes in every flowing fold,
    And swells the woven gold,
    That on the agitated air
Trembles, and glitters to the torches glare.   100

    A man and maid of aspect wan and wild,
Then, side by side, by bowmen guarded, came.
    O wretched father! O unhappy child!
Them were all eyes of all the throng exploring . . .
    Is this the daring man
    Who raised his fatal hand at Arvalan?
    Is this the wretch condemn'd to feel
    Kehama's dreadful wrath?
Then were all hearts of all the throng deploring,
    For not in that innumerable throng   110
Was one who lov'd the dead; for who could know
    What aggravated wrong

Provoked the desperate blow!
Far, far behind, beyond all reach of sight,
    In ordered files the torches flow along,
One ever-lengthening line of gliding light:
        Far ... far behind,
    Rolls on the undistinguishable clamour,
        Of horn, and trump, and tambour;
            Incessant as the roar   120
Of streams which down the wintry mountain pour,
        And louder than the dread commotion
            Of stormy billows on a rocky shore,
    When the winds rage over the waves,
        And Ocean to the Tempest raves.

    And now toward the bank they go,
    Where, winding on their way below,
        Deep and strong the waters flow.
        Here doth the funeral pile appear
With myrrh and ambergris bestrew'd,   130
        And built of precious sandal wood.
They cease their music and their outcry here;
        Gently they rest the bier:
    They wet the face of Arvalan,
No sign of life the sprinkled drops excite;
    They feel his breast, ... no motion there;
        They feel his lips, ... no breath;
    For not with feeble, nor with erring hand,
    The stern avenger dealt the blow of death.
    Then with a doubling peal and deeper blast,   140
The tambours and the trumpets sound on high,
        And with a last and loudest cry
        They call on Arvalan.

    Woe! woe! for Azla takes her seat
        Upon the funeral pile!
        Calmly she took her seat,
Calmly the whole terrific pomp survey'd;
        As on her lap the while
The lifeless head of Arvalan was laid.
        Woe! woe! Nealliny,   150
        The young Nealliny!
    They strip her ornaments away,
Bracelet and anklet, ring, and chain, and zone;

111

Around her neck they leave
The marriage knot alone, ...
That marriage band, which when
Yon waning moon was young,
Around her virgin neck
With bridal joy was hung.
Then with white flowers, the coronal of death,   160
Her jetty locks they crown.
O sight of misery!
You cannot hear her cries, ... all other sound
In that wild dissonance is drown'd; ...
But in her face you see
The supplication and the agony, ...
See in her swelling throat the desperate strength
That with vain effort struggles yet for life;
Her arms contracted now in fruitless strife,
Now wildly at full length   170
Towards the crowd in vain for pity spread, ...
They force her on, they bind her to the dead.

Then all around retire;
Circling the pile, the ministring Bramins stand,
Each lifting in his hand a torch on fire.
Alone the Father of the dead advanced
And lit the funeral pyre.

At once on every side
The circling torches drop,
At once on every side   180
The fragrant oil is pour'd,
At once on every side
The rapid flames rush up.
Then hand in hand the victim band
Roll in the dance around the funeral pyre;
Their garments flying folds
Float inward to the fire.
In drunken whirl they wheel around;
One drops, ... another plunges in;
And still with overwhelming din   190
The tambours and the trumpets sound;
And clap of hand, and shouts, and cries,
From all the multitude arise:
While round and round, in giddy wheel,

Intoxicate they roll and reel,
  Till one by one whirl'd in they fall,
And the devouring flames have swallow'd all.

Then all was still; the drums and clarions ceas'd;
  The multitude were hush'd in silent awe;
  Only the roaring of the flames was heard.   200

From Southey's note to line 172: *'They force her on, they
bind her to the dead'*

'Tis true, says Bernier, that I have seen some of them, which, at the sight of
the pile and the fire, appeared to have some apprehension, and that, perhaps,
would have gone back. Those demons, the Bramins, that are there with their
great sticks, astonish them, and hearten them up, or even thrust them in; as
I have seen it done to a young woman that retreated five or six paces from
the pile, and to another, that was much disturbed when she saw the fire take
hold of her clothes, these executioners thrusting her in with their long poles.

At Lahor, I saw a very handsome and a very young woman burnt; I believe
she was not above twelve years of age. This poor unhappy creature appeared
rather dead than alive when she came near the pile; she shook and wept
bitterly. Meanwhile, three or four of these executioners, the Bramins,
together with an old hag that held her under the arm, thrust her on, and made
her sit down upon the wood; and, lest she should run away, they tied her legs
and hands; and so they burnt her alive. I had enough to do to contain myself
for indignation. – BERNIER[30]

Pietro Della Valle conversed with a widow, who was about to burn herself
by her own choice. She told him, that, generally speaking, women were not
forced to burn themselves; but sometimes, among people of rank, when a
young woman, who was handsome, was left a widow, and in danger of
marrying again, (which is never practised among them, because of the
confusion and disgrace which are inseparable from such a thing) or of falling
into other irregularities, then, indeed, the relations of the husband, if they are
at all tenacious of the honour of the family, compel her to burn herself,
whether she likes it or no, merely to prevent the inconveniencies which might
take place.[31] ...

It would be easy to multiply authorities upon this point. Let it suffice to
mention one important historical fact: When the great Albuquerque had
established himself at Goa, he forbade these accursed sacrifices, the women
extolled him for it as their benefactor and deliverer, (*Commentarios de Alb.*
ii. 20,) and no European in India was ever so popular or so revered by the
natives.[32] Yet, if we are to believe the anti-missionaries, none but fools,

fanatics, and pretenders to humanity, would wish to deprive the Hindoo women of the right of burning themselves! 'It may be useful (says Colonel Mark Wilks,) to examine the reasonableness of interfering with the most exceptionable of all their institutions. It has been thought an abomination not to be tolerated, that a widow should immolate herself on the funeral pile of her deceased husband. But what judgment should we form of the Hindoo, who (if any of our institutions admitted the parallel) should *forcibly* pretend to stand between a Christian and the hope of eternal salvation? And shall we not hold him to be a driveller in politics and morals, a fanatic in religion, and a pretender in humanity, who would forcibly wrest this hope from the Hindoo widow?' – *Historical Sketches of the South of India*, vol. i. p. 499.[33]

Such opinions, and such language, may safely be left to the indignation and pity which they cannot fail to excite. I shall only express my astonishment, that any thing so monstrous, and so miserably futile, should have proceeded from a man of learning, great good sense, and general good feelings, as Colonel Wilks evidently appears to be....

From a late investigation, it appears, that the number of women who sacrifice themselves within thirty miles round Calcutta every year, is, on an average, upwards of two hundred. The Pundits[34] have already been called on to produce the sanction of their Shasters[35] for this custom. The passages exhibited are vague and general in their meaning, and differently interpreted by the same casts. Some sacred verses commend the practice, but none command it; and the Pundits refer once more to *custom*. They have, however, intimated, that if government will pass a regulation, amercing by fine every Brahmin who attends a burning, or every Zemindar[36] who permits him to attend it, the practice cannot possibly long continue; for that the ceremony, unsanctified by the presence of the priests, will lose its dignity and consequence in the eyes of the people.

The civilized world may expect soon to hear of the abolition of this opprobrium of a Christian administration, the female sacrifice; which has subsisted, to our certain knowledge, since the time of Alexander the Great.[37] – CLAUDIUS BUCHANAN.[38]

Extract 6: from James Mill, *The History of British India*, 3 vols (London: Baldwin, Craddock, Joy, 1817), 1: 304–10

Much attention has been attracted to the gentleness of Hindu manners. This people possess a feminine softness both in their persons and in their address. As the inhabitants of Europe were rough and impetuous in their rude and early state, and grew mild only as they grew civilized, the gentleness of Hindu manners has usually impressed their European visitors, particularly the English, with high ideas of their progress in civilization. It is, perhaps, a natural ground of presumption; but fallacious if taken as a conclusive proof. One of the circumstances which distinguish the state of commencing civilization is, that it is compatible with great ferocity, as well as great gentleness of manners. Nothing is more common than examples of both. Mildness of address is not always separated even from the rudest condition of human life, as the Otaheitans, and some other of the South-Sea islanders, abundantly testify. 'The savages of North America are affectionate in their carriage, and in their conversations pay a mutual attention and regard, says Charlevoix, more tender and more engaging, than what we profess in the ceremonial of polished societies.'[39]

The causes which seem to account for these effects are partly physical, and partly moral. Where the commodities of life, by a happy union of climate and soil, are abundant, gentleness of manners, as appears by the traditions respecting the golden or pastoral age, is by no means unnatural to men in the earliest period of improvement: The savage involved in a continual struggle with want, who sees himself and his children every day exposed to perish with hunger, is, by a sort of necessity, rapacious, harsh, unfeeling, and cruel. The species of polity under which the national character is formed is perhaps to a still greater degree the cause of the diversity which we now contemplate. Where the mind is free, and may vent its passions with little fear, the nation, while ignorant, and rude, is also fierce and impetuous: Where slavery prevails, and any departure from the most perfect obsequiousness is sure to be followed with the most direful consequences, an insinuating and fawning behaviour is the interest, and thence becomes the habit, of the people.

With the same causes are connected other leading features in the character of the Hindus. They are remarkably prone, for example, to flattery; the most prevailing mode of address from the weak to the strong, while they are still ignorant and unreflecting. The Hindus are full of dissimulation and false-hood, the universal concomitants of oppression. The vices of falsehood, indeed, they carry to a height almost unexampled, if we except their neighbours the Chinese, among the other races of men. Judicial perjury is more than common; it is almost universal. 'Perjury,' said Sir William Jones, to the Grand Jury at Calcutta, 'seems, to be committed by the meanest, and encouraged by some of the better sort among the Hindus and Mussulmans, with as little remorse, as if it were a proof of ingenuity, or even a merit.' – 'I have many reasons to believe, and none to doubt, that affidavits of every imaginable fact may as easily be procured in the streets and markets of Calcutta, especially from the natives, as any other article of traffic.' Speaking of the forms of an oath among the Hindus, he says, 'But such is the corrupt state even of their erroneous religion, that, if the most binding form on the consciences of men could be known and established, there would be few consciences to be bound by it.'[40]

I have not enumerated the religion of the Hindus as one among the causes of that gentleness, which has been remarked in their deportment. This religion has produced a practice, which has strongly engaged the curiosity of Europeans; a superstitious care of the life of the inferior animals. A Hindu lives in perpetual terror of killing even an insect; and hardly any crime can equal that of being unintentionally the cause of death to any of the more sacred animals. This feeble circumstance, however, is counteracted by so many gloomy and malignant principles, that their religion, instead of humanizing the character, must have had no inconsiderable effect in fostering that disposition to revenge, that insensibility to the sufferings of others, and often that active cruelty, which lurks under the smiling exterior of the Hindu. 'Although the killing of an animal of the ox kind,' says Buchanan, 'is by all Hindus considered as a kind of murder, I know no creature whose sufferings equal those of the labouring cattle of Hindustan.'[41] No other race of men are perhaps so little friendly, and beneficent to one another as the Hindus. 'Dysenteries,' says Dr. Tennant, speaking of the salt manufacturers, 'are, at one season, peculiarly fatal. The unhappy victims of this disorder are avoided as infectious by their companions, and suffered to pine without receiving either that aid or consolation, which compassion usually pays to the wretched.'[42] 'The Bengalese,' says another traveller, 'will seldom assist each other, unless they happen to be friends or relations, and then the service that they render only consists in carrying the sufferer to the water of the Ganges, to let him die there, or be carried away by the stream.'[43] Le Couteur remarks, that 'men accustomed from their infancy to abstain from every kind of cruelty towards brutes, ought naturally to be humane and benevolent towards their own species: And this would infallibly be the case, if the same religion had not hardened the hearts of the superior casts; for they hold those that are born their inferiors, as beings below even the most worthless animals: they take away the life of a man with less scruple than we kill a fowl. To strike a cow would be sacrilege; but a Bramin may put a man to death when he lists.'[44]

It commonly happens that in a rude period of society, the virtue of hospitality, generously and cordially displayed, helps to cast into the shade the viler passions which adhere to man in his uncultivated state. The unhappy circumstances, religious and political, of the Hindu, have eradicated even this, the virtue of a rude age, from his breast. The Hindus are notorious for the want of hospitality. After noticing, in various parts of his journey, the striking instances of this which he witnessed, Dr. Buchanan says in one passage, 'I mention these difficulties, which are very frequently met with by travellers in all parts of India where Europeans have not long resided, to show the inhospitable nature of its inhabitants.' For one of his sepoys, who was seized with an acute disease, and left in agony by the side of the road, he could not, except by force, in a large village, obtain a cot, though he was assured there was one in every house.[45]

The ancient literature of the Hindus affords many proofs that no inconsiderable degree of ferocity has at all times been mingled with the other ingredients of their character. The Yadavas, a sacred race, the kindred of Crishna, in a drunken fray, took arms, and butchered one another, to the utter extinction of the race. One of the most remarkable stories in the celebrated book, called *Hetopadesa*, is that of a man who cut off his wife's nose, because she would not speak to him.[46] The performance of that great religious ceremony, called a Jug, is so prevailing as to extort from the divinity whatever boon the true performer demands.[47] The following law makes provision against the most cool, intense, and persevering malignity of which human nature appears to be susceptible. 'If a man performs a jugg to procure the death of any innocent person, the magistrate shall fine him 200 puns of cowries.'[48] If the gentleness, too, of the punishment, about ten shillings, be a sign, the indignation, which so atrocious a purpose excites, is far from remarkable. That murder, by the most odious means, by poison, is looked upon in the same venial light, the following law bears equal testimony. 'If a man, to procure the death of any innocent person, by any contrivance, causes him to drink a potion, or otherwise meditates his death, the magistrate shall fine him 200 puns of cowries.' The cool reflection which attends the villany of the Hindu, has often surprised the European. Mr Holwell informs us, that, when he sat as a judge at Calcutta, he had often heard the most atrocious murders avowed and defended by the criminals, on the ground of its being now the Cali age, when men are destined to be wicked.[49]

Notwithstanding the degree to which the furious passions enter into the character of the Hindu, all witnesses agree in representing him as a timid being. With more apparent capacity of supporting pain than any other race of men and, on many occasions, a superiority to the fear of death which cannot be surpassed, this people run from danger with more trepidation and eagerness than has been almost ever witnessed in any other part of the globe.

Extract 7: from Abu Talib Ibn Muhammad Khan Isfahani, *The Travels of Mirza Abu Taleb Khan in Asia, Africa, and Europe, during the years 1799, 1800, 1801, 1802, and 1803, written by himself in the Persian Language*, trans. Charles Stewart, 3 vols (1810; London: Longman, 1814), 2: 128–38, 142–5, 147–50, 153–6

The first and greatest defect I observed in the English, is their want of faith in religion, and their great inclination to philosophy (atheism). The effects of these principles, or rather want of principle, is very conspicuous in the lower orders of people, who are totally devoid of honesty. They are, indeed, cautious how they transgress against the laws, from fear of punishment; but whenever an opportunity offers of purloining any thing without the risk of detection, they never pass it by. They are also ever on the watch to appropriate to themselves the property of the rich, who, on this account, are obliged constantly to keep their doors shut, and never to permit an unknown person to enter them. At present, owing to the vigilance of the magistrates, the severity of the laws, and the honour of the superior classes of people, no very bad consequences are to be apprehended; but if ever such nefarious practices should become prevalent, and should creep in among the higher classes, inevitable ruin must ensue.

The second defect, most conspicuous in the English character, is pride, or insolence. Puffed up with their power and good fortune for the last fifty years, they are not apprehensive of adversity, and take no pains to avert it. Thus, when the people of London, some time ago, assembled in mobs on account of the great increase of taxes and high price of provisions, and were nearly in a state of insurrection, – although the magistrates, by their vigilance in watching them, and by causing parties of soldiers to patrole the streets day and night, to disperse all persons whom they saw assembling together, succeeded in quieting the disturbance, – yet no pains were afterwards taken to eradicate the evil. Some of the men in power said, it had been merely a plan of the artificers to obtain higher wages (an attempt frequently made by the English tradesmen); others were of opinion that no remedy could be applied; therefore no further notice was taken of the affair. All this, I say, betrays a blind confidence, which, instead of meeting the danger and endeavouring to prevent it, waits till the misfortune arrives, and then attempts to remedy it. Such was the case with the late King of France, who took no step to oppose the Revolution, till it was too late.[50] This self-confidence is be be found, more or less, in every Englishman: it however differs much from the pride of the Indians and Persians.

Their third defect is a passion for acquiring money, and their attachment to worldly affairs. Although these bad qualities are not so reprehensible in them as in countries more subject to the vicissitudes of fortune, (because, in England, property is so well protected by the laws, that every person reaps the fruit of his industry, and, in his old age, enjoys the earnings or economy of his youth,) yet sordid and illiberal habits are generally found to accompany avarice and parsimony, and, consequently, render the possessor of them contemptible: on the contrary, generosity, if it does not launch into prodigality, but is guided by the hand of prudence, will render a man respected and esteemed.

The fourth of their frailties is a desire of ease, and a dislike to exertion: this, however, prevails only in a moderate degree, and bears no proportion to the apathy and indolence of the smokers of opium of Hindoostan and Constantinople; it only prevents them from perfecting themselves in science, and exerting themselves in the service of their friends, upon what they choose to call trivial occasions. I must, however, remark that friendship is much oftener cemented by acts of courtesy and good-nature, than by conferring permanent obligations; the opportunities of doing which can seldom occur, whereas the former happen daily....

Upon a cursory observation of the conduct of gentlemen in London, you would suppose they had a vast deal of business to attend to; whereas nine out of ten, of those I was acquainted with at the west end of the town, had scarcely any thing to do. An hour or two immediately after breakfast may be allotted to business, but the rest of the day is devoted to visiting and pleasure. If a person calls on any of these gentlemen, it is more than probable he is told by the servant, his master is not at home; but this is merely an idle excuse, to avoid the visits of people, whose business they are either ignorant of, or do not wish to be troubled with. If the suppliant calls in the morning, and is by chance admitted to the master of the house, before he can tell half his story, he is informed, that it is now the hour of business, and a particular engagement in the city requires the gentleman's immediate attendance. If he calls later in the day, the gentleman is just going out to pay a visit of consequence, and therefore cannot be detained: but if the petitioner, unabashed by such checks, continues to relate his narrative, he is set down as a brute, and never again permitted to enter the doors. In this instance, I again say that the French are greatly superior to the English: they are always courteous, and never betray those symptoms of impatience so conspicuous and reprehensible in the English character.

Their fifth defect is nearly allied to the former, and is termed irritability of temper. This passion often leads them to quarrel with their friends and acqaintances, without any substantial cause. Of the bad effects of this quality, strangers seldom have much reason to complain; but as society can only be supported by mutual forbearance, and sometimes shutting our eyes on the frailties or ignorance of our friends, it often causes animosities and disunion between the nearest relatives, and hurries the possessor into dilemmas whence he frequently finds it difficult to extricate himself.

The sixth defect of the English is their throwing away their time, in sleeping, eating, and dressing; for, besides the necessary ablutions, they every morning shave, and dress their hair; then, to accommodate themselves to the fashion, they put on twenty-five different articles of dress: all this, except shaving, is repeated before dinner, and the whole of these clothes are again to be taken off at night: so that not less than two complete hours can be allowed on this account. One hour is expended at breakfast; three hours at dinner; and the three following hours are devoted to tea, and the company of the ladies. Nine hours are given up to sleep; so that there remain just six hours, out of the twenty-four, for visiting and business. If they are reproached with this waste of time, they reply, 'How is it to be avoided?' I answer them thus: 'Curtail the number of your garments; render your dress simple; wear your beards; and give up less of your time to eating, drinking, and sleeping.'

Their seventh defect is a luxurious manner of living, by which their wants are increased a hundred-fold. Observe their kitchens, filled with various utensils; their rooms, fitted up with costly furniture; their side-boards, covered with plate; their tables, loaded with expensive glass and china; their cellars, stocked with wines from every quarter of the world; their parks, abounding in game of various sorts; and their ponds, stored with fish. All these expences are incurred to pamper their appetites, which, from long indulgence, have gained such absolute sway over them, that a diminution of these luxuries would be considered, by many, as a serious misfortune. How unintelligible to them is the verse of one of their own Poets:

'Man wants but little here below,
Nor wants that little long.'[51]

It is certain, that luxurious living generates many disorders, and is productive of various other bad consequences. . . .

The eighth defect of the English is vanity, and arrogance, respecting their acquirements in science, and a knowledge of foreign languages; for, as soon as one of them acquires the smallest insight into the principles of any science, or the rudiments of any foreign language, he immediately sits down and composes a work on the subject, and, by means of the Press, circulates books which have no more intrinsic worth than the toys bestowed on children, which serve to amuse the ignorant, but are of no use to the learned. This is not merely my own opinion, but was confirmed to me both by Greeks and Frenchmen, whose languages are cultivated in England with more ardour than any others. Such, however, is the infatuation of the English, that they give the author implicit credit for his profound knowledge, and purchase his books. Even those who are judges of the subject do not discountenance this measure, but contend, that a little knowledge is better than entire ignorance, and that perfection can only be acquired by degrees. This axiom I deny; for the portion of science and truth contained in many of their books is so small, that much time is thrown away in reading them: besides, erroneous opinions and bad habits are often contracted by the perusal of such works, which are more difficult to eradicate, than it is to implant correct ideas in a mind totally uncultivated.

Far be it from me to deprecate the transcendant abilities and angelic character of Sir William Jones; but his Persian Grammar, having been written when he was a young man, and previous to his having acquired any experience in Hindoostan, is, in many places, very defective; and it is much to be regretted that his public avocations, and other studies, did not permit him to revise it, after he had been some years in India.[52] Whenever I was applied to by any person for instruction in the Persian language, who had previously studied this grammar, I found it much more difficult to correct the bad pronunciation he had acquired, and the errors he had adopted, than it was to instruct a person who had never before seen the Persian alphabet. Such books are now so numerous in London, that, in a short time, it will be difficult to discriminate or separate them from works of real value.

A ninth failing prevalent among the English is selfishness. They frequently endeavour to benefit themselves, without attending to the injury it may do to others: and when they seek their own advantage, they are more humble and submissive than appears to me proper; for after they have obtained their object, they are ashamed of their former conduct, or dislike the continuance of it so much, that they frequently break off the connection. Others, restrained by a sense of propriety, still keep up the intercourse, and endeavour to make the person they have injured, or whom they have deceived by promises, forget the circumstance, by their flattering and courteous behaviour. . . .

The tenth vice of this nation is want of chastity; for under this head I not only include the reprehensible conduct of young women running away with their lovers, and others cohabiting with a man before marriage, but the great degree of licentiousness practised by numbers of both sexes in London, evinced by the multiplicity of public-houses and bagnios[53] in every part of town. I was credibly informed, that in the single parish of Mary-la-bonne,[54] which is only a sixth part of London, there reside sixty thousand courtezans; besides which, there is scarcely a street in the metropolis where they are not to be found. The conduct of these women is rendered still more blameable, by their hiring lodgings in or frequenting streets which from their names ought only to be the abode of virtue and religion; for instance, 'Paradise Street,' 'Modest Court,' 'St. James's Street,' 'St. Martin's Lane,' and 'St. Paul's Churchyard.' The first of these is to be the residence of the righteous; the second implies virtue; and the others are named after the holy Apostles of the Blessed Messiah. Then there is 'Queen Anne Street,' and 'Charlotte Street;' the one named after the greatest, the other after the best, of Queens. I however think, that persons who let the lodgings are much more reprehensible than the unfortunate women themselves.

The eleventh vice of the English is extravagance, that is, living beyond their incomes by incurring useless expences, and keeping up unnecessary establishments. Some of these I have alluded to, under the head of luxuries; but to those are now to be added the establishments of carriages, horses, and servants, two sets of which are frequently kept, one for the husband, the other for his wife. Much money is also lavished in London, on balls, masquerades, routs, &c. Sometimes the sum of £.1000 is thus expended in one night's entertainment. . . .

Their twelfth defect is a contempt for the customs of other nations, and the preference they give to their own; although theirs, in fact, may be much inferior. . . .

In London, I was frequently attacked on the apparent unreaonableness and childishness of some of the Mohammedan customs; but as, from my knowledge of the English character, I was convinced it would be folly to argue the point philosophically with them, I contented myself with parrying the subject. Thus, when they attempted to turn into ridicule the ceremonies used by the pilgrims on their arrival at Mecca, I asked them, why they supposed the ceremony of baptism, by a clergyman, requisite for the salvation of a child, who could not possibly be sensible what he was about? When they reproached us for eating with our hands; I replied, 'There is by this mode no danger of cutting yourself or your neighbours; and it is an old and a true proverb, "The nearer the bone, the sweeter the meat": but, exclusive of these advantages, a man's own hands are surely cleaner than the *feet of a baker's boy*; for it is well known, that half the bread in London is kneaded by the feet.' By this mode of argument, I completely silenced all my adversaries, and frequently turned the laugh against them, when they expected to have refuted me and made me appear ridiculous.

SELECT BIBLIOGRAPHY

Bayly, C. A., *Imperial Meridian: The British Empire and the World 1780–1830* (London: Longman, 1989). Study of the British Empire in the context of Asian and Islamic regimes.

Blackburn, Robin, *The Overthrow of Colonial Slavery 1776–1848* (London: Verso, 1988). Account of liberation struggles against slavery in the Americas and anti-slavery movement in Europe.

Drescher, Seymour, *Capitalism and Antislavery: British Mobilization in Comparative Perspective* (London: Macmillan, 1986). Comparative study of anti-slavery movement; discusses the case of Saartjie Baartman.

Ferguson, Moira, *Subject to Others: British Women Writers and Colonial Slavery 1670–1834* (New York and London: Routledge, 1992). Traces the history of women's anti-slavery writing and examines the place of Elizabeth Heyrick in that tradition.

Leask, Nigel, *British Romantic Writers and the East: Anxieties of Empire* (Cambridge: Cambridge University Press, 1992). Reads the work of Byron, Shelley and

De Quincey in terms of British involvement in the East; examines the influence of Southey on Shelley.

McCalman, Iain, 'Anti-Slavery and Ultra-Radicalism in Early Nineteenth-Century England: The Case of Robert Wedderburn', *Slavery and Abolition* 7(2) (September 1986): 99–117. Argues that anti-slavery ideas were widespread in plebeian, ultra-radical circles. For more information on Wedderburn's milieu see the introduction to McCalman's edition of Robert Wedderburn, *The Horrors of Slavery and Other Writings* (Edinburgh: Edinburgh University Press, 1991).

Majeed, Javed, *Ungoverned Imaginings: James Mill's The History of British India and Orientalism* (Oxford: Oxford University Press, 1992). A study of the aesthetics and politics of the work of orientalist scholars and poets: William Jones, Robert Southey, Thomas Moore and James Mill.

Said, Edward W., *Culture and Imperialism* (London: Chatto and Windus, 1993). Analyses nineteenth- and twentieth-century literature in relation to the history of empire, decolonization and independence.

—— *Orientalism* (1978; Harmondsworth: Penguin, 1991). Wide-ranging discussion of European and American representations of the East; a founding text in the study of colonial discourse.

Schwab, Raymond, *The Oriental Renaissance: Europe's Rediscovery of India and the East 1680–1880*, trans. Gene Patterson Black and Victor Reinking (New York: Columbia University Press, 1984). An account of the impact of orientalist scholarship on European culture.

Stepan, Nancy, *The Idea of Race in Science: Great Britain 1800–1900* (London: Macmillan, 1982). Charts the development of racial theory and science in nineteenth-century Britain; places the ideas of William Lawrence in context.

Stokes, Eric, *The English Utilitarians and India* (Oxford: Oxford University Press, 1959). Demonstrates how India became the testing ground for utilitarian ideas and highlights the importance of James Mill.

5

NATION AND STATE

Simon Edwards

Issues of national identity arising from the roles of Scotland and Ireland within an expanded British state are at the heart of a significant strand of the writing of the period, particularly of its prose fiction. This section focuses on some of the political, cultural and intellectual concerns raised by this writing. Although the immediate social, economic and political conditions differed widely between Ireland and Scotland, there was also a remarkable exchange of cultural and literary energy among writers from both countries.[1]

The period begins with the passage of the Act of Union between the nominally separate kingdoms of Ireland and England in 1800. The transfer of parliamentary representation from Dublin to Westminster had momentous political and constitutional consequences, not only in the immediately following decades, but throughout the nineteenth century and down, indeed, to our own time.[2] Modelled, in part, on the 1707 Act of Union between Scotland and England, it might have looked, from one perspective, like the culmination of the modern British state, whose seeming apotheosis was reached by the defeat of Napoleon at the battle of Waterloo in 1815. More plausibly, however, it could be interpreted as an essentially defensive measure, which, in the wake of the 1798 rebellion of the United Irishmen, led by the Protestant Wolfe Tone, was intended to secure the most vulnerable part of the British Isles from the danger of French invasion.[3] While its terms were intended to propitiate the interests of the almost wholly Protestant Anglo-Irish land-owning class — the Ascendancy — it was also expected to facilitate the modernization of the notoriously backward Irish economy, in the manner of Scotland's in the previous century.

The Prime Minister, Pitt, who introduced the legislation into the English Commons in 1799, had certainly considered the necessity of some form of Catholic emancipation, if only to guarantee the loyalty of the vast majority of the Irish to the new regime.[4] His resignation in 1801, in the face of royal opposition to emancipation, was simply the first of a series of constitutional crises endemic to the new Union. Another immediate effect was the abortive revolt led by Robert Emmet in 1803.[5] Thereafter the revolutionary impulse in Ireland was diverted into

Ribbonism, a popular movement of agrarian protest analogous in many ways to contemporary unrest in the English countryside associated with Luddism and 'Captain Swing'. Ribbonism, nevertheless, was able to draw on the proto-nationalist sentiment which had characterized the Defender movement of the 1790s, while it anticipated the later whole-hearted commitment to Irish independence of the Fenian movement.[6]

Perhaps the most striking consequence of this agitation was the growth of a new kind of political organization, led by the Dublin lawyer, Daniel O'Connell (1775–1847). O'Connell's distinctive strategy was the mobilization of popular support for Catholic emancipation to be achieved by constitutional means. The formation of the mass membership Catholic Association in 1824 eventually led to O'Connell himself standing successfully for parliament in 1828. Although his electoral support came largely from Catholic voters, he was unable to take his seat without renouncing his faith. That a bill removing Catholic disabilities was finally passed in 1829 (by an administration led by the Anglo-Irish Duke of Wellington) confirmed the deeper crisis in post-war Tory political hegemony, leading the way to the Whig election victory of 1830 and the introduction of parliamentary reform. The Irish political agenda too shifted radically. O'Connell was now to become the leader of a parliamentary group seeking repeal of the Act of Union itself.

O'Connell's parliamentary strategy was soon to be accompanied, if not over-taken, by a new generation of nationalist spokesmen – the so called Young Ireland movement led by Thomas Davis.[7] It was clear, by the end of this period, that there had existed in Ireland, as elsewhere in Europe, only a fine line between the constitutional aspirations of bourgeois nationalism and the revolutionary invoca-tion of popular sovereignty.[8]

Some of the contradictory lineaments of Irish politics and culture can be found in the work of Sydney Owenson (later Lady Morgan). Her first novel, *The Wild Irish Girl* (1806), was significantly sub-titled *A National Tale*. Her fictional treatment of Irish material had been anticipated by Maria Edgeworth's *Castle Rackrent* (1800).[9] Whereas Edgeworth's first essay in Irish fiction might have seemed to serve as a literary footnote to the Act of Union, an ambiguous celebration of the passing of a corrupt and venal old order, Owenson's treatment made the divisions in Irish society far more explicit. The novel's clumsy and rambling courtship plot is the vehicle for a series of encounters between Mortimer, the heir to a vast Anglo-Irish estate, travelling the country *incognito*, and the pervasive culture of an older dispossessed Gaelic aristocracy. Mortimer eventually marries the 'Wild Irish Girl', Glorvina, heiress to the Irish title of the estate, thus enabling the property to be 'restored' to her in her husband's name. Such a marriage suggests a wished-for reconciliation between two aristocratic orders, but the novel itself reinforces the complete incompatibility of two competing social and cultural codes. Thus it effectively undermines the project of the Union which the novel's nominal eighteenth-century setting predates. Glorvina presides, together with her father and an articulate and cultured priest (not to mention her fatefully seductive harp), over a coherent but wholly different world. If Irish civilization is subject to erosion, its features are too distinctive for it to disappear. Indeed the systematic recollection of historical and cultural difference emphasizes the role of the Irish past in determining the present, the impossibility of its incorporation into an Anglocentric Protestant vision of modernity.[10] This problem is focused in **extract 1**, when Mortimer and his priestly mentor, Father John, cross the 'imaginary line' between Connaught and Ulster, that divides the largely Catholic western province from the province most intensively settled by Protestant immigrants.[11] In an attempt at narrative balance it is the priest who provides the tentative *apologia* for Ulster's untypical social, economic and, crucially, *ethnic* formation, and Mortimer who immediately wishes to return. The introduction of 'Wee Wully', a dourly provincial Scot, with his boast of never having gone more than twenty miles from his home, clearly directs the reader's response. The precise rendering of Wully's dialect speech signals further that the Ulsterization of the rest of Ireland is a remote and untenable prospect.[12]

In **extract 2**, Owenson strikes an almost apocalyptic note at the end of her 1825 essay on 'Absenteeism' for *The New Monthly Magazine*. Landlord absenteeism had come to be seen as the key symptom in the diagnosis of contemporary Irish ailments. Consistently active in radical causes, Owenson sets out the case for both Catholic emancipation and the repeal of the Union. Such drastic measures would, however, leave little or no place for the Ascendancy world with whose values she still identifies. Thus, paradoxically, in her closing peroration she seems to make the case most eloquently *for* absenteeism! The new Ireland was not to be found under the aegis of a revitalized Gaelic aristocracy working harmoniously with responsible Protestant patriots, but reveals itself in a 'race of vulgar upstarts, or uneducated and capricious despots, spreading a barbarous *morgue* over the once elegant society of the metropolis, and banishing peace and security from the mountain and the plain'. Elsewhere 'the landholder, wearied by his contests with the clergy, and intimidated by the armed and masked opposition of his tenancy' can choose only to retreat. If the Whig hauteur of this explicit disdain for Catholic bourgeoisie and peasantry alike comes a little oddly from the daughter of a provincial theatre-manager, it is also a measure of the political dead-end that confronts any Anglo-Irish solution to the problem. Owenson's conclusion seems a fatalistic resignation to a mire of degraded modernity that echoes that of Swift a century earlier, as much as it anticipates that of Yeats a century later.[13]

Within the long tradition of Irish exile and emigration, it may be instructive to balance Owenson's assertion that 'absenteeism is less a crime than a misfortune', with some examination of the fortunes of her contemporary Thomas Moore (1779–1852). The Catholic son of a Dublin grocer, he found his way as an expatriate with the astonishing success of his now little-considered but well-remembered *Irish Airs and Melodies* (1807–34). Not only did these songs grace the English drawing-room for over a century (among the best known are 'The Minstrel Boy', 'Oft in the Stilly Night' and 'Believe Me, If All Those Endearing Young Charms'), but he was also the author of the best-selling 'orientalist' poem *Lallah Rookh* (1817), whose popularity rivalled anything by either Scott or Byron (whose biographer he was to become). We may want to see Moore's exile, in Owenson's terms, as the flight of a sensitive soul from the 'fat, contented ignorance' of contemporary Dublin. Alternatively he might be cast as the cultural epitome of an Irish diaspora driven as much by economic *opportunity* in the first decades of the century, as it was by economic necessity during the Great Famine of the 1840s. Moore had some aspirations as a satirical poet, producing verse on contemporary Irish political themes, from a position of moderate constitutionalism. **Extract 3** appeared as an appendix to two such poems, *Corruption* and *Intolerance*, published in 1808. It is, at once, playful and bitter, as much about the myths as the realities of Irish history, and, of course, the difficulty of separating them. While this brief essay, with its quirky classical scholarship, manages to suggest the pleasures of elegiac withdrawal that are so manifest in the *Airs and Melodies* themselves (the quality that gave them their wide appeal), it also more profoundly asks what are the appropriate cultural forms for a putatively dynamic modern nation, with Moore, himself, at a loss to provide an answer.

If the status and function of Irish culture, whether ancient or modern, seemed both urgent and uncertain within the political cul-de-sac into which the nation had been driven, then the buoyancy of contemporary Scottish culture, by contrast, is all the more notable. Both the legacy of the past as well as the distinctive features of the modern found their way into diverse literary forms. It was as though James MacPherson's by now long-exploded *Ossian* legends (1761–63) had cleared the way of Jacobite lament, and the real dynamics of Scottish history and society could be confronted, although largely if not always from within the Union.[14]

Scotland had proved, throughout the revolutionary years either side of 1800, in Bruce Lenman's words, 'the most deferential of the British provinces'.[15] The resignation of the Pitt government in 1801 had taken with it the notorious Henry Dundas, the Tory politician responsible for ensuring the compliance of the vast majority of Scotland's forty-five Westminster MPs.[16] There was, however, little shift in the balance of power north of the border and Dundas returned briefly to office as the Earl of Melville. He survived a charge of impeachment and in 1807 was succeeded by his son Robert. Nevertheless Scottish intellectual and cultural life was charged with the expectation of imminent transformation of the whole political system, a source of both promise and anxiety. This was, in part, a result of the very success of Scotland's incorporation into the Union, its economy relatively booming in each of the agricultural, mercantile and industrial spheres. If neither Whig nor Tory could countenance the dissolution of the Union, or conceive a role for a radical popular politics, the intellectual legacy of the Scottish Enlightenment had without doubt generated a unique self-consciousness about the nature of national identity within the broad parameters of modern historical progress.[17] Such self-conscious-ness was galvanized by the admission of Ireland to the Union, as well as by events in mainland Europe with its new political agenda of national liberation.[18]

The vitality and energy of Scottish culture was to be found in four competing periodical journals. Francis Jeffrey's *Edinburgh Review* was founded in 1802 and by 1813 had a subscription of 12,000 (comparing favourably with the daily circulation of the London *Times* at 8,000 in the same period). Its increasing radicalism led to the founding of the Tory *Quarterly Review* under Scott's aggrandizing publisher Archibald Constable. The end of the Napoleonic wars saw the launch of the pro-reform *Scotsman* in 1817, to be followed almost immediately by the aggressively Tory *Blackwood's Edinburgh Magazine* under the direction of John Wilson (or 'Christopher North').[19] It was from this fertile ground that the reputation not only of Scott emerged, but also that of a number of distinctively Scottish writers. These included James Hogg, 'The Ettrick Shepherd', whose peasant farmer origins made him a plausible heir to Robert Burns;[20] John Galt, whose 'philosophical histories' provided a fictional chronicle of the changing social fabric of south-west Scotland, and, by his own claim, were conceived prior to Scott's own first excursion into the historical novel;[21] and the young Thomas Carlyle.[22] Within this milieu literary experiment, antiquarian historical interests and questions of poetic judgement were pursued alongside explicitly political debate and commentary with equal, if not greater, acerbity.

As **extract 5** suggests, the most potent author to emerge from this veritable literary renaissance was Walter Scott. If the first three decades of the century as a whole see the growth of a new kind of English novel in which issues of national history and identity, popular life, cultural difference and political synthesis are repeatedly addressed, then this genre was crucially seized and developed in the historical fiction of Scott.[23] From the publication of his first novel, *Waverley*, in 1814, his prolific output was not merely to determine in many ways the develop-ment of European fiction as a whole, but to contribute, in part unwittingly, to the new rationale of the *patria* as an ethnically and linguistically cohesive nation, with both a mythic origin and destiny. The revolutionary 'people' of the late eighteenth century were remade as the waiting 'peoples' of the early nineteenth, a plethora of histories and aspirations, some already engaged in struggle, others still in the process of invention.[24]

While obviously in no way a patron in the political sense, Scott can be seen as performing a role in the cultural sphere comparable to that played by his close personal friends Dundas and the Duke of Buccleuch (1746–1812), the largest land-owner in the Scottish lowlands, in the political sphere. He sponsored and facilitated countless projects – from the antiquarian philologist John Jamieson's seminal *Dictionary of the Scottish Language* (1808) with its *Supplement* of 1825, to his notorious stage-management of the 1822 state visit to Edinburgh, a great and grotesque gathering of the 'clans' offering their loyalty to George IV, the first

Hanoverian monarch to cross the border.[25] Nor did Scott's involvement in this eminently clubbable male world preclude enthusiastic support for numerous women writers, not least the widely admired dramatist Joanna Baillie (1762–1851).

John Lockhart's *Peter's Letters to His Kinsfolk* (1819), putatively written by a visiting Welshman, offers an extended commentary on the Edinburgh literary scene. It reveals not only a sharp eye for contemporary controversy, but attempts, as **extracts 4–5** suggest, to account more fully for the origins and significance of a modern national culture. Lockhart (1794–1854) was a young lawyer actively involved in the *Blackwood's* circle. He was later to marry Scott's daughter and write his biography. In 1817 he visited Goethe at Weimar, at *Blackwood*'s expense, and, on his return to Scotland, published a translation of Schlegel's *On the History of Literature* (1818).[26] Enthusiasm for the heady admixture of philosophical, political and aesthetic theory to be found in German literature was not confined to Scottish writers. There is no doubt, however, that Lockhart's Tory sympathies made him susceptible to the note of reactionary nationalism to be found in Schlegel's work.

Such reactionary political theory in the context of Scotland's continuing membership of the Union could generate some striking paradoxes, as **extract 6**, by Scott himself, indicates. In response to a financial crisis in the autumn of 1825, the government proposed to suppress the issue of all bank notes below the value of £5. While this may have been relevant to the eight hundred or so small English banks, it ignored the relative stability of the Scottish banking system. Indeed the three large joint-stock banking companies in Scotland had proved adept in the supply and control of paper money on which the Scottish economy was dependent. It was only in England that something like seventy banks had failed in the winter of 1825/6. Scott, however, had borrowed heavily from English creditors and was left spectacularly bankrupt in the wake of the crisis, with debts of £104,000.[27] This personal embarrassment may have been the prime incentive for his decision to campaign against the introduction of the new legislation in Scotland. The extract is taken from the second of a series of 'letters' published in the name of Malachi Malagrowther. Based on Sir Mungo Malagrowther, a cantankerous courtier in an earlier novel, *The Fortunes of Nigel* (1822), this persona allows Scott to retain a distance from the full force of his anti-English rhetoric. Nevertheless, as the argument develops, some of the intolerable strains latent within the Union are made apparent. Analogies are drawn with the far more combustible Anglo-Irish union, as well as the problematic nature of metropolitan authority in France 'during the Revolution, in all its phases'. The extract concludes with an invocation of the American Revolution as the type of an explicit breach with imperial power. Scott's persistent appeal to the idea of imperial unity suggests that his patriotism is still rooted in the politics of *ancien régime* Europe. Nevertheless, his historical and political senses are both too keen for him not to articulate here, however indirectly, a local version of the national aspirations that were to undermine the Restoration settlement in Europe throughout the nineteenth century. Of his wider literary achievement, it may not be too much of an exaggeration to say that in providing a fictionalized history of Scotland's recent past, the *Waverley* novels helped to mould the 'unconscious' of European politics in the decades which followed. The record of their countless translations, adaptations and imitations remains the most outstanding testimony of Scotland's contribution to world history.[28]

Extract 1: from *The Wild Irish Girl: A National Tale: In Three Volumes,* By Miss Owenson (London: Richard Philips, 1806), pp. 89–96

Letter XXVII
To J. D. Esq. M.P.[29]

THE priest is gone on his embassy. The rain, which batters against the casement of my little hotel, prevents my enjoying a ramble. I have nothing to read, and I must write, or yawn myself to death.

Yesterday, as we passed the imaginary line which divides the province of Connaught from that of Ulster, the priest said, 'As we now advance northwards, we shall gradually lose sight of the genuine Irish character, and those ancient manners, modes, customs, and language, with which it is inseparably connected. Not longer after the chiefs of Ireland had declared James the First universal monarch of their country, a sham plot was pretended, consonant to the usual ingratitude of the House of Stuart, by which six entire counties became forfeited, which James with a liberal hand bestowed on his favourites; so that this part of Ireland may in some respects be considered as a Scottish colony, and in fact, Scotch dialect, Scotch manners, Scotch modes, and the Scotch character, almost universally prevail.[30] Here the ardor of the Irish constitution seems abated, if not chilled. Here the *cead-mile failta*[31] of Irish cordiality seldom sends its welcome home to the stranger's heart. The bright beams which illumine the gay images of Milesian[32] fancy are extinguished; the convivial pleasures, dear to the Milesian heart, scared at the prudential maxims of calculating interest, take flight to the warmer regions of the south; and the endearing socialities of the soul, lost and neglected amidst the cold concerns of the counting-house and the *bleach green*,[33] droop and expire in the deficiency of that nutritive warmth on which their tender existence depends. So much for the shades of the picture, which however possesses its lights, and those of no dim lustre. The north of Ireland may be justly esteemed the palladium[34] of Irish industry and Irish trade, where the staple commodity[35] of the kingdom is reared and manufactured; and while the rest of Ireland is devoted to that species of agriculture,[36] which, in lessening the necessity of human labour, deprives man of subsistence; while the wretched native of the Southern provinces (where little labour is required, and consequently little hire given) either famishes in the midst of a helpless family, or begs his way to England, and offers those services there in harvest time, which his own country rejects or wants not; here, both the labourer and his hire rise in the scale of political consideration: here more hands are called for than can be procured; and the peasant, stimulated to exertion by the rewards it reaps for him, enjoys the fruit of his industry, and acquires a relish for the comforts and conveniences of life. Industry, and this taste for comparative luxury, mutually react; and the former, while it bestows the means, enables them to gratify the suggestions of the latter; while their wants, nurtured by enjoyment, afford fresh allurement to continued exertion. In short, a mind not too deeply fascinated by the florid virtues, the warm overflowings of generous and ardent qualities, will find in the Northerns of this island much to admire and esteem; but on the heart they make little claim, and from its affections they receive but little tribute.'[37]

'Then in the name of all that is warm and cordial,' said I, 'let us hasten back to the province of Connaught.'

'That you may be sure we shall,' returned Father John, 'for I know none of these sons of trade; and, until we once more find ourselves within the pale of Milesian hospitality, we must set up at a sorry inn, near a tract of the sea coast, called the Magilligans, and where one *solitary fane*[38] is raised to the once tutelar deity of Ireland; in plain English, where one of the last of the race of *Irish bards*[39] shelters his white head beneath the fractured roof of a wretched hut.' Although the evening sun was setting on the western wave when we reached the inn, yet, while our fried eggs and bacon were preparing, I proposed to the priest that we should visit the old bard before we put up our horses. Father John readily consented, and we inquired his address.

'What the *mon wi the twa heads?*'[40] said our host. I confessed my ignorance of this hydra epithet, which I learnt was derived from an immense wen on the back of his head.

'Oh!' continued our host, 'A wull be telling you weel to gang[41] tull the old Kearn[42] and one of our wains[43] wull show the road. Ye need nae fear, trusting yoursels to our wee Wully, for he os an uncommon kanie chiel.'[44] Such was the dialect of this Hibernian[45] Scot, who assured me he had never been twenty miles from his 'aine wee hame.'

Extract 2: from Lady Morgan [Sydney Owenson], 'Absenteeism', in *The New Monthly Magazine* (London, 1825): 152–9

Previously to the Act of Union, Absenteeism, though encouraged by the geographical position of the country, and promoted by some inveterate habits derived from ancient abuse, was principally confined, among the native Irish, to a few individuals whose ill understood vanity tempted them to seek for a consequence abroad, which is ever denied to the unconnected stranger, a consequence which no extravagant expense can purchase. With a few exceptions, therefore, the malady was confined to the great English proprietors of forfeited estates, whose numbers must in the progress of events have been diminished, by the dissipations inseparable from unbounded wealth, and the growth of commercial and manufactural fortunes. It might, in some cases, indeed, be both a vice, and a ridicule, in the absent; but had the nation in other respects been well used and well governed, it would have been of no serious evil to those who remained at home. But the Act of Union, whatever may be its other operations, meritorious or vicious, at once converted a local disease into a national pestilence. The centre of business and of pleasure, the mart of promotion, and the fountain of favour, were by this one fatal act at once removed into a foreign land; ambition, avarice, dissipation and refinement, all combined to seduce the upper classes into a desertion of their homes and country: and as each succeeding ornament of the Irish capital abandoned his hotel, as each influential landlord quitted his castle in the country, or his house in the city, a new race of vulgar upstarts, of uneducated and capricious despots, usurped their place, spreading a barbarous *morgue*[46] over the once elegant society of the metropolis, and banishing peace and security from the mountain and the plain.

Many whom temptation could not hitherto seduce from home, were now forced by fear to fly; and every passion, every motive combined to drive from the happy land, all those who were possessed of the means of flight. It is in vain that patriotism struggles and conscience arrests the departing step of those who yet linger behind in painful vacillation. Self-preservation must and will in the end prevail. Whatever is educated, whatever is tasteful, whatever is liberal, will too probably fly a land, where the insolence of official rank supplies the amenity of an admitted aristocracy, and where vulgar wealth, acquired by political subserviency, and too frequently unaccompanied by knowledge, holds talent at arms' length, and rejects wit from its coteries as dangerous to its own dull supremacy and hostile to the repose of its own '*fat contented ignorance.*' Philanthropists, disgusted with the perpetual spectacle of hopeless wretchedness and irredeemable despair, will seek relief by flying the misery they cannot mitigate; the enlightened and the liberal will turn with horror from the country where laws of exception[47] have been adopted into the permanent code, and where necessitated violence is only met by judicial severity and legal murder. The landholder, wearied by his contests with the clergy, and intimidated by the armed and masked opposition of his tenantry, will be contented to purchase repose by abandoning at once the soil and its produce, to the proctors, the police-men and their chiefs. The *sbirri*[48] of Ireland will alone find in a land, thus every way accursed, the elements congenial to their existence, as the reptiles and insects subsist in that putrefaction, which spreads disease and death among the nobler animals.

In the present political prospect of Ireland, the eye of philosophy and philanthropy turns on every side in search of a principle of regeneration, and turns in vain. On every side a circle of recurrent cause and effect, like the mystic emblem of the Egyptians, points to an eternity of woe, and to endless cycles of misgovernment and resistance. As long as the actual system continues, (as long as every cause is forced to concur in rendering Ireland uninhabitable,) so long will it be impossible to organize any plan for civilizing, tranquillizing, and enriching the country. It is an empty and an idle boast in the British House of Commons, that it devotes its successive nights to the debating of Irish affairs, so long as the religious division of the people and the proconsular[49] government founded upon that division are to be recognized as sound policy or Christian charity. The half measures which have hitherto been adopted, far from proving beneficial, and composing the contentions of hostile factions, have served only to increase discontent and disarm inquiry.[50] Nor can the ministers be entitled to any praise for generosity who dare not, in the first place, be just. In spite, therefore, of all their professions of zeal and compassion for the national distress; in spite of all their parliamentary tamperings with the national abuses, they must still remain answerable for the greater part of the absenteeship which they strenuously hold up as the giant ill, over which they have no controul, and for the existence of which they imagine themselves not responsible.

The grand principle of '*divide et impera*'[51] has produced both the religious question and the question between landlords and tenants, which are the hinges on which all the misfortunes of Ireland turn. To commence the work of regeneration in earnest, that principle must be fairly and honestly abandoned: when this is done, and not before, absenteeship, with every other evil which has grown out of the monstrous anarchical system, that has so long subsisted, will gradually disappear; and proprietors in Ireland, as in other countries, will inhabit their country, when their country becomes inhabitable. – '*Ube bene, ibi patria*'[52] is a maxim not altogether unreasonable; and, surely, if in any circumstances it is entitled to toleration, it is in that land where the greater the patriotism and virtue, the less chance is there of social comfort and rational happiness. To the absentees themselves we would willingly appeal with every invocation that can bind the conscience or awaken the heart. But the appeal were worse than idle, it would in fact be injurious, by pointing to effects and disengaging the attention from causes. In the present condition of affairs, absenteeism is a necessitated evil!! In the absentees it is less a crime than a misfortune; and with respect to the government it is so far from being a justification of its acts, that it has become a pregnant and a pointed conclusion of its ignorance of all sound principle, or its heartless indifference to all those interests which the unhappy destiny of 'the *most unhappy country under heaven*,' has committed to its charge.

Extract 3: [Thomas Moore], Appendix to *Corruption and Intolerance: Two Poems with Notes Addressed to an Englishman by an Irishman* (London, 1808), pp. 59–64

The following is part of a Preface which was intended by a friend and countryman of mine for a collection of Irish airs[53] to which he had adapted English words. As it has never been published, and is not inapplicable to my subject, I shall take the liberty of subjoining it here.

'Our history, for many centuries past, is creditable neither to our neighbours or ourselves, and ought not to be read by any Irishman who wishes either to love England or to feel proud of Ireland. The loss of independence very early debased our character, and our feuds and rebellions, though frequent and ferocious, but seldom displayed that generous spirit or enterprise, with which the pride of an independent monarchy so long dignified the struggles of Scotland. It is true this island has given birth to heroes who, under more favourable circumstances, might have left in the hearts of their countrymen recollections as dear as those of a Bruce or a Wallace;[54] but success was wanting to consecrate resistance, their cause was branded with the disheartening name of treason, and their oppressed country was such a blank among nations, that, like the adventures of those woods which Rinaldo[55] wished to explore, the fame of their actions was lost in the obscurity of the place where they achieved them.

> errando in quelli boschi
> Trovar potria strane avventure e molte,
> Ma come i luoghi i fatti ancor son foschi
> Che non se'n ha notizia le piu volte.[56]

'Hence it is that the annals of Ireland, through a long lapse of six hundred years,[57] exhibit not one of those shining names, not one of those themes of national pride, from which poetry borrows her noblest inspiration, and that history, which ought to be the richest garden of the Muse, yields nothing to her here but weeds and cypress. In truth, the poet who would embellish his song with allusions to Irish names and events, must be content to seek them in those early periods when our character was yet unalloyed and original, before the impolitic craft of our conquerors had divided, weakened, and disgraced us; and the only traits of heroism which he can venture at this day to commemorate, with safety to himself, or, perhaps, with honour to the country, are to be looked for in those times when the native monarchs of Ireland displayed and fostered virtues worthy of a better age; when our Malachies wore collars of gold which they had won in single combat from the invader, and our Briens[58] deserved the blessings of a people by all the most estimable qualities of a king. It may be said indeed that the magic of tradition has shed a charm over this remote period, to which it is in reality but little entitled, and that most of the pictures, which we dwell on so fondly, of days when this island was distinguished amidst the gloom of Europe, by the sanctity of her morals, the spirit of her knighthood, and the polish of her schools, are little more than the inventions of national partiality, that bright but spurious offspring which vanity engenders upon ignorance, and with which the first records of every people abound. But the sceptic is scarcely to be envied who would pause for stronger proofs than we already possess of the early glories of Ireland; and were even the veracity of all these proofs surrendered, yet who would not fly to such flattering fictions from the sad degrading truths which the history of later times presents to us?

'The language of sorrow however is, in general, best suited to our Music, and with themes of this nature the poet may be amply supplied. There is not a page of our annals which cannot afford him a subject, and while the national Muse of other countries adorns her temple with trophies of the past, in Ireland her altar, like the shrine of Pity at Athens, is to be known only by the tears that are shed upon it; "lacrymis altaria sudant."[59]

'There is a well-known story, related of the Antiochians under the reign of Theodosius,[60] which is not only honourable to the powers of music in general, but which applies so peculiarly to the mournful melodies of Ireland, that I cannot resist the temptation of introducing it here. – The piety of Theodosius would have been admirable, if it had not been stained with intolerance; but his reign affords, I believe, the first example of a disqualifying penal code enacted by Christians against Christians.[61] Whether his interference with the religion of the Antiochians had any share in the alienation of their loyalty is not expressly ascertained by historians; but severe edicts, heavy taxation, and the rapacity and insolence of the men whom he sent to govern them, sufficiently account for the discontents of a warm and susceptible people. Repentance soon followed the crimes into which their impatience had hurried them, but the vengeance of the Emperor was implacable, and punishments of the most dreadful nature hung over the city of Antioch, whose devoted inhabitants, totally resigned to despondence, wandered through the streets and public assemblies, giving utterance to their grief in dirges of the most touching lamentation.[62] At length, Flavianus, their bishop, whom they sent to intercede with Theodosius, finding all his entreaties coldly rejected, adopted the expedient of teaching these songs of sorrow, which he had heard from the lips of his unfortunate countrymen, to the minstrels who performed for the Emperor at table. The heart of Theodosius could not resist this appeal; tears fell fast into his cup while he listened, and the Antiochians were forgiven. – Surely, if music ever spoke the misfortunes of a people, or could ever conciliate forgiveness for their errors, the music of Ireland ought to possess those powers!'

135

Extract 4: from [John Lockhart], *Peter's Letters to His Kinsfolk*, by Peter Morris, M. D., 2 vols (Edinburgh: Blackwood, 1819), 2: 156–162

Letter XLII

TO THE SAME

Dear Williams,[63]

I trust, that among the many *literateurs* of Edinburgh, there will ere long be found some person to compose a full and detailed history of this city, considered as a great mart of literature. I do not know of any other instance, in the whole history of the world, of such a mart existing and flourishing in a place not the seat of a government, or residence of a court, or centre of any very great political interest. The only place which at all approaches to Edinburgh in this view is Weimar;[64] for the residence of so small a prince as the Grand Duke can scarcely be considered as conferring anything like what we would understand by the character of a capital. But even there it can scarcely be said that any great mart of literature exists, or indeed existed even at the time when Wieland, Schiller and Goëthe[65] lived together under the wing of the palace. Books were written there in abundance, and many books were nominally published there; but the true centre from which they were diffused over Germany was always Leipsick.[66]

Till within these twenty years, I suppose there was no such thing in Edinburgh as the great trade of Publishing. Now and then some volume of sermons or so issued from the press of some Edinburgh typographer, and after lying for a year or two upon the counter of some of their booksellers, was dismissed into total oblivion, as it probably deserved to be. But of all the great literary men of the last age, who lived in Edinburgh, there was no one who ever thought of publishing his books in Edinburgh. The *trade* here never aspired to anything beyond forming a very humble appendage of understrappers to the *trade* of the Row.[67] Even if the name of an Edinburgh bookseller did appear upon a title-page, that was only a compliment allowed him by the courtesy of the great London dealer, whose instrument and agent he was. Every thing was conducted by the Northern Bibliopoles[68] in the same timid spirit of which this affords a specimen. The dulness of their atmosphere was never enlivened by one breath of daring. They were all petty retailers, inhabiting snug shops, and making a little money in the most tedious and uniform way imaginable. As for risking the little money they did make upon any bold adventure, which might have tripled the sum, or swept it entirely away, this was a thing of which they had not the most remote conception. In short, in spite of Hume and Robertson,[69] and the whole generation of lesser stars, who clustered around those great luminaries, the spirit of literary adventure had never approached the bibliopoles of

Edinburgh. They never dreamed of making fortunes for themselves, far less of being the means of bestowing fortunes upon others, by carrying on operations in the large and splendid style of mercantile enterprize....

The first manifestation of the new state of things was no less an occurrence than the appearance of the first Number of the Edinburgh Review – a thing which, wherever it might have occurred, must have been a matter of sufficient importance, and which appearing here, was enough not only to change the style of bookselling, and the whole ideas of booksellers, but to produce almost as great a revolution in minds not so immediately interested in the result of the phenomenon. The projectors of this Journal – both writers and publishers I should imagine – were quite satisfied that nothing could be done without abundance of money. Whoever wrote for their book must submit to be paid for doing so, because they would have no distinction of persons. But, indeed, I never heard it suspected, that any one objected to receiving on the publication of an article, not only the honour of the thing, but a bunch of bank-notes into the bargain. If a man does not want money himself, he always knows abundance of people that do; and, in short, the root of all evil is a medicament, which requires little sweetening of the cup, either to the sick or the sound palate.

The prodigious impetus given to the *trade* of Edinburgh by the first application of this wonderful engine, has never since been allowed to lose any part of its energy. The Review, in the first place, of itself alone, has been sufficient to keep all fear of stagnation far enough from the scene in which it makes its appearance. And from the Review, as might well have been foreseen, a kindred impulse has been continually carried into every region of the literary world – but most of all into the heart of the literature and the notions of the literary men of Edinburgh. Very shortly after the commencement of the Review, Mr Walter Scott began to be an author; and even without the benefit of its example, it is probable that he would have seen the propriety of adopting some similar course of procedure. However this might have been, ever since that time the Edinburgh Reviewers and Mr Walter Scott have between them furnished the most acceptable food for the reading public, both in and out of Scotland – but no doubt most exclusively and effectually in their own immediate neighbourhood; and both have always proceeded upon the principle of making the reading public pay handsomely for their gratification, through their fore-speakers, interpreters and purveyors, the booksellers. It would be unfair, however, to omit mentioning what I firmly believe, that the efforts – even the joint efforts of these great authors, would not have availed to anything like the extent to which they have in reality reached, had they not been so fortunate as to meet with a degree of ardour and tact, quite correspondent to their own, among the new race of booksellers, who had started into life along with themselves – above all, in

Mr Constable, the original publisher of the Edinburgh Review – the publisher of most of Mr Scott's works, and, without doubt, by far the greatest publisher Scotland has ever produced.

There is no doubt that this person is deserving of infinite credit for the share he has had in changing the whole aspect of Edinburgh, as a seat of literary merchandize – and, in truth, making it, instead of no literary mart at all, a greater one than almost any other city in Europe. What a singular contrast does the present state of Edinburgh, in regard to these matters, afford, when compared with what I have been endeavouring to describe as existing in the days of the Creeches![70] Instead of Scotch authors sending their works to be published by London booksellers, there is nothing more common now-a-days, than to hear of English authors sending their books to Edinburgh, to be published in a city, than which Memphis or Palmyra[71] could scarcely have appeared a more absurd place of publication to any English author thirty years ago. One that has not examined into the matter would scarcely be able to believe how large a proportion of the classical works of English literature, published in our age, have made their first appearance on the counters of the Edinburgh booksellers. But we all know the practical result of this, videlicet,[72] that at this moment an Edinburgh title-page is better than almost any London one – and carries a greater authority along with it. For my part, if ever I should take it into my head to publish a book, I should undoubtedly endeavour to get it published in Edinburgh. No book can be published there, and totally neglected. In so small a town, in spite of the quantity of books published in it, the publication of a new book is quite sure to attract the attention of some person, and if it has the least interest, to be talked of in company. If the book be a very interesting one in any way, its popularity extends with the most wonderful rapidity – and, ere a few days have elapsed, the snow-ball has grown so large, that it can be hurled to a distance with steady and certain assurance of hitting its mark. And, indeed, it is only in consequence of the frequency with which all this has occurred, that the imprimatur of an Edinburgh bookseller has come to be looked upon with so much habitual respect even in the south. This is surely a very remarkable change; and, for all that I can hear, both authors and booksellers are indebted for it to nothing more than the genuine sagacity of the one individual I have mentioned. I believe it should also be observed, that the establishment of the press of Ballantyne,[73] at the very same instant, almost, as the commencement of the Review, and the publication of the Lay of the Last Minstrel,[74] helped to push on Scottish publications, or, indeed, Scottish literature. Before that press was set up in Edinburgh, I am told, nobody could venture a book to be printed in Edinburgh; afterwards, the Edinburgh press gained the same sort of celebrity as the Edinburgh title-pages.

Extract 5: from [John Lockhart], *Peter's Letters to His Kinsfolk*, 2: 348–61

[From] Letter LV

You have often told me that Walter Scott has been excelled by several other poets of his time, in regularity and beauty of composition; and so far I have agreed, and do still agree with you. But I think there can be no doubt, that, far more than any other poet, or any other author of his time, he is entitled to claim credit for the extent and importance of the class of ideas to which he has drawn the public attention; and if it be so, what small matters all his deficiencies or irregularities are, when put in the balance against such praise as this. At a time when the literature of Scotland – and of England too – was becoming every day more and more destitute of command over everything but the mere speculative understanding of men – this great genius seems to have been raised up to counteract, in the wisest and best of all ways, this unfortunate tendency of his age, by re-awakening the sympathies of his countrymen for the more energetic characters and passions of their fore-fathers. In so doing he employed, indeed, with the skill and power of a true master, and a true philosopher, what constitutes the only effectual means of neutralising that barren spirit of lethargy into which the progress of civilization is in all countries so apt to lull the feelings and imaginations of mankind. The period during which most of his works were produced, was one of mighty struggles and commotions throughout all Europe, and the experience of that eventful period is sufficient to prove, that the greatest political anxieties, and the most important international struggles, can exert little awakening influence upon the character and genius of a people, if the private life of its citizens at home remains limited and monotonous, and confines their personal experience and the range of their thoughts. The rational matter-of-fact way in which all great public concerns are now-a-days carried forward, is sufficient to throw a damp upon the most stirring imagination. Wars are begun and concluded more in reliance upon the strength of money, than on the strength of minds and of men – votes, and supplies, and estimates, and regular business-like dispatches, and daily papers, take away among them the greater part of that magnificent indistinct-ness, through which, in former times, the great games of warfare and statesmanship used alike to be regarded by those whose interests were at stake. Very little room is left for enthusiasm, when people are perpetually perplexed in their contemplations of great actions and great men, by the congratulating pettinesses of the well disposed on one side, and the carping meannesses of the envious, and the malevolent, and the little-minded, on the other. The circle within which men's thoughts move, becomes every day a narrower one – and they learn to travel to all their conclusions, not over the free and generous ranges of principle and feeling, but along the plain, hard, dusty high-way of calculation. Now, a poet like Walter Scott, by enquiring into and representing the modes of life in earlier times, employs the imagination of his countrymen, as a means of making them go through the personal experience of their ancestry, and of making them acquainted with the various courses of thought and emotion, by which their forefathers had their genius and characters drawn out – things to which, by the mechanical arrangements of modern life and society, we have been rendered too much strangers. Other poets, such as Byron, have attempted an analogous operation, by carrying us into foreign countries, where society is still comparatively young – but their method is by no means so happy or so complete as Scott's, because the people among whom they seek to interest us, have national characters totally different from our own – whereas those whose minds he exhibits as a stimulus to ours, are felt at once to be great kindred originals, of which our every-day experience shows us copies, faint indeed, but capable of being worked into stronger resemblance. If other poets should afterwards seek and collect their materials from the same field, they may perhaps be able to produce more finished compositions, but the honour of being the Patriarch of the National Poetry of Scotland, must always remain in the possession of Walter Scott. Nay, whatever direction the genius of his countrymen may take in future years, the benefit of his writings must ever be experienced in the great resuscitation of slumbering elements, which they have produced in the national mind. Perhaps the two earliest of his poems, the Lay of the Last Minstrel and Marmion,[75] are the most valuable, because they are the most impregnated with the peculiar spirit of Scottish antiquity. In his subsequent poems, he made too much use of the common materials and machinery employed in the popular novels of *that* day, and descended so far as to hinge too much of their interest upon the common resources of an artfully constructed fable. In like manner, in those prose Tales – which I no more doubt to be his than the poems he has published with his name – in that delightful series of works, which have proved their author to be the nearest kinsman the creative intellect of Shakespeare has ever had – the best are those, the interest of which is most directly and historically national – Waverley and Old Mortality.[76] The whole will go down together, so long as any national character survives in Scotland – and themselves will, I nothing question, prolong the existence of national character there more effectually, than any other stimulus its waning strength is ever likely to meet with. But I think the two I have mentioned, will always be considered as the brightest jewels in this ample crown of unquenched and unquenchable radiance. What Shakespeare has done for the civil wars of the two Roses, and the manifestations of national mind produced by the influence of the old baronial feuds – what the more than dramatic Clarendon[77] has done for the great period of contest between the two majestic sets of principles, upon whose union, matured and tempered, the modern constitution of England is founded – the same service has been rendered by the author of these Tales (whosoever he may be), to the most interesting times in the history of the national mind of Scotland – the times, when all the various elements of her character, religious and political, were exhibited in their most lively fermentation of sharpness and vigour. As for the complaints which have been made of unfairness and partiality, in the views which he has given of the various parties – I think they are not only exaggerated, but altogether absurd. It is, indeed, very easy to see to which side the Poet's own early prejudices have given his mind a leaning – but I think it is no less easy to see that the romance of his predilections has been tempered and chastened by as fine a mixture of sober reflection and generous candour, as ever entered into the composition of any man of high and enthusiastic feeling. There is too much chivalry about the man to allow of his treating his *foes* unfairly; and had he been really disposed to injure any set of men, he had weapons enough at his disposal, very different from any which even his detractors can accuse him of having employed. But enough of such fooleries; they are only fit for those who have uttered them – a set of persons, by the way, who might have been expected to bear a little innocent ridicule with a little more Christian equanimity, after so ample experience of the '*Cachinno monstrarier.*'[78]

Altogether, it must be allowed that the situation of Scotland, as to literature, is a very peculiar one. No large crop of indigenous literature sprung out of its own feelings at the time when the kindred spirit of England was in that way so prolific. The poets it produced in the former times were almost all emigrants, and took up the common stock of ideas that were floating in England; – or at least their works, like those of Thomson,[79] had no relation to their own country in particular, or its modes of feeling. It is a difficult question how two countries, standing in the relation of England and Scotland, should manage with their respective talents and histories. It cannot be doubted that there is a very considerable difference in their national genius – and indeed, the Scots seem to resemble the English much more in their power of thought than in their turn of character. Their first remarkable exhibition of talent was entirely in the line of thought – Hume – Smith, and the rest of that school are examples. The Scots dialect never having been a written language, at least to any important extent, and there being no literary monuments belonging exclusively to Scotland, of course the associations of the literary men were formed on English models and on English works. Now, after two nations have been long separate in their interests, and have respectively nourished their own turn of thinking – they may at last come to be united in their interests, but their associations cannot be so pliable, nor can they be so easily amalgamated. An union of national interests *quoad*[80] external power relates chiefly to the future – whereas, associations respect the past. And here was an unfortunate circumstance of separation between the Scots literati and the mass of the Scottish people. – The essence of all nationality, however, is a peculiar way of thinking, and conceiving, which may be applied to subjects not belonging to the history of one's own country, although it certainly is always most in place when exhibited in conjunction with the scenery and accompaniments of Home. In Scotland, there are many things that must conspire to wean men from the past – the disuse of their old dialect – the unpleasant nature of some of the events that have befallen them – the neighbourhood of triumphant and eclipsing England, which, like an immense magnet, absolutely draws the needles from the smaller ones – the Reformation, above all, which, among them, was conducted in a way peculiarly unfortunate, causing all the old religious associations to be considered as detestable and sinful; and gradually sinking into oblivion a great many ancient ideas of another class, which were entwined with these, and which were shaken off also as a matter of necessity, *ne pars sincera trahatur.*[81]

Puritanism, by its excessive exclusiveness, always brings along with it a nakedness and barrenness of mind in relation to all human attachments, and the temporal concerns of life. But human nature, in despite of Puritanism, can never be utterly extinguished. It still demands some human things for our affections to lean upon – some thoughts to be dear to our imaginations, and which we may join our countrymen in loving – for common attachments widely diffused, must always tend to civilize and improve human nature, and awaken generous and social habits of feeling. Shakespeare observes in Coriolanus, that, during the time of war, citizens always feel more benevolent towards each other; and the reason, no doubt is, that war reminds them in what respects their interests and feelings concur. Puritanism weighs too hard upon human nature, and does not tend to draw out its best aspect. It makes every man too much the arbiter of his opinions and their champion – hence too much self-love. It makes him look with too much jealousy and anxiety upon his neighbours, as persons in error, or capable of leading him into error – or as differing in their convictions from those at which he himself has had the happiness to arrive. Hence a want of cheerfulness, confidence, and settled good nature. – Lastly, Puritanism leaves a man alone to face and fight the devil upon the strength of his own virtue and judgment, which, I dare say, Colonel Harrison[82] himself would feel to be as much as he was able for. Puritans confine their imaginations entirely to the Scriptures, and cut themselves off from the early Romish legends of saints – the true mythology of Christianity – the only part of it, at least, which poetry and the other fine arts can, without too great a breach of reverence, mould and adapt to their own purposes. Some of them surely are exquisite in beauty, and afford room

142

for all manner of play of fancy. I speak, you will remember, entirely with an eye to literature. Whatever may be the orthodox opinions on these subjects, why should poetry refuse to invest them with preternatural attributes, or to take advantage of the fine poetical situations which sometimes occur in those old histories?

Again, although the history of Scotland has not been throughout filled with splendid or remarkable events, fitted to show off the national character in the most luminous and imposing points of view, yet few persons will refuse to consider the Scots as a nation remarkable – most remarkable – for national endowments. It would be difficult to say in what elements adapted to make a nation shine in literature they are at all deficient. Now, when the character of a nation has once fully developed itself in events or in literature, its posterity are too apt to consider its former achievements or writings as an adequate expression or symbol of what exists in themselves, and so to remain contented without making any farther exertions – and this, I take it, is one of the main causes of what appears externally in the history of nations, to be barrenness, degeneracy, and exhaustion of intellectual power, – so that it may perhaps be one of the advantages which Scotland possesses over England and many other countries, that she has not yet created any sufficient monuments of that 'mightiness for good or ill' that is within her.

If a remainder of her true harvest is yet to be reaped – if any considerable body of her yet unexpended force is now to make its appearance in literature, it will do so under the most favourable circumstances, and with all appliances to boot, which the present state of intellectual cultivation in Europe can furnish, both in the way of experience, and as objects for examination and reflection. The folly of slighting and concealing what remains concealed within herself, is one of the worst and most pernicious that can beset a country, in the situation wherein Scotland stands. Although, perhaps, it is not now the cue of Scotland to dwell very much on her own past history, (which that of England has thrown too much into the shade,) yet she should observe what fine things have been made even of this department, by the great genius of whom I have spoken above – and learn to consider her own national character as a mine of intellectual wealth, which remains in a great measure unexplored. While she looks back upon the history of England, as upon that of the country to which she has suspended and rendered subordinate her fortunes, yet she should by no means regard English literature, as an expression of her mind, or as superseding the examination of what intellectual resources remain unemployed within her own domains of peculiar possession.

The most remarkable literary characters which Scotland produced last century, showed merely (as I have already said) the force of her intellect, as applied to matters of reasoning. The generation of Hume, Smith, &c., left matters of feeling very much unexplored, and probably considered Poetry merely as an elegant and tasteful appendage to the other branches of literature, with which they themselves were more conversant. Their disquisitions on morals were meant to be the vehicles of ingenious theories – not of convictions of sentiment. They employed, therefore, even in them, only the national intellect, and not the national modes of feeling.

The Scottish literati of the present day have inherited the ideas of these men, and acted upon them in a great measure – with scarcely more than the one splendid exception of Walter Scott. While all the rest were contenting themselves with exercising and displaying their speculative acuteness, this man had the wisdom – whether by the impulse of Nature, or from reflection, I know not – to grapple boldly with the feelings of his countrymen. The habits of self-love, so much pampered and indulged by the other style, must have opposed some resistance to the influence of works such as his – I mean their more solid, and serious and abiding influence upon the characters and minds of those who read them; but these are only wreaths of snow, whose cold flakes are made to be melted when the sun shines fairly upon them. His works are altogether the most remarkable phenomenon in this age of wonders – produced among a people, whose taste had been well nigh weaned from all those ranges of feeling, on which their main inspiration and main power depend – they have of themselves been sufficient to create a more than passionate return of faith and homage to those deserted elements of greatness, in all the better part of his countrymen. I consider him, and his countrymen should do so, as having been the sole saviour of all the richer and warmer spirit of literature in Scotland. He is, indeed, the *Facillime Princeps*[83] of all her poets, past and present, and I more than question the likelihood of his having hereafter any 'Brother near the throne.'[84]

Extract 6: from [Walter Scott], 'A Second Letter to the Editor of the Edinburgh Weekly Journal from Malachi Malagrowther Esq.', in *Thoughts on the Proposed Change of Currency and Other Late Alterations As They Affect, or Are Intended to Affect the Kingdom of Scotland* (Edinburgh: Blackwood, 1826), pp. 74–82

I mentioned in my former Letter[85] another circumstance, of which I think my country has reason to complain. It is that sort of absolute and complete state of tutelage to which England seems disposed to reduce her sister country, subjecting her in all her relations to the despotic authority of English Boards, which exercise an exclusive jurisdiction in Scottish affairs, without regard to her local peculiarities, and with something like contempt of her claims as a country united with England, but which certainly has never resigned the right of being at least consulted in her own concerns.

I mentioned the restrictions, and, as I conceive them, degrading incapacities, inflicted on our Revenue Boards, – I might extend the same observations to the regulations in the Stamp-Office;[86] – and I remember, when these were in progress, that it was said in good society, that the definitive instructions (verbal, I believe) communicated to the able officer upon whom the examination and adjustment of the alterations in that department devolved, and who was sent down hither on purpose, were to this purport: – 'That he was to proceed in Scotland without more regard to the particular independence of that country than he would feel in Yorkshire.' These, however, were matters interesting the general revenue – the servants of the Crown had a right to regulate them as they pleased. But if they were regulated with a purposed and obvious intention to lessen the consequence of Scotland, throw implied discredit on her natives, as men unworthy of trust, and hold her recollections and her feelings at nought, they make links in a chain which seems ready to be wound around us whenever our patience will permit.

This, sir, is an unwise, nay, an unsafe proceeding. An old chain, long worn, forms a callosity on the limb which bears it, and is endured, with whatever inconvenience, as a thing of custom. It is not so with restraints newly imposed. These fret – gall – gangrene – the iron enters first into the flesh, and then into the soul. I speak out what more prudent men would keep silent. I may lose friends by doing so; but he who is like Malachi Malagrowther, old and unfortunate, has not many to lose, and risks little in telling truths before, when men of rising ambition and budding hopes would leave them to be discovered by the event.

But, besides such matters of punctilio, Mr Journalist, there has been in England a gradual and progressive system of assuming the management of affairs entirely and exclusively proper to Scotland, as if we were totally unworthy of having the management of our own concerns. All must centre in London. We could not have a Caledonian Canal,[87] but the Commissioners must be Englishmen, and meet in London; – a most useful canal they would have made of it, had not the lucky introduction of steam-boats – *Deus ex machina*[88] – come just in time to redeem them from having made the most expensive and most useless undertaking of the kind ever heard of since Noah floated his ark! We could not be intrusted with the charge of erecting our own kirks, (churches in the Highlands,) or of making our roads and bridges in the same wild districts, but these labours must be conducted under the tender care of men who knew nothing of our country, its wants and its capabilities, but who, nevertheless, sitting in their office in London, were to decide, without appeal, upon the conduct of the roads in Lochaber! – Good Heaven, sir! To what are we fallen? – or rather, what are we esteemed by the English? Wretched drivellers, incapable of understanding our own affairs; or greedy peculators, unfit to be trusted? On what ground are we considered either as the one or the other?

But I may perhaps be answered, that these operations are carried on by grants of public money; and that, therefore, the English – undoubtedly the only disinterested and public-spirited and trust-worthy persons in the universe – must be empowered exclusively to look after its application. Public money forsooth!!! I should like to know whose pocket it comes out of. Scotland, I have always heard, contributes FOUR MILLIONS to the public revenue. I should like to know, before we are twitted with grants of public money, how much of that income is dedicated to Scottish purposes – how much applied to the general uses of the empire – and if the balance should be found to a great amount on the side of Scotland, as I suspect it will, I should like still farther to know how the English are entitled to assume the direction and disposal of any pittance which may be permitted, out of the produce of our own burthens, to revert to the peculiar use of the nation from which it has been derived? If England was giving us alms, she would have a right to look after the administration of them, lest they should be misapplied or embezzled. If she is only consenting to afford us a small share of the revenue derived from our own kingdom, we have some title, methinks, to be consulted in the management, nay, intrusted with it.

This assumption of uncalled-for guardianship accelerates the circulation a little, and inclines one to say to his countrymen,

> Our blood has been too cold and temperate,
> Unapt to stir at such indignities –.[89]

You could not keep a decent servant in your family, sir, far more a partner, if you obviously treated such a person as a man in whom no confidence was to be reposed even in his own department. We shall in due time, I suppose, be put all under English control, deprived even of the few native dignitaries and office-holders we have left, and accommodated with a set of English superintendants in every department. It will be upon the very reasoning of Goneril before alluded to: –

> 'What need you five-and-twenty, ten, or five,
> To follow in a house where twice so many
> Have a command to tend you? –'

Patrick, will you play Regan and echo,

> ' – What need *one* ?'[90]

Take care, my good fellow! For you will scarce get a great share in our spoils, and will be shortly incapacitated, and put under a statute of lunacy, as well as ourselves.

But what will England take by this engrossing spirit? Not the miserable candle-ends and cheese-parings – these, I dare say, she scorns. The mere pleasure, then, of absolute authority – the gratification of humour exacted by a peevish and petted child, who will not be contented till he has the toy in his own hand, though he break it the next moment. Is any real power derived by centering the immediate and direct control of everything in London? Far from it. On the contrary, that great metropolis is already a head too bulky for the empire, and, should it take a vertigo, the limbs would be unable to support it. The misfortune of France, during the Revolution, in all its phases, was, that no part of the kingdom could think for itself or act for itself; all were from habit necessitated to look up to Paris. Whoever was uppermost there, and the worst party is apt to prevail in a corrupted metropolis, were, without possibility of effectual contradiction, the uncontrolled and despotic rulers of France – *absit omen!*[91]

Again, would the British empire become stronger, were it possible to annul and dissolve all the distinctions and peculiarities, which, flowing out of circumstances, historical events, and difference of customs and climates, make its relative parts still, in some respects, three separate nations, though intimately incorporated into one empire? Every rope-maker knows, sir, that three distinct *strands*, as they are called, incorporated and twisted together, will make a cable ten times stronger than the same quantity of hemp, however artificially combined into a single twist of cord. The reason is obvious to the meanest capacity. If one of the strands happen to fail a little, there is a threefold chance that no imperfection will occur in the others at the same place, so that the infirm strand may give way a little, yet the whole cord remain trustworthy. If the single twist fail at any point, all is over. For God's sake, sir, let us remain as Nature made us, Englishmen, Irishmen, and Scotchmen, with something like the impress of our several countries upon each! We would not become better subjects, or more valuable members of the common empire, if we all resembled each other like so many smooth shillings. Let us love and cherish each other's virtues – bear with each other's failings – be tender to each other's prejudices – be scrupulously regardful of each other's rights. Lastly, let us borrow each other's improvements, but never before they are needed and demanded. The degree of national diversity between different countries, is but an instance of that general variety which Nature seems to have adopted as a principle through all her works, as anxious, apparently, to avoid, as modern statesmen to enforce, anything like an approach to absolute 'uniformity.'

It may be said that some of the grievances I have complained of are mere trifles. I grant they are, – excepting in the feelings and intentions towards Scotland which they indicate. But, according to Bacon's maxim,[92] you will see how the wind sits by flinging up a feather, which you cannot discern by throwing up a stone. Affronts are almost always more offensive than injuries, although they seldom are in themselves more than trifles. The omitting to discharge a gun or two in a salute, the raising or striking of a banner or sail, have been the source of bloody wars. England lost America about a few miserable chests of tea – she endangered India for the clipping of a mustachio.[93]

SELECT BIBLIOGRAPHY

Cairns, David and Shaun Richards, *Writing Ireland: Colonialism, Nationalism and Culture* (Manchester: Manchester University Press, 1988). Highly polemical deployment of modish theory.

Calder, Angus, *Revolving Culture: Notes from the Scottish Republic* (London: Tauris, 1994). Provocative essays on national literary and political themes.

Colley, Linda, *Britons: Forging the Nation 1707–1837* (New Haven: Yale University Press, 1992). Brilliantly suggestive but deals far more fully with Scotland's role in the forging of British identity than Ireland's.

Craig, David, *Scottish Literature and the Scottish People 1680–1830* (London: Chatto, 1961). Ground-breaking study in its time, but its populist political perspective may seem dated in comparison with Crawford (see below).

Crawford, Robert, *Devolving English Literature* (Oxford: Clarendon Press, 1992). Dedicated 'To Scotland', but situates late eighteenth- and early nineteenth-century Scottish writing in an extremely broad picture of modern English-language writing.

Eagleton, Terry, *Heathcliff and the Great Hunger: Studies in Irish Culture* (London: Verso, 1995). Extremely well-grounded in contemporary Irish historiographical controversies (such as 'nationalist' versus 'revisionist') with an outstanding chapter on the Anglo-Irish novel.

Foster, R. F., *Modern Ireland: 1600–1972* (Harmondsworth: Allen Lane, 1988). Perhaps the best general history of the topic with a full and helpful 'Bibliographical Essay' for further reading.

Hobsbawm, E. J., *Nations and Nationalism since 1780: Programme, Myth, Reality* (Cambridge: Cambridge University Press, 1990). A superb introduction to the wider contexts of national histories and cultures.

Hobsbawm, Eric and Terence Ranger, eds, *The Invention of Tradition* (Cambridge: Cambridge University Press, 1983). Contains splendid 'debunking' essay on Scottish Highland traditions by Hugh Trevor-Roper and one of the most accessible accounts of Welsh national culture in the period by Prys Morgan, in 'From a

Death to a View: the Hunt for the Welsh Past in the Romantic Period'.

Kelly, Gary, *English Fiction of the Romantic Period 1789–1830* (London: Longman, 1989). Extremely thorough account of much of the fiction of the period, though oddly omits to discuss the work of the Irish novelist John Banim (1798–1842) in relation to the 'national tale'.

Lenman, Bruce P., *Integration and Enlightenment: Scotland 1746–1832* (London: Edward Arnold, 1981). Splendid, if brief, introductory account.

Lukács, Georg, *The Historical Novel* (1936), trans. H. and S. Mitchell (London: Merlin, 1962). Still the indispensible starting-point for any consideration of Scott and the development of the genre.

McCormack, W. J., *Ascendancy and Tradition in Irish Literary History 1793–1939* (Oxford: Clarendon, 1985). Painstaking readings of Irish fiction 'in' Irish history.

Smout, T. C., *A History of the Scottish People, 1560–1830* (London: Collins, 1969). Fine account that usefully identifies a wide range of original source material.

Thom, Martin, *Republics, Nations and Tribes* (London: Verso, 1995). Teeming with ideas and insights, although it touches only marginally on British writers of the period.

6

GENDER

Susan Matthews

The first three decades of the nineteenth century saw the disappearance from the public sphere of the radical rhetoric of women's rights that was so important in the early 1790s. In 1792 Mary Wollstonecraft had published *A Vindication of the Rights of Woman*. Wollstonecraft criticized the limited education of contemporary women, but defended women's innate rationality and their potential, using an argument based on the Christian assumption of equality between the souls of both sexes. But as counter-revolutionary anxieties grew in the later 1790s, Wollstonecraft's speculation about gender roles and possibilities for change became associated with dangerous radical politics. By 1800 the debate about the roles and duties of women, particularly middle-class women, was increasingly dominated by the Evangelical campaign against Wollstonecraft (who had died in childbirth in 1797) led by such figures as Hannah More and William Wilberforce.[1] Women were prominent in many spheres. They played an active role in the campaign for the abolition of slavery, and across a range of political persuasions were involved in such concerns as education, Owenite organizations and Catholic emancipation.[2] Much was made in the radical press of the fact that some of those injured at Peterloo in 1819 were women, and women were also active in support of the war effort in the first half of this period. Women were particularly active as writers, especially as novelists and poets. But discussion of gender was dominated by an assertion of the need for separate spheres, and it was the *domestic* woman that was most often celebrated in fiction and promoted in conduct manuals.

Just those authors of conduct literature who Wollstonecraft subjected to withering scorn in her 1792 *Vindication* (Fordyce, Dr Gregory, among others) continued to be reissued in new editions. Much of the conduct literature published in the first three decades of the nineteenth century is in the form of reissues of works dating from as early as the 1760s.[3] The 1822 edition of Dr Gregory's 1774 *A Father's Legacy to his Daughters* is prefaced by a note that admits:

> Dr Gregory's little work, which has, for nearly half a century, sustained itself, during all the vicissitudes of literary fashion, is deficient only in that, which is abundant in almost every similar manual – quantity: – the printer

has hitherto, with no little difficulty and the aid of thickened paper and wide spaces, made a volume of it.[4]

The conduct literature for women published in this period suggests a continuity with earlier more conservative notions of femininity. Yet there are other indications that models of gender were in fact changing in these years.

Reactions to Wollstonecraft's death in 1797, and more particularly, the controversy about her life created by the publication the next year by William Godwin (1756–1836) of his *Memoirs of the Author of the Vindication of the Rights of Woman* provide a striking contrast to reactions to the deaths twenty-odd years later of two other women very much in the public eye. Godwin's sympathetic *Memoirs* of his wife provoked outrage and contributed, it seems, to the disappearance of Wollstonecraft's name and works from public debate. Godwin revealed that Wollstonecraft was not married to the father of her first child, and had also attempted suicide after being betrayed by him. This news dominated the public response to Godwin's *Memoirs*, and Wollstonecraft's morals were widely criticized not only in right-wing journals, like the *Anti-Jacobin*, but even in the sympathetic *Monthly Review*. Godwin produced a second, revised edition, also in 1798, in which he rephrases crucial passages in the account of Mary's relationship with her lover, and also in the final paragraphs in which he describes her mental qualities (**extract 1**). The revised version describes Mary in terms of femininity and emphasizes gender difference in the added paragraph which begins: 'A circumstance by which the two sexes are particularly distinguished from each other, is, that the one is accustomed more to the exercise of its reasoning powers, and the other of its feelings.' Godwin, as in the first edition, celebrates Mary Wollstonecraft as a woman of feeling. But the changes made no difference to the tide of universal condemnation. Twenty years later, in 1817, the public received with universal sympathy and sorrow the news of the death in childbirth of a woman who had defied her father in her choice of husband. Even more strikingly, in 1820, there was a national movement in support of a woman accused of adultery who wished to fight her husband's attempts to divorce her. The royal status of these two women, the Princess Charlotte who died in 1817 and Queen Caroline who was at the centre of a national scandal in 1820, is of course significant. Neither was tainted, like Wollstonecraft, by the association with radical politics, and Caroline's husband was the notoriously rakish and unpopular Prince Regent, later George IV. Yet the fact that the lives and deaths of these two women were received so differently to Wollstonecraft may also reveal changes in the degree to which women's behaviour (as opposed to gender ideology) could be flexibly interpreted in the post-war years. The issue of adultery is singled out by Hannah More in her 1799 *Strictures on the Modern System of Female Education* (**extract 2**) in her references to Wollstonecraft's posthumous novel *The Wrongs of Woman*, but the charge of adultery, highly plausible in the case of Queen Caroline, was vigorously countered by the women of Britain in the campaign of 1820.

Gender ideology at this time is perhaps most visible in its treatment of femininity: there was no corresponding flood of conduct books on male behaviour. Yet there were clearly parallel concerns about male identities. The Evangelical campaign, aimed primarily at women of rank, and set up to counter Wollstonecraft's influence, was echoed by an attempt to describe corresponding forms of masculinity. Religious identity seems to have been key to the formation of a new middle-class identity in these years. The Evangelical writer, Thomas Gisborne, a friend, like Hannah More, of William Wilberforce, and like her an author of conduct literature for women, wrote *Enquiry into the Duties of Men in the Higher and Middle Classes of Society* (1794) which was reissued in six editions by 1811. Gisborne stresses the domestic duties of men as husbands and as fathers, seeing these roles as common to men belonging to diverse professions or ranks. Although Gisborne sees male identity as determined by profession whereas women's roles are determined by marital status, his account of male duties is much closer to his account of women's duties than might have been expected. As Davidoff and Hall argue:

> Many of the values associated with evangelical Christianity – the stress on moral earnestness, the belief in the power of love and a sensitivity to the weak and helpless – ran counter to the worldly assumptions and pursuits of the gentry. Masculine nature, in gentry terms, was based on sport and codes of honour derived from military prowess, finding expression in hunting, riding, drinking and 'wenching'. Since many of the early Evangelicals came from gentry backgrounds they had to consciously establish novel patterns of manhood.[5]

William Cowper's poetry provided a central reference point for Evangelical images of masculinity: Cowper seems to develop the late eighteenth-century fashion for sensibility which produced images of men of feeling, and his version of masculinity, and that of Evangelicalism generally, was in some ways very close to that of femininity.[6] The newly defined middle-class identity, which developed through an earnest sense of religious identity, brought masculinity close to femininity, stressing the domestic duties of both sexes. Yet there were also writers, such as William Hazlitt (1778–1830), who saw Cowper as insufficiently manly.[7] Other writers suggested that the national culture was at risk from the feminization of the public sphere. The Swiss painter and Professor of Painting at the Royal Academy, Henry Fuseli (1741–1825), appealed in his 1801 Academy Lectures (**extract 3**) to values which draw on the epic and heroic in art to introduce a new sense of manly virtue and artistic greatness to the nation.[8] When he argues that 'the ambition, activity, and spirit of public life is shrunk to the minute detail of domestic arrangements – every thing that surrounds us tends to show us in private, is become snug, less, narrow, pretty, insignificant' he seems to fight back against the idealization of the domestic that dominates these years, for both women and (for Evangelicals) men too. Keats's anxieties about the feminization of the market for literature, and especially poetry, revealed in his changes to the text of the 'Eve of St Agnes' (1820), are not unique to him but are shared in concerns about manliness in the work of Byron and Hazlitt.[9]

The contested nature of masculinity can be seen in images of the soldier in these years. Wollstonecraft, paradoxically, uses the soldier in the 1792 *Vindication* to describe a person who is vain, coquettish and uneducated, concerned more with dress than intellect, seeing the ill-educated women of her time as being like soldiers. The role of the militia in *Pride and Prejudice* seems to suggest an analysis like Wollstonecraft's, and may respond in part to the figure of the dandy in the Regency years, a figure for whom dressing up and a certain sexual indeterminacy are key.[10] But in the war years, the figure of the soldier generally provided a positive image of masculinity. The statue of Achilles in Hyde Park erected by exclusively female subscription in 1822 in honour of the Duke of Wellington (1769–1852) chooses the language of classical heroism with a subject from the *Iliad*. The classical figure by Sir Richard Westmacott was a copy of one of the ancient Horse Tamers on the Quirinal hill, Rome, regarded as one of the greatest classical monuments, a subject sketched by Henry Fuseli in 1810–15 in a plan for a monument to seafarers.[11] It was the first public nude statue to be erected in London, and was attacked in the press for indecency, gaining the names of the 'Ladies Fancy Man' or 'Ladies Trophy'. Elizabeth Vassall Fox, Lady Holland, remarked in a letter to her son of 1822:

> A difficulty has arisen, and the artist had submitted to the female subscribers whether this immense colossal figure should preserve its antique nudity or should be garnished by a fig leaf. It was carried for the leaf by a majority ... the names of the *minority* have not transpired.[12]

It was the men of the committee who insisted on the provision of a fig leaf. A series of contemporary engravings depict this controversy, often showing women viewing the statue. In George Cruikshank's 1822 print 'Making Decent' (see plate 5), the Evangelical William Wilberforce is shown covering the genitals with his hat. The statue is also described for a male audience in a report from the *Gentleman's Magazine* of 1822 (**extract 7**) which focuses on the context of classical statuary and its celebration of heroism. The cult of the heroic male, whether in the form of Byron, Napoleon, Nelson or Wellington, is clearly a product of the war years, yet is challenged in the Regency period by the image of the fop and the dandy.[13]

The texts in this section display a number of recurrent though often contradictory concerns. Even though gender difference (as in Godwin's two attempts to distinguish between Mary's mind and his own) tends to be seen as natural, there is a continuing concern with education and particularly the difficult task of determining the appropriate education for girls. The contradiction between the assumed naturalness of femininity and the need to inculcate it carefully can be traced back to the important account of a girl's education provided by Jean-Jacques Rousseau in *Émile* (1762). Rousseau's fictionalized treatise on the education of nature ends with an account of the education of Sophie, as a wife for Rousseau's imaginary pupil, Émile. This model of education widely irritated even sympathetic English female readers. It is a model to answer and rebut for the novelist and writer for children, Maria Edgeworth (1762–1848), from her earliest publication, *Letters for Literary Ladies* (1795) to *Harry and Lucy Concluded* (1825). In the latter (**extract 8**), Edgeworth presents gender difference as innate, but also suggests that a practical scientific education can be of benefit to women.[14] Her preface explains that 'the young brother is employed to teach his sister what he has learned, either from his father, or from books'. And whereas 'Harry's abilities and knowledge will perhaps appear a little above his age', Lucy 'may at times seem too childish and volatile'. Maria Edgeworth had in fact undertaken the education of her own younger brother, Henry, and had defended female education explicitly in *Letters for Literary Ladies*. But in her 1825 text, Edgeworth is perhaps even more cautious than in her 1795 work about retaining both hierarchy and difference in her presentation of gender. Lucy in the 1825 text is attracted to literature and shows herself to be fascinated by metaphor, in contrast to the literal concern for accuracy manifested by her brother. Whereas Wollstonecraft in the 1792 *Vindication* centred her account of female equality in women's ability to reason (and in later texts represented strong feeling as productive of clear reasoning) a more orthodox opposition between feeling and imagination as female qualities and reason and exactness as male ones returned in Godwin's *Memoir* and in Edgeworth's later model of education.

The assumption that women were particularly susceptible to the effects of reading and to imaginative literature was widespread in these years. A striking example of this occurs in the passage from Hannah More's *Strictures on the Modern System of Female Education* (**extract 2**) which sees the ability of women to resist the attractions of foreign literature as key to both the moral and political strength of the nation. French literature and the German theatre are seen as posing a moral threat to women and to Britain. More's attack on Rousseau, Goethe, Schiller and Kotzebue was highly influential at the time and caused Alexander Tytler, who had translated Schiller's *The Robbers* in 1792, to add a postscript to his second edition regretting his translation.[15]

Perhaps the most consistent concern of writers on gender was the distinction between private and public life. Godwin, opening his memoir of Wollstonecraft, is clearly aware of the distinction but celebrates his wife as a woman belonging in the public sphere of great men:

It has always appeared to me, that to give to the public some account of the life of a person of eminent merit deceased, is a duty incumbent on survivors. It seldom happens that such a person passes through life, without being the subject of thoughtless calumny, or malignant misrepresentation. It cannot happen that the public at large should be on a footing with their intimate acquaintance, and be the observer of those virtues which discover themselves principally in personal intercourse.[16]

The hostile response to the memoir focused on very private events that Godwin had made public. In contrast, the Dissenting minister John Evans, who preached in 1817 on the death of the Princess Charlotte (**extract 4**), singles out for praise not only her education (which he speculates may have been guided by a work by Hannah More) but also the retirement from public life of the princess and her husband, Prince Leopold: 'And now this *august pair* withdrew from the glare of public observation, to participate of the pure and unsullied blessings of domestic life. Having received the customary gratulations, they sunk into a sort of enviable obscurity.'[17] This focus on the world, and the court, as a corrupt place from which the good individual retires is particularly appropriate to the Dissenting perspective, but Evans's account of the domestic woman has much in common with the idealized lives of domestic women eulogized in many a published funeral oration.

The doctrine of separate spheres, by which women were believed to belong in domestic life, also emphasized the responsibility of the private woman to the public sphere. As Hannah More so clearly stresses in 1799 (**extract 2**), it is by retiring into private life that 'women of rank and fortune' have the power to improve the moral quality of the public life they are removed from. Domestic women become the embodiment of higher and purer moral virtues than men, and their influence over men becomes a force which, as More argues, can save the nation in its hour of need. Women are frequently enjoined to remain in private, but public culture is also clearly fascinated by images of these idealized domestic women.

The power of journals and newspapers to publicize women's lives can be seen in the speed and extent with which the events of royal women's lives became part of those of men and women throughout the country.[18] Edmund Burke, in a famous passage in his 1791 *Reflections on the Revolution in France*, had celebrated the figure of Marie Antoinette and lamented the threat to her privacy when her bedroom was entered and she was taken to Paris. Burke's rhetoric was echoed frequently during the Queen Caroline affair, as in the address of the women of Nottingham published by Cobbett's *Political Register* (**extract 5**). But the English female royalty in this period show an even greater power than Marie Antoinette to provide images of ordinary women's lives. The news of the death of Princess Charlotte seems to have touched a huge number of English men and women.[19]

The Queen Caroline affair of 1820 (the subject of **extracts 5 and 6**) again shows the power of female royalty to capture the imaginations of the women of the nation. Caroline was the separated wife of the king and mother of Princess Charlotte (who was born nine months after possibly the only night the couple spent together). On his accession to the throne, George IV tried to prevent Caroline from becoming queen.[20] Insisting on a divorce but unable to appeal to the ecclesiastical courts, in part because of the light this would have thrown on his own sexual conduct, George brought a 'Bill of Pains and Penalties' to the House of Lords. The 'Trial of Queen Caroline' consisted in the debate on this bill, and when the bill was withdrawn Caroline's supporters saw this as victory. Hazlitt wrote that 'It was the only question I have ever known that excited a thorough popular feeling. It struck its roots into the heart of the nation; it took possession of every house or cottage in the kingdom'.[21]

The divorce action became a great radical cause, exploited by Cobbett and others who saw that it allowed an expression of hostility to the monarch. But it also became a women's cause for women of all political positions. The intense public agitation was shortlived, yet the issue focused women's attention on the sexual double standard (because of the public nature of George's affairs), on property rights within marriage (since Caroline was denied a palace on her return to London) and on the rights of access, since Caroline had been denied access to her daughter, Princess Charlotte. Despite rumours of an affair with her Italian butler in her years abroad, Caroline became an unlikely symbol of women's sexual purity and virtue. The campaign in support of the queen produced widespread female involvement in political action. There were at least seventeen exclusively female petitions, two of which are included as **extract 5**. Caroline in her replies presents herself as a woman of feeling and sensibility and links her own image with the idealized image of her daughter:

> With the most gentle delicacy the female inhabitants of the town of Nottingham and its vicinity have touched those springs of grief in my heart which will ever continue painfully to vibrate at the recollection of the near and dear relatives of whom I have been bereaved, and particularly of that departed saint in whose talents and whose virtues the women have lost a model of the most estimable excellence.

In doing so she draws, just as Godwin did in his account of Wollstonecraft, on a gendered language of feeling and virtue but also appeals to the national sense of women as mourners to which Byron's early poetry also appealed in the period of the Napoleonic wars.

Extract 1: from William Godwin, *Memoirs of the Author of a Vindication of the Rights of Woman*, second edition (London: Joseph Johnson, 1798), pp. 199–206

The loss of the world, in this admirable woman, I leave to other men to collect; my own I well know, nor can it be improper to describe it. I do not here allude to the pleasures I enjoyed in her conversation: these increased every day, in proportion as we knew each other better, and as our mutual confidence increased. They can be measured only by the treasures of her mind, and the virtues of her heart. But this is a subject for meditation, not for words. What I purposed alluding to, was the improvement that I have for ever lost.

A circumstance by which the two sexes are particularly distinguished from each other, is, that the one is accustomed more to the exercise of its reasoning powers, and the other of its feelings. Women have a frame of body more delicate and susceptible of impression than men, and, in proportion as they receive a less intellectual education, are more unreservedly under the empire of feeling. Feeling is liable to become a source of erroneous decisions, because a mind not accustomed to logical analysis, cannot be expected accurately to discriminate between the simple dictates of an ingenuous mind, and the factitious sentiments of a partial education. Habits of deduction enable us to correct this defect. But habits of deduction may generate habits of sophistry; and scepticism and discussion, while they undermine our prejudices, have sometimes a tendency to weaken or distort our feelings. Hence we may infer one of the advantages accruing from the association of persons of an opposite sex: they may be expected to counteract the principal mistake into which either is in danger to fall.

Mary and myself perhaps each carried farther to its common extent the characteristic of the sexes to which we belonged. I have been stimulated, as long as I can remember, by the love of intellectual distinction; but, as long as I can remember, I have been discouraged, when casting the sum of my intellectual value, by finding that I did not possess, in the degree of some other persons, an intuitive sense of the pleasures of the imagination. Perhaps I feel them as vividly as most men; but it is often rather by an attentive consideration, than an instantaneous survey. They have been liable to fail of their effect in the first experiment; and my scepticism has often led me anxiously to call in the approved decisions of taste, as a guide to my judgment, or a countenance to my enthusiasm. One of the leading passions of my mind has been an anxious desire not to be deceived. This has led me to view the topics of my reflection on all sides, and to examine and re-examine without end the questions that interest me. Endless disquisition however is not always the parent of certainty.

What I wanted in this respect, Mary possessed in a degree superior to any other person I ever knew. Her feelings had a character of peculiar strength and decision; and the discovery of them, whether in matters of taste or of moral virtue, she found herself unable to control. She had viewed the objects of nature with a lively sense and an ardent admiration, and had developed their beauties. Her education had been fortunately free from the prejudices of system and bigotry, and her sensitive and generous spirit was left to the spontaneous exercise of its own decisions. The warmth of her heart defended her from artificial rules of judgment; and it is therefore surprising what a degree of soundness pervaded her sentiments. In the strict sense of the term, she had reasoned comparatively little; and she was therefore little subject to diffidence and scepticism. Yet a mind more candid in perceiving and retracting error, when it was pointed out to her, perhaps never existed. This arose naturally out of the directness of her sentiments, and her fearless and unstudied veracity.

A companion like this, excites and animates the mind. From such an one we imbibe, what perhaps I principally wanted, the habit of minutely attending to first impressions, and justly appreciating them. Her taste awakened mine; her sensibility determined me to a careful development of my feelings. She delighted to open her heart to the beauties of nature; and her propensity in this respect led me to a more intimate contemplation of them. My scepticism in judging, yielded to the coincidence of another's judgment; and especially when the judgment of that other was such, that the more I made experiment of it, the more was I convinced of its rectitude.

The improvement I had reason to promise myself, was however yet in its commencement, when a fatal event, hostile to the moral interests of mankind, ravished from me the light of my steps, and left to me nothing but the consciousness of what I had possessed, and must now possess no more!

While I have described the improvement I was in the act of receiving, I believe I have put down the leading traits of her intellectual character from whom it flowed.

Extract 2: from Hannah More, *Strictures on the Modern System of Female Education*, 2 vols (London: T. Cadell and W. Davies, 1799), 2: 4–9, 30–49

[From Chapter 1: 'Address to Women of Rank and Fortune, on the effects of their influence on society – Suggestions for the exertions of it in various instances.']

[pp. 4–9] In this moment of alarm and peril, I would call on them with a 'warning voice,' which should stir up every latent principle in their minds, and kindle every slumbering energy in their hearts; I would call on them to come forward, and contribute their full and fair proportion towards the saving of their country. But I would call on them to come forward, without departing from the refinement of their character, without derogating from the dignity of their sex: I would call them to the best and most appropriate exertion of their power, to raise the depressed tone of public morals, to awaken the drowsy spirit of religious principle, and to re-animate the dormant powers of active piety. They know too well how imperiously they give the law to manners, and with how despotic a sway they fix the standard of fashion. But this is not enough; this is a low mark, a prize not worthy of their high and holy calling. For, on the use which women of the superior class may be disposed to make of that power delegated to them by the courtesy of custom, by the honest gallantry of the heart, by the imperious controul of virtuous affections, by the habits of civilized states, by the usages of polished society: on the use, I say, which they shall hereafter make of this influence, will depend, in no low degree, the well-being of those states, and the virtue and happiness, nay perhaps the very existence of that society.

At this period, when our country can only hope to stand by opposing a bold and noble *unanimity* to the most tremendous confederacies against religion and order, and governments, which the world ever saw; what an accession would it bring to the public strength, could we prevail on beauty, and rank, and talents, and virtue, confederating their several powers, to come forward with a patriotism at once firm and feminine for the general good! I am not sounding an alarm to female warriors, or exciting female politicians: I hardly know which of the two is the most disgusting and unnatural character. Propriety is to a woman what the great Roman critic says action is to an orator; it is the first, the second, the third requisite. A woman may be knowing, active, witty, and amusing; but without propriety she cannot be amiable. Propriety is the centre in which all the lines of duty and of agreeableness meet. It is to character what proportion is to figure, and grace to attitude. It does not depend on any one perfection; but it is the result of general excellence. It shows itself by a regular, orderly, undeviating course; and never starts from its sober orbit into any splendid eccentricities; for it would be ashamed of such praise as it might extort by any aberrations from its proper path. It renounces all commendation but what is characteristic; and I would make it the criterion of true taste, right principle, and genuine feeling, in a woman, whether she would be less touched with all the flattery of romantic and exaggerated panegyric, than with that beautiful picture of correct and elegant propriety, which Milton draws of our first mother, when he delineates

'Those thousand *decencies* which daily flow
From all her words and actions.'[22]

Even the influence of religion is to be exercised with discretion. A female Polemic wanders almost as far from the limits prescribed to her sex, as a female Machiavel or warlike Thalestris.[23] Fierceness and bigotry have made almost as few converts as the sword, and both are peculiarly ungraceful in a female. Even *religious* violence has human tempers of its own to indulge, and is gratifying itself when it would be thought to be 'working the righteousness of God.'[24] But the character of a consistent Christian is as carefully to be maintained, as that of a fiery disputant is to be avoided; and she who is afraid to avow her principles, or ashamed to defend them, has little claim to that honourable title.

[pp. 30–49] In animadverting farther on the reigning evils which the times more particularly demand that women of rank and influence should repress, Christianity calls upon them to bear their decided testimony against every thing which is notoriously contributing to the public corruption. It calls upon them to banish from their dressing rooms, (and oh, that their influence could banish them from the libraries of their sons and husbands!) that sober and unsuspected mass of mischief, which, by assuming the plausible names of Science, of Philosophy, of Arts, of Belles Lettres, is gradually ministering death to the principles of those who would be on their guard, had the poison been labelled with its own pernicious title. Avowed attacks upon revelation are more easily resisted, because the malignity is advertised. But who suspects the destruction which lurks under the harmless or instructive names of *General History*, *Natural History*, *Travels*, *Voyages*, *Lives*, *Encyclopedias*, *Criticism*, and *Romance*? Who will deny that many of these works contain much admirable matter; brilliant passages, important facts, just descriptions, faithful pictures of nature, and valuable illustrations of science? But while 'the dead fly lies at the bottom,' the whole will exhale a corrupt and pestilential stench.

Novels, which used chiefly to be dangerous in one respect, are now become mischievous in a thousand. They are continually shifting their ground, and enlarging their sphere, and are daily becoming vehicles of wider mischief. Sometimes they concentrate their force, and are at once employed to diffuse destructive politics, deplorable profligacy, and impudent infidelity. Rousseau was the first popular dispenser of this complicated drug, in which the deleterious infusion was strong, and the effect proportionably fatal.[25] For he does not attempt to seduce the affections but through the medium of the principles. He does not paint an innocent woman, ruined, repenting, and restored; but with a far more mischievous refinement, he annihilates the value of chastity, and with pernicious subtlety attempts to make his heroine appear almost more amiable without it. He exhibits a virtuous woman, the victim not of temptation but of reason, not of vice but of sentiment, not of passion but of conviction; and strikes at the very root of honour by elevating a crime into a principle. With a metaphysical sophistry the most plausible, he debauches the heart of woman, by cherishing her vanity in the erection of a system of male virtues, to which, with a lofty dereliction of those that are her more peculiar and characteristic praise, he tempts her to aspire; powerfully insinuating, that to this splendid system chastity does not necessarily belong: thus corrupting the judgment and bewildering the understanding, as the most effectual way to inflame the imagination and deprave the heart.

The rare mischief of this author consists in his power of seducing by falsehood those who love truth, but whose minds are still wavering, and whose principles are not yet formed. He allures the warmhearted to embrace vice, not because they prefer vice, but because he gives to vice so natural an air of virtue: and ardent and enthusiastic youth, too confidently trusting in their integrity and in their teacher, will be undone, while they fancy they are indulging in the noblest feelings of their nature. Many authors will more infallibly complete the ruin of the loose and ill disposed; but perhaps (if I may change the figure) there never was a net of such exquisite art and inextricable workmanship, spread to entangle innocence and ensnare inexperience, as the writings of Rousseau: and, unhappily, the victim does not even struggle in the toils, because part of the delusion consists in imagining that he is set at liberty.

Some of our recent popular publications have adopted all the mischiefs of this school, and the principal evil arising from them is, that the virtues they exhibit are almost more dangerous than the vices. The chief materials out of which these delusive systems are framed, are characters who practise superfluous acts of generosity, while they are trampling on obvious and commanded duties; who combine sentiments of honour with actions the most flagitious: a high-tone of self-confidence, with a perpetual breach of self-denial: pathetic apostrophes to the passions, but no attempt to resist them. They teach that no duty exists which is not prompted by feeling: that impulse is the main spring of virtuous actions, while laws and principles are only unjust restraints; the former imposed by arbitrary men, the latter by the absurd prejudices of timorous and unenlightened conscience.[26] In some of the most splendid of these characters, compassion is erected into the throne of justice, and justice is degraded into the rank of plebian virtues. Creditors are defrauded, while the money due to them is lavished in dazzling acts of charity to some object that affected their senses; which fits of charity are made the sponge of every sin, and the substitute of every virtue: the whole indirectly tending to intimate how very *benevolent people are who are not Christians.* From many of these compositions, indeed, Christianity is systematically, and always virtually excluded; for the law and the prophets and the gospel *can* make no part of a scheme in which this world is looked upon as all in all; in which poverty and misery are considered as evils arising solely from the dispensations of God: this poverty is represented as the greatest of evils, and the restraints which tend to keep the poor honest, as the most flagrant injustice. The gospel can have nothing to do with a system in which sin is reduced to a little human imperfection, and Old Bailey crimes are softened down into a few engaging weaknesses; and in which the turpitude of all the vices a man himself commits, is done away by his *candour* in tolerating all the vices committed by others.

But the most fatal part of the system to that class whom I am addressing is, that even in those works which do not go all the lengths of treating marriage as an unjust infringement on liberty, and a tyrannical deduction from general happiness; yet it commonly happens that the hero or heroine, who has practically violated the letter of the seventh commandment, and continues to live in the allowed violation of its spirit, is painted as so amiable and so benevolent, so tender or so brave; and the temptation is represented as so *irresistible*, (for all these philosophers are fatalists,) the predominant and cherished sin is so filtered and purged of its pollutions, and is so sheltered and surrounded, and relieved with shining qualities, that the innocent and impressible young reader is brought to lose all horror of the awful crime in question, in the complacency she feels for the engaging virtues of the criminal.

But there is a new and strong demand for the exertion of that power I am humbly endeavouring to direct to its true end. Those ladies who take the lead in society are loudly called upon to act as the guardians of public taste as well as public virtue, in an important instance. They are called upon to oppose with the whole weight of their influence, the irruption of those swarms of publications that are daily issuing from the banks of the Danube; which, like their ravaging predecessors of the darker ages, though with far other arms, are overrunning civilized society. Those readers, whose purer taste has been formed on the correct models of the old classic school, see with indignation and astonishment the Vandals once more overpowering the Greeks and Romans. They behold our minds, with a retrograde but rapid motion, hurried back to the reign of 'chaos and old night,'[27] by wild and mis-shapen superstitions; in which, with that *consistency* which forms so striking a feature of the new philosophy, those who deny the immortality of the soul are most eager to introduce the machinery of ghosts; and by terrific and unprincipled compositions, which unite the taste of the Goths with the morals of Bagshot[28]

Gorgons, and Hydras, and Chimeras dire![29]

The writings of the French infidels were some years ago circulated in England with uncommon industry, and with some effect: but the good sense and good principles of the far greater part of our countrymen resisted the attack, and rose superior to the trial.[30] Of the doctrines and principles here alluded to, the dreadful consequences, not only in the unhappy country where they originated and were almost universally adopted, but in every part of Europe where they have been received, have been such as to serve as a beacon to surrounding nations, if any warning can preserve them from destruction. In this country the subject is now so well understood, that every thing which issues from the *French* press is received with jealousy; and a work, on the first appearance of its exhibiting the doctrines of Voltaire and his associates, is rejected with indignation.

But let us not on account of this victory repose in confident security. The modern apostles of infidelity and immorality, little less indefatigable in dispersing their pernicious doctrines than the first apostles were in propagating gospel truths, have only changed their weapons, but they have by no means desisted from the attack. To destroy the principles of Christianity in this island, appears at the present moment to be their grand aim. Deprived of the assistance of the French press, they are now attempting to attain their object under the close and more artificial veil of German literature.[31] Conscious that religion and morals will stand or fall together, their attacks are sometimes levelled against the one and sometimes against the other. With occasional strong professions of attachment to both of them, the feelings and the passions of the reader are engaged on the side of some one particular vice, or some one objection to revealed religion. Poetry as well as prose, romance as well as history; writings on philosophical as well as political subjects, have thus been employed to instil the principles of *Illuminatism*,[32] while incredible pains have been taken to obtain able translations of every book which it was supposed could be of use in corrupting the heart, or misleading the understanding. In many of these translations, the strongest passages, which, though well received in Germany, would have excited disgust in England, are wholly omitted, in order that the mind may be more certainly, though more slowly prepared for the full effect of the poison at another period.

Let not those to whom these pages are addressed deceive themselves, by supposing this to be a fable; but let them inquire most seriously whether I speak the truth, when I assert that the attacks of infidelity in Great Britain are at this moment principally directed against the female breast. Conscious of the influence of women in civil society, conscious of the effect which female infidelity produced in France, they attribute the ill success of their attempts in this country to their having been hitherto chiefly addressed to the male sex. They are now sedulously labouring to destroy the religious principles of women, and in too many instances they have fatally succeeded. For this purpose not only novels and romances have been made the vehicles of vice and infidelity, but the same allurement has been held out to the women of our country, which was employed by the original tempter to our first parent – Knowledge. Listen to the precepts of the new German enlighteners, and you need no longer remain in that situation in which Providence has placed you! Follow their examples, and you shall be permitted to indulge in all those gratifications which custom, not religion, has too far overlooked in the male sex!

We have hitherto spoken only of the German *writings*; but as there are multitudes who never read, equal pains have been taken to promote the same object through the medium of the stage: and this weapon is, of all others, that against which it is at the present moment the most important to warn my countrywomen. As a specimen of the German drama, it may not be unseasonable to offer a few remarks on the admired play of the *Stranger*.[33] In this piece the character of an *adultress*, which, in all periods of the world, ancient as well as modern, in all countries heathen as well as Christian, has hitherto been held in detestation, and has never been introduced but to be reprobated, is for the first time presented to our view in the most pleasing and fascinating colours. The heroine is a woman who forsook a husband, the most affectionate and the most amiable, and lived for some time in the most criminal commerce with her seducer. Repenting at length of her crime, she buries herself in retirement. The talents of the poet during the whole piece are exerted in attempting to render this woman the object, not only of the compassion and forgiveness, but of the esteem and affection, of the audience. The injured husband, convinced of his wife's repentance, forms a resolution, which every man of true feeling and Christian piety will probably approve. He forgives her offence, and promises her through life his advice, protection, and fortune, together with every thing which can alleviate the misery of her situation, but refuses to replace her in the situation of his wife. But this is not sufficient for the *German* author. His efforts are employed, and it is to be feared but too successfully, in making the audience consider the husband as an unrelenting savage, while they are led by the art of the poet anxiously to wish to see an adultress restored to that rank of women who have not violated the most solemn covenant that can be made with man, nor disobeyed one of the most positive laws which has been enjoined by God.

About the same time that this first attempt at representing an adultress in an exemplary light was made by a German dramatist, which forms an aera in manners; a direct vindication of adultery was for the first time attempted by a *woman*, a professed admirer and imitator of the German suicide Werther.[34] The Female Werther, as she is styled by her biographer, asserts in a work, intitled 'The Wrongs of Woman,' that adultery is justifiable, and that the restrictions placed on it by the laws of England constitute part of the *wrongs of woman*.[35]

But let us take comfort. These fervid pictures are not yet generally realised. These atrocious principles are not yet adopted into common practice. Though corruptions seem to be pouring in upon us from every quarter, yet there is still left among us a discriminating judgment. Clear and strongly marked distinctions between right and wrong still subsist. While we continue to cherish this sanity of mind, the case is not desperate. Though the crime above alluded to, the growth of which always exhibits the most irrefragable proof of the dissoluteness of public manners; though this crime, which cuts up order and virtue by the roots, and violates the sanctity of vows, is awfully increasing,

> 'Till senates seem,
> For purposes of empire less conven'd
> Than to release the adult'ress from her bonds;[36]

yet, thanks to the surviving efficacy of a holy religion, to the operations of virtuous laws, and the energy and unshaken integrity with which these laws are *now* administered; and still more perhaps to a standard of morals which continues in force, when the principles which sanctioned it are no more; this crime, in the female sex at least, is still held in just abhorrence; if it be practised, it is not honourable; if it be committed, it is not justified; we do not yet affect to palliate its turpitude; as yet it hides its abhorred head in lurking privacy; and reprobation hitherto follows its publicity.

But on YOUR exerting your influence, with just application and increasing energy, it may in no small degree depend whether this corruption shall still continue to be resisted. For, from admiring to adopting, the step is short, and the progress rapid; and it is in the moral as in the natural world, the motion, in the case of minds as well as of bodies, is accelerated on a nearer approach to the centre to which they are tending.

O ye to whom this address is particularly directed! an awful charge is in this instance, committed to your hands; as you shrink from it or discharge it, you promote or injure the honour of your daughters and the happiness of your sons, of both which you are the depositaries. And, while you resolutely persevere in making a stand against the encroachments of this crime, suffer not your firmness to be shaken by that affectation of charity, which is growing into a general substitute for principle. Abuse not so noble a quality as Christian candour, by misemploying it in instances to which it does not apply. Pity the wretched woman you dare not countenance; and bless HIM who has 'made you to differ.'[37] If unhappily she be your relation or friend, anxiously watch for the period when she shall be deserted by her betrayer; and see if, by your Christian offices, she can be snatched from a perpetuity of vice. But if, through the Divine blessing on your patient endeavours, she should ever be awakened to remorse, be not anxious to restore the forlorn penitent to that society against whose laws she has so grievously offended; and remember, that her soliciting such a restoration, furnishes but too plain a proof that she is not the penitent your partiality would believe; since penitence is more anxious to make its peace with heaven, than with the world. Joyfully would a truly contrite spirit commute an earthly for an everlasting reprobation! To restore a criminal to public society, is perhaps to tempt her to repeat her crime, or to deaden her repentance for having committed it; while to restore a strayed soul to God will add lustre to your Christian character, and brighten your eternal crown.

Extract 3: from Henry Fuseli, *Royal Academy Lectures* (1801), Lecture XI, in John Knowles, ed., *The Life and Writings of Henry Fuseli, Esq*, 3 vols (London, 1831), 3: 47–50[38]

The efficient cause, therefore, why higher Art at present is sunk to such a state of inactivity and languor that it may be doubted whether it will exist much longer, is not a particular one, which private patronage, or the will of an individual, however great, can remove; but a general cause, founded on the bent, the manners, habits, modes of a nation, – and not of one nation alone, but of all who at present pretend to culture. Our age, when compared with former ages, has but little occasion for great works, and that is the reason why so few are produced:[39] – the ambition, activity, and spirit of public life is shrunk to the minute detail of domestic arrangements – every thing that surrounds us tends to show us in private, is become snug, less, narrow, pretty, insignificant. We are not, perhaps, the less happy on account of all this; but from such selfish trifling to expect a system of Art built on grandeur, without a total revolution, would only be less presumptuous than insane.

What right have we to expect such a revolution in our favour?

Let us advert for a moment to the enormous difference of difficulty between forming and amending the taste of a public – between legislation and reform: either task is that of Genius; both have adherents, disciples, champions; but persecution, derision, checks will generally oppose the efforts of the latter, whilst submission, gratitude, encouragement, attend the smooth march of the former. No madness is so incurable as wilful perverseness; and when men can once, with Medea,[40] declare that they know what is best, and approve of it, but must, or choose to follow the worst, perhaps a revolution worse to be dreaded than the disease itself, must precede the possibility of a cure. Though, as it has been observed, the fourteenth and fifteenth centuries granted to the artists little more than the attention due to ingenious craftsmen; they were, from the object of their occupations and the taste of their employers, the legitimate precursors of M. Agnolo and Raffaello, who did no more than raise their style to the sublimity and pathos of the subject.[41] These trod with loftier gait and bolder strides a path, on which the former had sometimes stumbled, often crept, but always advanced: the public and the artist went hand in hand – but on what spot of Europe can the young artist of our day be placed to meet with circumstances equally favourable? Arm him, if you please, with the epic and dramatic powers of M. Agnolo and Raffaello, where are the religious and civic establishments, where the temples and halls open to receive, where the public prepared to call them forth, to stimulate, to reward him?

Idle complaints! I hear a thousand voices reply! You accuse the public of apathy for the Arts, while public and private exhibitions tread on each other's heels, panorama opens on panorama, and the splendour of galleries dazzles the wearied eye, and the ear is stunned with the incessant stroke of the sculptor's hammer, and our temples narrowed by crowds of monuments shouldering each other to perpetuate the memory of Statesmen who deluded, or of Heroes who bled at a Nation's call! Look round all Europe – revolve the page of history from Osymandias to Pericles, from Pericles to Constantine[42] – and say what age, what race stretched forth a stronger arm to raise the drooping genius of Art? Is it the public's fault if encouragement is turned into a job, and dispatch and quality, as objects of the artist's emulation? – And do you think that accidental and temporary encouragement can invalidate charges founded on permanent causes? What blew up the Art, will in its own surcease terminate its success.

Extract 4: from John Evans, *The Vanity of Human Expectations: A Tribute of Respect to the Beloved Memory of the Princess Charlotte* (London, 1817)[43]

ECCLESIASTES, I.1.2

The Words of the Preacher, the Son of David, King of Jerusalem, – VANITY OF VANITIES, SAITH THE PREACHER, VANITY OF VANITIES, ALL IS VANITY –

– But *who* of us regards the royal preacher – verily none – until some disastrous occurrence arise, which awakens the faculties, rouses the imagination, and penetrates the heart. The PREACHER, however neglected and despised, utters salutary truths, involving the immediate and eternal welfare of mankind. The present mournful occasion must render every mind susceptible of powerful impressions. The recent awful event is of a nature to banish every emotion of levity – and to excite the individual of any reflection to exclaim – *Vanity of vanities, saith the Preacher, Vanity of vanities, all is vanity!*

The *death* of THE PRINCESS CHARLOTTE in the bloom of youth – in the vigour of her age – in the maturity of her accomplishments – in the possession of every blessing that could render life desirable – proclaims the extreme *vanity* of the human condition: it is indeed the common lot of mortality.

It is but a few years ago that the birth of this AMIABLE PERSONAGE was announced to us by the thundering of cannon, the blaze of illumination, and other ebullitions of public joy! We congratulated ourselves on the security of an heir to the crown. We were pleased with the addition of another member to the Brunswick Family. The constitutional principles which seated them on the throne, ought to be had in everlasting remembrance. Hence our ancestors, suffering in the sacred cause of civil and religious liberty, hailed the accession of the race of Brunswick as an event of no ordinary magnitude. Indeed the expiration of the last reigning member of the *Stuart Dynasty* was the prevention of an act of tyranny meditated against the liberties of the country. By the death of Queen Anne, and the introduction of the House of Brunswick, Protestant Dissenters were rescued from an impending evil, whilst the nation was emancipated from the yoke of slavery.

The education of this distinguished heir to the British Throne was such as to lead us to entertain hopes of her becoming a blessing to the community. No pains were spared to invigorate her understanding and to ameliorate her heart. If any opinion can be formed from a work entitled, *Hints towards forming the Character of a young Princess*, dedicated to the learned prelate who had the care of her education, proper sentiments were inculcated, and a suitable spirit recommended. The topics are selected with judgment – and illustrated with peculiar facility. A considerable knowledge of human nature is evinced – and our national records elucidated with ability. A paragraph near the close of the publication indicates the temper in which it is written, and the laudable ends it had in view. The passage is brief but impressive, 'And may we not rest persuaded, (says this intelligent authoress,) that if there is a spectacle which our *Almighty Ruler* beholds with peculiar complacency on earth, and will recompense with a crown of distinguished brightness in heaven, it is a SOVEREIGN DOING JUSTLY, LOVING MERCY, AND WALKING HUMBLY WITH GOD.'[44]

Speaking of the education of Princes and Statesmen – 'I call that a complete and generous education,' says the immortal Milton, 'which fits a person to perform *justly, skilfully,* and *magnanimously* all the offices both of public and private life – of PEACE and WAR.' With the particulars of the education of the Princess I am unacquainted; nor, had I a knowledge of them, would it be proper to introduce them on this occasion. Suffice it just to say – that she was initiated into some of the ancient, and most of the modern, languages; that the ample scroll of history, 'rich with the spoils of time,'[45] was unfolded before her inquisitive mind, and that the principles of the British Constitution were held up in all their justness and beauty. And, judging from the following pleasing anecdote, there is reason to believe that RELIGION was inculcated as the purifier of the heart, the regulator of life, and the precursor of a glorious immortality!

Here I shall beg leave to introduce an interesting anecdote of *the Princess* (then between five and six years old), taken from the Journal of Dr. Porteus, the late venerable Bishop of London[46] – 'Yesterday (the 6th of August, 1801) I passed a very pleasant day at Shrewsbury-House, near Shooters' Hill, the residence of the Princess Charlotte of Wales. The day was fine, and the prospect extensive and beautiful, taking in a large reach of the Thames, which was covered with vessels of various sizes and descriptions. We saw a good deal of *the young Princess*. She is a most captivating and engaging child, and considering the high station she may hereafter fill, a most interesting and important one. She repeated to me several of her hymns with great correctness and propriety; and on being told that when she went to South End, in Essex, as she afterwards did for the benefit of sea-bathing, she would then be in my diocese, *she fell down on her knees and begged my blessing.* I gave it her with all my heart, and with my earnest secret prayers to God that she might adorn her illustrious station with every Christian grace, and that if ever she became to be *Queen* of this truly great and glorious country, she might be the means of diffusing virtue, piety, and happiness through every part of her dominions!'

The entrance into life of this *youthfull Princess*, we all recollect, was at an age somewhat earlier than what terminates the minority of the subject. Intelligent and sprightly, cheerful and accomplished, she was introduced into the first circle of rank, fashion, and beauty. Blessed with a firmness of mind which induced her to think and act for herself – she would avow her sentiments on every proper occasion. Possessed of an open temper and frank disposition, she conciliated the affection of those who had the felicity of being most acquainted with her. She also had a spirit of promptitude and decision which, under the controul of good sense, would have been productive of the best consequences. Without energy the business of life cannot be prosecuted, nor with a listless hand is the rod of empire swayed to any good purpose among the nations of the earth.

When this *illustrious Princess* entertained an idea of entering the most important connection of human life, she conducted herself in a manner honourable to her character and feelings. Royal marriages are not unfrequently dictated by reasons of state, utterly regardless of personal attachment. But here a noble example was set to the British nation. Rejecting the first proffered lover, she chose the man of her affection – the idol of her heart. In this truly august union the feelings of nature were venerated: pure affection was not immolated at the shrine of unfeeling interest or of an adventitious glory.

Soon followed her *union* with an illustrious Protestant Prince, endeared to us by the acknowledged good qualities of his head and of his heart. It was deemed by competent judges an appropriate connection. It met the wishes of all parties – it had resting upon it the blessing of the whole nation! Well do

I recollect the account communicated in the public prints of the solemniza-
tion of this ROYAL MARRIAGE, celebrated with the pomp and splendor
usually accompanying such an event. Her person, her habiliments, her
attendants, were minutely pourtrayed – it was a brilliant spectacle – glowing
with life and animation.

And now this *august pair* withdrew from the glare of public observation,
to participate of the pure and unsullied blessings of domestic life. Having
received the customary gratulations, they sunk into a sort of enviable
obscurity. Her illustrious consort, interfering with no political parties, led
a life without offence; whilst the Princess cherished those virtues which,
mild and unassuming, enter into the essence of connubial felicity. LOVING
and BELOVED, the pure stream of domestic affection ran on clear and
unperturbed to the very last, without annoyance or interruption.
Uncontaminated by the fascinations of rank, and unseduced by the
frivolities of fashion, she might be held up as a model of connubial fidelity.
In this retirement, however, it is said that she frequently spoke of *Elizabeth*
as the model for a British Queen; and it has been remarked, that in her
ample forehead, large blue eye, and steady stately countenance, there was
a strong similitude to the portraits of Elizabeth in the days of her youth
and beauty.

At length it was announced to the British nation, that its just hopes would
not be disappointed; this happy Princess gave indications of future progeny
– a circumstance received by all descriptions of people with exaltation. In the
commonest ranks of life increase of family is deemed a desirable event. The
pleasing imagery of a *fruitful vine* is employed by the Psalmist to represent
the augmentation of the human race:[47] but the present case had too deep an
interest attached to it not to be deemed a matter of high importance. Upon
the *first born* of an heir to the throne, revolve, as on an axis, the hopes of the
nation! It is a circumstance of general notoriety, of pleasing interest, – of
universal joy. The eyes of the nation were turned toward this object with an
intenseness which, the interest created, could alone justify. All ranks and
degrees of people eagerly anticipated the event.

And NOW arrives the important hour, and of a memorable day
renowned in the annals of our country, the *fifth* of November – when
hopes long indulged, and expectations fervently wrought, are on the verge
of gratification. But awful are the dispensations of Providence – manifold
and pungent the sorrows of mortality! The event is fatal – terminating
in the death of MOTHER and CHILD – the lamp of life is extinguished
– one common grave is thrown open for their reception, and thus closes
the agonizing scene. The shock vibrated throughout the whole circle of
civilized society –

There is an outward pomp, a garb of woe,
That sometimes follows SOVEREIGNS to the tomb;
There is a soul-felt grief that sighs at home
And presses on the heart – the great, the low,
Alike feel this, and oh! *lamented shade*,
To *thy* dear loss shall every rite be paid,
And the sad tear of fond affection flow!
'Tis not the sable garb – the room of state –
The minute bell that tells the fatal tale.
She, she is gone for whom we felt elate,
'Tis the *fond wife*, the *mother*, we bewail,
Young, loving, and belov'd – the good the great;
She was a NATION's hope – a NATION's pride,
With *her* that pride has fled – those hopes have died!

VANITY OF VANITIES, SAITH THE PREACHER, VANITY OF VANITIES, ALL IS VANITY!

But the last painful ceremony remains to be performed – the consignment of THE PRINCESS and her *Babe* to the tomb. At the close of this mournful day, lo! the funereal torches begin to blaze – the mourners gather together – the attendants fall into the procession, and the long sable train, with measured step, follow the *lifeless body*, borne along through the vaulted aisle, preceded and accompanied by the emblazoned pomp of heraldry, to its last retreat. They arrive at the destined spot – the lamented remains are consigned to its final abode, whilst the officiating minister, concluding the solemn service, utters amidst the profoundest grief, these well known accents – *Ashes to ashes, dust to dust, in sure and certain hope of a resurrection to eternal life!* Nor at such a crisis will the awful monition of the Prophet cease to vibrate in the ears of the illustrious mourners, returning homewards meditating on mortality and immortality. *The voice said cry, and he said, What shall I cry? All flesh is grass, and all the goodness thereof is as the flower of the field – the grass withereth, the flower fadeth, but the word of our God shall stand for ever.*[48]

Such was the brief but interesting career of our BELOVED PRINCESS; we have traced her from her cradle to her grave! Few in a situation so critical and exalted have acquitted themselves so well. But I must repress the inclination I feel to linger over the recital of her departed virtues. She was a kind, generous, and completely domesticated being. For her the blandishments of a court possessed no peculiar attractions; SHE sought, in conjunction with her endeared partner, the shade where, alas! she has terminated her *virtuous* and *peaceful* life, in an uncorrupting and uncorrupted retirement.

Extract 5: from *Cobbett's Weekly Political Register* 37 (5 and 19 August 1820): 333–6

DOCUMENTS RELATING TO HER MAJESTY THE QUEEN

The following Address to the Queen has been presented from the Female Inhabitants of Nottingham:–

'TO HER MOST GRACIOUS MAJESTY, QUEEN CAROLINE
    The humble Address of the Female Inhabitants of the town of Nottingham and its vicinity.

'We, your Majesty's most dutiful and loyal subjects, the Female Inhabitants of Nottingham, beg leave to congratulate you on your safe arrival in this country, after so long an absence, and to hail you Queen of these Kingdoms!

Beloved as you are by a great people, who have long preserved for you a faith unshaken, we dare not boast an unrivalled attachment; but we can truly say, that amidst this general glow of beating hearts, none are more loyal, none love you better, and none pray oftener for your present and future happiness, than the females of Nottingham. When you were far distant we remembered the unhappy exile; and when the accusers of your honour rung in our ears (as they fondly hoped) the death-bell of your innocence, we never for a moment believed their slanders, but felt at every charge, as we are sure we shall always feel, a more than common indignation.

You bring with you such powerful recommendations to protection, as no generous bosom can resist – your father is no more – your brother fell in battle – the chief solace of your cares, your amiable daughter, was soon, too soon snatched away![49] – and your great protector, our late venerable monarch, soon followed her.[50]

All in whom the spirit of the days of chivalry are not utterly extinct, all who would not immolate the best impulses of our nature on the altar of modern policy, will rally round their Queen, and save her alike from foreign emissaries and spies, and domestic persecutors.[51]

We desire to assure you of our continued fidelity, and to express a hope that ere long, you will have defeated the machinations of your enemies, be restored to all the honours of your illustrious station, and that neither sea nor land will again separate you from an admiring people.' – (Signed by 7,800 females.)

To which her Majesty returned the following most gracious answer:–
    'I should be deficient in sensibility if I had not felt the warmest gratitude, and more than ordinary delight when I received from the Female Inhabitants of the town of Nottingham and its vicinity, an Address which is remarkable for the amiable spirit which it breathes, and for the fervour of attachment to my person and rights which it displays. I am proud of being the Queen of women of such

generous sentiments; and I am happy to remark that such sentiments indicate an increased and increasing cultivation of the female mind.

To be conscious that the hearts of so large a portion of my own sex are vibrating with emotions of affection for his Majesty's Royal Consort, that they are sympathising with her sorrows, and deprecating her wrongs, and that her happiness is the object of their pious supplications, cannot but awaken in my breast the most pleasurable sensations. The same spirit of devotedness to the fair fame, to the lawful rights, and to the general interests of a persecuted Queen, which animates the female inhabitants of Nottingham, is, I trust, diffused through a large majority of their countrywomen. They will consider the honour of her Majesty as reflected upon themselves – they will best know how to appreciate the slanders by which I have been assailed, and the indignities by which I have been oppressed.

With the most gentle delicacy the female inhabitants of the town of Nottingham and its vicinity have touched those springs of grief in my heart which will ever continue painfully to vibrate at the recollection of the near and dear relatives of whom I have been bereaved, and particularly of that departed saint in whose talents and whose virtues the women have lost a model of the most estimable excellence, and the nation in general a future sovereign, under whose fostering care that liberty would have flourished which gives happiness to the people and security to the Throne.'

ADDRESS OF THE MARRIED LADIES

'MADAM – Whilst thousands and tens of thousands of our fellow-subjects are approaching your Majesty with assurances of homage and affection – whilst addresses even from the remoter parts of the kingdom are laid at your feet – permit us, your Majesty's neighbours, as wives, and the mistresses of families, in and near the metropolis, to approach you. We are unaccustomed to public acts, and uninfluenced by party feelings; yet we cannot be excluded from offering to your Majesty's notice our sympathy and devotion. Grateful to the Constitution under which it is our happiness to live – saved also by our rank in the middle classes of society, from the dangers attendant on high rank or poverty, and protected by our husbands, we may hardly be supposed judges of all the value of your Majesty's conduct; but, Madam, we admire your magnanimity, and we adore that womanly feeling which has made your Majesty treat with contempt every offer, the tendency of which was to compromise your honour, and we thank you for it in the name of our sex.

Had your Majesty been treated with the respect due to your exalted rank, our hearts would have throbbed with ardent interest in your cause, and with love to your person; and, leaving to our husbands and sons all public expression of feeling, we should have confined ours to our domestic circles; but now, Madam, the indignation we feel for the cruel treatment of your Majesty bursts every barrier between us, and we hasten to express at your feet the warm, the almost overwhelming interest with which we are inspired: and be assured, Madam, our judgments are quite as much enlisted in your Majesty's service as our feelings: for, added to the dreadful charges against you, are not new crimes found out by your enemies? and new modes of judging them, unknown alike to common law and common sense? Under these circumstances, scarcely less than a miracle, we think, can procure your justification, refused as your Majesty has been every means of fairly meeting the accusations against you. We commit your Majesty's cause to the integrity of your own great mind; to the zeal, to the honour, and the ability of your legal advisers, who will have for their reward a nation's gratitude; but, above all, to our all-seeing and merciful God – to that God whom no one can prevent our addressing, and teaching our children to address, in fervent prayers for your protection.

And now, Madam, in simplicity of style, and sincerity of heart, we beg to subscribe ourselves

Your Majesty's dutiful, affectionate, and loyal subjects and servants.'

Her Majesty was graciously pleased to return the following answer:–

'In this honest and affectionate address from my female neighbours, who are wives and mothers of families in and near the metropolis, I gratefully acknowledge the sympathy which they express for my many sorrows, and the indignation which they feel for my unnumbered wrongs. The approbation of my own sex must be ever dear to my heart; and it must be more particularly gratifying when it is the approbation of mothers of families in and near this enlightened metropolis.

When my honour is attacked, every loyal Englishwoman must feel it as an imputation upon her own. The virtues of sovereigns are not circumscribed in their influence or insulated in their operations. They put in motion a wide circle of the imitative propensity in the subordinate conditions of life. Thus the virtues of the great become the property of the people; and the people are interested in preserving them from slanderous contamination.

The present procedure against me is like a wilful attempt on the part of blind phrenzy or improvident malice to destroy the moral character of the monarchy. To lessen this moral character in public estimation is not merely to degrade the Queen, but to shatter into atoms that reverential respect which gives strength to the sceptre and dignity to the Sovereign.

I shall never sacrifice that honour which is the glory of a woman, and the brightest jewel of a Queen, for any earthly consideration. All the possessions in the world would be purchased too dear if they were obtained at the price of self-condemnation. I can never be debased while I observe the great maxim of respecting myself.

In this era of ceaseless change, and of violent agitation, when whole nations

seem tossed, like individuals, on the ocean of storms, no circumstances, however menacing, shall shake the constancy of my attachment to the English
nation, or estrange my affections from the general good of the community. The
future is wisely covered with an opaque cloud; but whatever may be my destiny, I will cherish in all vicissitudes, and preserve in all fortunes, that resignation to the Divine will, which in proportion as it becomes an habitual sentiment
of the mind, improves all its virtues, and elevates the general character.'

Extract 6: from Madame D'Arblay [Frances Burney] to Mrs Lock (15 August 1820), in Charlotte Barrett, ed., *Diary and Letters of Madame D'Arblay*, 6 vols (London: Macmillan, 1905), 6: 386–8[52]

We are all, and of all classes, all opinions, all ages, and all parties, absolutely
absorbed by the expectation of Thursday.[53] The Queen has passed the
bottom of our street twice this afternoon in an open carriage, with Lady Ann
and – Alderman Wood![54] – How inconceivable that among so many
adherents, she can find that only Esquire! – And why she should have any,
in her own carriage and in London, it is not easy to say. There is a universal
alarm for Thursday; the letter to the King breathes battle direct to both
Houses of Parliament as much as to His Majesty. Mr. Wilberforce is called
upon, and looked up to, as the only man in the dominions to whom an
arbitration should belong. Lord John Russell positively asserts that it is not
with Lord Castlereagh and the Ministers that conciliation or non-concilia-
tion hang, but with Mr. Wilberforce and his circle.[55] If I dared hope such was
the case, how much less should I be troubled by the expectance awakened for
to-morrow – it is now Wednesday that I finish my poor shabby billet.
Tremendous is the general alarm at this moment; for the accused turns
accuser, public and avowed, of King, Lords and Commons, declaring she will
submit to no award of any of them.

What would she say should evidence be imperfect or wanting, and they
should *acquit* her?

It is, however, open war, and very dreadful. She really invokes a revolution
in every paragraph of her letter to her Sovereign and lord and husband.

I know not what sort of conjugal rule will be looked for by the hitherto
Lords and Masters of the World, if this conduct is abetted by them....

The heroine passed by the bottom of our street yesterday, in full pomp
and surrounded with shouters and vociferous admirers. She now dresses
superbly every day, and has always six horses and open carriage. She seems
to think now she has no chance but from insurrection, and therefore all her
harangues invite it. Oh Dr. Parr![56] – how my poor brother[57] would have
blushed for him! he makes these orations with the aid of Cobbett! – and the
council, I suppose. Of course, like Croaker in *The Good-Natured Man*, I
must finish with 'I wish we may all be well this day three months!'[58]

Plate 4

Plate 5

**Extract 7: from *The Gentleman's Magazine and Historical Chronicle*
17 (1822): 70–1**

STATUE TO THE DUKE OF WELLINGTON, &C. IN HYDE PARK

The Ladies of England having resolved to erect a Monument in honour of the Duke of Wellington and his brave Companions in victory – the brothers, sons, lovers, and husbands of many of those from whom the tribute so nobly and so gratefully comes, – about ten thousand pounds were voluntarily and speedily raised. It is extraordinary that a work, which has excited not only by its magnitude, but by its excellence, the admiration of the greatest Artists of modern times, should not have been mentioned either by Pausanias or any other ancient writer upon Art; and that all we can tell of it is, that this splendid original from which our Statue is cast (attributed to Phidias, and existing on the Quirinal Hill at Rome), was removed from the Baths of Constantine in the Papacy of Sixtus V, and erected on its present site under the direction of Fontana. The horse which accompanies the Statue, was discovered near it, and applied to form a groupe. It has been held by many connoisseurs not to be in unison with the grandeur of form displayed in the Statue. Some enlightened Antiquaries have conjectured that it was raised in honour of Achilles. Others have imagined it to represent Castor; but there seems to be little ground for this supposition, unless the Statue was positively connected with the horse: it wants the bonnet, the usual appendage of the Dioscuri. As the Statue simply has been adopted by Mr. Westmacott, he appears to have preferred the former opinion, and to have armed him with the short Greek sword and shield.

The height of the Statue as it stands, is rather more than eighteen feet. It is erected upon a basement and plinth of Dartmoor grey granite, surmounted on a pedestal of red granite from Peterhead (near Aberdeen, and exceedingly beautiful); the whole, with the mound, from the line of the road, being thirty-six feet in height. The site is just within the angle where, after entering by the gate at Hyde Park Corner, the carriage roads divide; the one leading to Oxford-street, the other to the Serpentine. The Statue fronts the corner, and the head is turned almost directly towards the residence of the Hero whose glories it commemorates in the following inscription in bronze letters on the pedestal:–

TO ARTHUR DUKE OF WELLINGTON, AND HIS BRAVE COMPANIONS IN ARMS, THE STATUE OF ACHILLES, CAST FROM CANNON TAKEN IN THE BATTLES OF SALAMANCA, VITTORIA, TOULOUSE, AND WATERLOO,[59] IS INSCRIBED BY THEIR COUNTRY-WOMEN.

Upon the base (not yet affixed) will appear the following Inscription:
PLACED ON THIS SPOT, ON THE XVIII DAY OF JUNE

MDCCCXXII. BY COMMAND OF HIS MAJESTY GEORGE III.

The Statue was brought upon the ground on the Anniversary of the Victory of Waterloo; and the time since has been employed in the difficult task of elevating and placing it upon the pedestal. The mechanical means used in transporting it from the foundry and effecting this its final position were necessarily of immense power; for we learn that its weight cannot be estimated at less than 33 or 34 tons!! The thickness of the metal varies from about an inch at the head, to 1½ and 2 inches, as the figure descends; and as it was impossible to extract the core from its internal frame, a great addition is thus made to its weight. The core consists of a composition of plaster, cow-dung, and other materials. In its composition twelve 24 pounders were melted; but as the metal of cannon is too brittle to be wrought into such shapes, it was requisite to add about one-third more of metal, whose fusion would render the work, if we may say so, pliant and perfect. The whole is thus equal to eighteen 24-pounders.

In antient Greece, the honoured Victors of the Olympic Games, on returning crowned to their native cities, were not permitted to enter them by the common way and gate; to distinguish them above all their compatriots, a breach was made in the wall, by which they were borne home in triumph. By one of those *accidents* which seem to be *fate*, the Ladies' Statue to the Duke of Wellington, when brought to its destination, was found to be too mighty for the gates by which it should have entered, and it became necessary to breach the wall for the admission of this trophy of a Victor more glorious than ever threw lustre on the resplendent annals of immortal Greece.

Extract 8: from Maria Edgeworth, *Harry and Lucy Concluded* (London, 1825), pp. 1–10

'Mamma, do you recollect, two years ago, when my father was explaining to us the barometer and thermometer, and when he showed us several little experiments?' said Lucy, and she sighed.

'Yes, my dear, I remember that time very well,' said her mother; 'but why do you sigh?'

'Because I was very happy *then*,' said Lucy.

'And are not you happy now, my dear?'

'Yes, mamma, but not so very happy as I was then, because now I do not *go on* with Harry as I used to do.'

'How so? I hope that you have not had any quarrel with your brother?'

'Quarrel! oh no, mamma, it would be impossible to quarrel with Harry, he is so good-natured; and he is as fond of me as ever, I believe. But yet, I do not know how it is, we do not suit each other quite so well as we did.

We are not so much together; I do not know all he is doing, nor go on with all he is thinking of, as I used to do.'

'My dear Lucy, you and your brother have been learning different things for some time past; and as you grow older, this must be; your different employments must separate you during a great part of the day; and so much the better, you will be the more glad to be together in your hours of amusement. Do not you find this?'

'Yes, I do, mamma,' said Lucy, 'but – ' and after this *but*, she sighed again. 'But now we are not amused always in the same way. Harry has grown so excessively fond of mechanics, and of all those scientific things, which he is always learning from my uncle and papa.'

'I thought, Lucy, that you were fond of those things too?' said her mother.

'So I am, mamma; only I am not nearly so fond of them as I was formerly: I do not exactly know why; but, in the first place, I suppose, because I do not understand them now nearly so well as Harry does: he has got very far before me.'

'True,' answered her mother, 'you have been learning other things, which it is more necessary for a girl to know.'

'Yes, mamma, I remember your saying just after that happy barometer time, that I thought of nothing but experiments; papa said, that must not be. Then I was not allowed to go into his room with Harry in the mornings. However, I learned more of arithmetic, and drawing, and dancing, and music, and work.'

'And you grew fond of these; so much the better,' said her mother. 'This does not make you less happy, does it?'

'No, no, mamma; but then came the time when Harry and I were quite separated. That long – long – long time, when you were ill, mamma, and when I was at my aunt Pierrepoint's: while I was with her, I read nothing but stories and poetry, and I heard my aunt and people who were there reading plays. She used to praise me for understanding wit, and for repeating poetry. Then I grew very fond of them. But Harry is so grave always about wit, he never understands it at first; and at last he says, "Is that all?" – As to similes, they always interrupt him.'

'*They* interrupt him!' said her mother, 'perhaps, Lucy, *you* interrupt him.'

'Sometimes, perhaps, I do, mamma; but he always finds out that similies [sic] are not exact. This is very provoking. I wonder why he is so much fonder of exactness than I am.'

'Probably because in science, which he has been learning, he finds at every step the use, the necessity of exactness. He could not go on without it in measuring or in reasoning.'

'Mamma, I understand the use of exactness in some things. In drawing in perspective, and in proportion, by a scale, as you taught me. Harry came to me the other day, and asked me to draw a cart for him; and I was glad to find a cart for him; and I was glad to find that I could help him in something.'

'And I dare say he will be glad to help you in his turn. You each know different things, which you can learn from one another, and in which you can be of mutual assistance. This is just as it should be between friends.'

'Thank you, mamma, you make me feel happy again. I will ask Harry to bring me up to him in all he has been learning, as fast as possible, that we may go on together as we used to do, if you have no objection, mamma.'

'Do so, my dear Lucy; but I warn you, that you should not expect to go fast; you must be content to go slowly, and you must submit to be inferior to your brother for some time. This may mortify you, my dear, but it cannot be avoided, you must bear it.'

SELECT BIBLIOGRAPHY

Bainbridge, Simon, *Napoleon and English Romanticism* (Cambridge: Cambridge University Press, 1995). Traces the complex reactions to the figure of Napoleon in the poetry of the period.

Colley, Linda, *Britons: Forging the Nation 1707–1837* (1992; London: Pimlico Press, 1994). See chapter on 'Womanpower' which focuses on the role of women in the public sphere.

Curran, Stuart, 'Women Readers, Women Writers', in *The Cambridge Companion to British Romanticism*, ed. Stuart Curran (Cambridge: Cambridge University Press, 1993). Wide-ranging account of the work of women writers in the period.

Davidoff, Leonore and Catherine Hall, *Family Fortunes: Men and Women of the English Middle Class 1780–1850* (London: Hutchinson, 1987). Especially good on the role of religion, the rise of Evangelicalism and the Queen Caroline affair.

Laqueur, T.W., 'The Queen Caroline Affair: Politics as Art in the Reign of George IV', *Journal of Modern History* 54 (1982): 417–66. Examines the implications of the crisis in terms of politics and representation.

Moers, Ellen, *The Dandy: From Brummell to Beerbohm* (Lincoln: University of Nebraska Press, 1978). Very useful on the Regency figure of the Dandy.

Porter, Roy and Lesley Hall, *The Facts of Life: The Creation of Sexual Knowledge in Britain, 1650–1950* (New Haven and London: Yale University Press, 1995). A study of sexual advice books.

Richardson, Alan, *Literature, Education and Romanticism: Reading as Social*

Practice 1780–1832 (Cambridge: Cambridge University Press, 1994). The best account of debates over education in the period.

Ross, Marlon B., *The Contours of Masculine Desire: Romanticism and the Rise of Women's Poetry* (Oxford: Oxford University Press, 1989).

Sales, Roger, *Jane Austen and Representations of Regency England* (London: Routledge, 1996). Good on public and literary reactions to the figure of the Prince Regent.

Taylor, Barbara, *Eve and the New Jerusalem: Socialism and Feminism in the Nineteenth Century* (London: Virago, 1983). A study of the Owenite socialists.

7

LITERARY INSTITUTIONS

Catherine Boyle and Zachary Leader

This section discusses the complex interaction of authors, publishers, patrons, booksellers, libraries, reviewers and readers in the production of literature in the years 1800–30. These years saw important shifts in the price of books: in the first half of the period, during the Napoleonic wars, prices were high; with the resumption of trade across the Channel after 1815 (and a reduction in the price of paper), prices fell.[1] The consequence was a boom in book production, and 'the market', a newly identifiable reading public, became a conscious preoccupation of writers and publishers alike.[2] How that market shaped published writing has only recently become the concern of scholars of the Romantic period: the image of the literary work as personal rather than social – the creation of solitary, autonomous geniuses – has been hard to shake.[3] Yet even while fiercely professing independence, writers typically draw on a range of institutional collaborators, or are affected by them. Though the role of the nominal author in literary creation is dominant, it is not exclusive; nor, as we shall see, are institutional influences always negligible or unwelcome to authors.

The first of these influences is exerted by the publisher, often also the bookseller. It is the publisher who selects books for publication and makes sure they reach an audience, not merely through production, but through advertising, wholesaling of editions, usually at his (or occasionally her[4]) own expense, purchase or lease of copyright, and financing (purchasing paper, hiring printers and binders). In Philip Gaskell's words: 'His position was pivotal because he was not only the organizer but also the financier and indeed the speculator of the book trade.'[5] Though money could be made from publishing, few made fortunes (losing fortunes was more common, as in the spectacular £250,000 loss suffered by Archibald Constable in 1825).[6] With rare exceptions, most literary works were published in editions of 500–1,500 copies and sold, especially in the case of novels, chiefly to libraries. The resulting profits were modest.[7] However, that authors themselves, even poets, could make money out of writing was clear, as the examples of Scott, Byron, Samuel Rogers, Felicia Hemans, Charlotte Smith and Letitia Landon, among others, attest. When, in 1818, Keats declared to his guardian, Richard Abbey, his intention to 'gain his living' as a poet, the declaration was neither foolish nor unreasonable, especially if Keats was prepared to attend to the market.[8] Of the many wounding moments in John Gibson Lockhart's notorious *Blackwood's Edinburgh Magazine* review of *Endymion* (1818), the first product of Keats's determination to 'overwhelm' himself in poetry, the most alarming may well have been Lockhart's 'small prophecy that his bookseller will not again venture £50 upon any thing he can write'.[9]

Keats's 'bookseller' was the firm of Taylor and Hessey, whose authors included Coleridge, Walter Savage Landor, William Hazlitt, Leigh Hunt, Thomas De Quincey, Charles Lamb, George Darley, Thomas Hood, Francis Cary, Thomas Carlyle and John Clare.[10] These authors joined the firm, founded in 1806 by John Taylor (1781–1864) and James Hessey (1785–1870), after 1816, when it greatly expanded the publishing, as opposed to bookselling, side of its business, and they made the firm's name in the literary world. Financial survival, though, derived from the publication not of literary but of moral, religious and educational works, in particular a series of conduct books written by Mrs Ann Taylor and Miss Jane Taylor of Ongar (no relations to Taylor the publisher).[11] Without the success of these conduct books the firm could not have published its literary titles, especially those of authors like Keats, whose initial volumes sold poorly, or Hazlitt and Hunt, who were embroiled in sales-inhibiting political controversies.[12]

Taylor and Hessey's complex and controversial relations with the Northamptonshire poet, John Clare (1793–1864), as revealed in correspondence, a brief review of Clare's first volume, *Poems Descriptive of Rural Life and Scenery* (1820), and Taylor's Introduction to the volume (which makes clear his efforts to market Clare as 'peasant poet', efforts Clare himself aided and approved) make up the subject matter of the initial texts of this section (**extracts 1–10**). Though Clare's reliance on his publishers was extreme (school pretty much ended for him when he was 10, and throughout his life he had problems, in several senses, conforming to conventions of spelling, punctuation and grammar), this extremity throws into relief evolving institutional relations and pressures experienced by most writers in the period, even well-educated and aristocratic writers, like Byron, who affected indifference to the market.[13] The function of these extracts is to highlight the role of the publisher, the periodical and the patron in literary production.

By 1800 the publisher had supplanted the patron as chief poetical midwife, though the patron was still a presence – in Clare's case an important one. Clare was brought to Taylor's attention by Taylor's cousin, the Stamford bookseller Edward Drury. But his career was also helped by the early intervention of a wealthy and influential patron, Lord Radstock (1753–1825), a retired admiral, friend of Nelson, ex-Naval Governor of Newfoundland and prominent Evangelical. It was Radstock who in 1819 arranged a subscription list among rich and titled friends to afford Clare a steady yearly income. When Radstock took exception to lines from *Poems Descriptive* attacking wealth and station (the lines in question come from

'Helpstone' and 'Dawnings of Genius') he did so with brutal directness, threatening to denounce the poet publicly. As the correspondence between Clare, Taylor and Radstock's friend and emissary, Eliza L. Emmerson, suggests, the result was a struggle for influence between publisher and patron, one Clare negotiated with considerable tact, while also acknowledging Taylor's ultimate indispensability.

If the patron's influence over the poet was in decline in the early decades of the nineteenth century, the degree of authority the publisher was meant to exercise in shaping and marketing the work of an author was not yet clear. Hence Clare's startling insistence in the correspondence upon *Taylor*'s independence (Taylor handled editorial matters for the firm, Hessey handled bookselling), even when rejecting poems Clare especially favours. Hence also Taylor's several attempts to identify or demarcate roles, as when he announces, in a letter to Clare of 29 September 1820, that 'my province qualifies me to cut out but not to introduce anything', or when elsewhere he frets over the authority Clare cedes him (for example, by submitting twice the number of poems any publisher could afford to print at any one time, even in a two-volume format, or by submitting obviously imperfect, unfinished and barely legible manuscripts).[14] The current view of the role Taylor and Hessey played in the production of Clare's poems is that it was oppressive or exploitative, as in Andrew Motion's clever conflation 'enclosing lands, banishing nomadic wanderers, planting hedges and putting in punctuation'.[15] **Extracts 1–10** suggest a more complicated and nuanced history.

Taylor and Hessey, like other publishers of the period, were determined not merely to meet but to shape the tastes and interests of the market. As publishers they assisted their authors both by publishing and paying for their writings (either by outright purchase of copyright, profit sharing, royalty agreements or commission publishing), and by actively marketing the books they produced and sold. When Marilyn Butler declares of the period that 'it is through journalism that writing becomes a viable way of making a living', she may be thinking as much of publicity as of commissions.[16] In the early decades of the nineteenth century publishers made use of journalism to draw attention to their books in several ways: by puffing authors in newspapers (a practice that seems to have been counter-productive in Clare's case); by arranging favourable notices (as when Clare's friend Octavius Gilchrist reviewed *Poems Descriptive* in the *Quarterly Review* of May 1820[17]); and, more directly, by founding, seeking to control or purchasing specific journals or specialized literary reviews.

In 1821, after the bruising reception given to Keats's first two volumes of poetry, Taylor and Hessey made just such a purchase: of the *London Magazine*, the principal liberal rival to *Blackwood's Edinburgh Magazine* and the *Quarterly Review*. The aims of this purchase were several: to counter the power of critical orthodoxy; to provide the firm's authors a venue, or voice; and to make money, since by the 1820s periodical publication had become the main source of publishers' profits. The purchase was no innovation: Constable, for example, had started the *Edinburgh*

Review in 1802, and John Murray, his London agent (also, eventually, the publisher of Byron, Crabbe and Austen, among others), had started the *Quarterly Review* in 1809. As Clare's correspondence makes clear, his early writings were much influenced by these periodicals, not only indirectly, through suggestions and revisions from his publishers, but through his own often anxious attention to reviewers.[18]

The influence of another sort of literary institution, the circulating library, was especially associated with fiction. 'Miss Edgeworth's New Novel is enclosed', Taylor writes to Hessey in 1814, 'Johnsons printed 3000 and could deliver only half what were subscribed for – When shall we pick up a Miss Edgeworth?'[19] They never did, but then neither did they publish lesser novelists; Taylor and Hessey were too fastidious or highbrow for novels, publishing only two in the firm's lifetime, despite the success of both. But novels were the wave of the future. When the price of books fell after 1815 the market for poetry declined, in part because readers could at last afford more immediate and disposable – also less demanding – pleasures, the sort often found, or thought to be found, in novels. Those readers who continued to find the price of novels prohibitive (in 1815, the average three-volume novel sold for a guinea, the average single volume of poetry sold for five shillings[20]) rented them from circulating libraries, whose influence expanded rapidly in the period.

Circulating libraries were private businesses, often run by booksellers. By 1801 there were a thousand such libraries in England, at least one in every major city or town. In addition to renting books (for an annual subscription fee, at the most two guineas), they sold luxury items such as perfume, cosmetics, silverware and toys; organized raffles; and provided a place for readers to meet, gossip, read newspapers or play cards.[21] Most libraries offered a range of books, but from the start novels dominated their trade. The most important and controversial of these libraries, with a catalogue listing over 20,000 titles, was run by the London bookseller William Lane. Lane was the proprietor of the Minerva Press, begun in 1790, the leading publisher of Gothic fiction in England, and he was also the principal wholesaler of complete, prepackaged circulating libraries, offering entrepreneurial customers a range of models from 100 volumes to 10,000.[22]

Extract 11, concerning circulating libraries, is from the opening pages of a Minerva Press novel of 1802 entitled *Nobility Run Mad, or Raymond and His Three Wives*. Like many Minerva Press publications its author was anonymous, a signal (like the more obvious pseudonym 'A Lady') that the novel was written by a woman for women. The primacy of women in the novel-writing field during the first decades of the nineteenth century was universally acknowledged, but it was also being gradually undermined, as Gaye Tuchman has argued, by male authors.[23] The excerpt from *Nobility Run Mad* reflects the ambivalence women themselves felt towards both circulating libraries and the fiction they promoted: it describes one such library in attractive terms, but also suggests that its popularity might be part of the 'degeneracy of the age'. In like manner, the brief anonymous notice of the novel reprinted here from the *Annual Review* of 1802 (**extract 12**) praises its 'considerable beauties' while also questioning its propriety.

As the fortunes of the novel boomed after 1815, those of poetry began to fade, and by 1830 almost no publishers would publish it, at least not in single volumes. The periodicals played a role in this decline, particularly the more catholic publications (like *Blackwood's* or the *London Magazine*) which combined essays, reviews, short fiction and poetry. *Poole's Index to Periodical Literature* lists over twenty such publications launched between the years 1815 to 1832, what a contemporary observer called 'a grand army of reviews, of all shapes and prices, from five-shillings down to fourpence, in many of which was to be had the cream of from five to five-and-twenty authors together, carefully skimmed for your sipping palate'.[24] The taste for 'sipping' or 'skimming' which periodicals satisfied (or helped to create) was further fed by the last of the institutions introduced here, the literary Annual. The effect this taste had on the poetry of the 1820s and 1830s was also noteworthy.

Literary Annuals were lavishly produced gatherings of verse, prose and engraved plates, published in advance of the Christmas season.[25] The first of their kind, *Forget Me Not*, appeared in 1823, edited by the art publisher and bookseller Rudolph Ackermann. Two years later it had nine rivals, and by 1831 there were sixty-two. The excerpt from John Wilson's archly florid 'Monologue, or Soliloquy on the Annuals' (**extract 13**), written under the pseudonymn 'Christopher North', and published in 1829 in *Blackwood's*, makes their popularity clear. The most successful Annuals regularly sold in six figures, despite a sale price of twelve shillings, more than twice that of the average poetry volume. 'The Annuals are now the only books bought for presents to young ladies', wrote Robert Southey in 1828, 'in which way poems formerly had their chief vent.'[26]

Because the Annuals paid so well, almost all the major poets of the period – Felicia Hemans, Letitia Landon, Charlotte Smith, Thomas Moore, Robert Southey, Samuel Rogers, Coleridge, Wordsworth, Byron, Scott – appeared in them, often in improbable conjunctions.[27] In 1829, for example, Coleridge, Wordsworth and Southey appeared in *The Keepsake*, the most lavish and popular of all Annuals, alongside Percy Shelley, Mary Shelley and Thomas Moore. Coleridge was offered £50 for two short poems, which he described as 'more than all, *I* ever made by all my Publications'.[28] The aesthetic, as opposed to financial, impact of the Annuals, though, was often less welcome. In Peter Manning's words, 'the seemingly neutral notion of taste the *Keepsake* promoted subsumed divisive distinctions – radical and conservative, libertine and pious – into serene solidarity'.[29] The effect of the Annuals was to encourage the limiting view that poetry was decorative, decorous, sentimental, quietist. When Clare published in the Annuals, for example, it made him value Taylor. 'The Ballad that I wrote to the "Souvenir"', he complains to Taylor, 'is so polished and altered that I did not scarcely know it was my own ... I feel a disgust to write for such things but I did it for the sake of making a little money.'[30]

From the start the Annuals were addressed to a genteel female audience; they were 'drawing-room' or 'parlour' books, items of display and decoration like the gems, flowers and fine objects after which they were named: the *Bijou*, the *Cameo*, the *Forget-Me-Not*, the *Iris*, the *Amethyst*. The most prominent and influential poet of the Annuals was Letitia Elizabeth Landon or L. E. L., who began contributing to them in 1824 and was most closely associated with *Fisher's Drawing Room Scrap-Book*, which she edited from 1832 until her death in 1838.[31] The poems in *Fisher's Scrap-Book*, like those in many Annuals, took second place to the prints; they were in effect 'illustrations' of them. The prints were chosen not by the poet but the publisher, and as Landon explains in her Introduction to the 1832 volume, were 'selected rather for their pictorial excellence than their poetic capabilities'.

Hence the frequent oddity or unexpectedness of the connections between print and poem, as in several of the examples reproduced here. Jerome McGann has argued for the constitutive or thematically appropriate character of this oddity, the way it points to the poet's compromised or secondary role in the poem's creation.[32] Landon's poems in *Fisher's Scrap-Book* and elsewhere foreground failed hopes, loss, defeat and disillusion, themes common to much poetry written in the 1820s and 1830s, and not just poetry written by women; so, too, McGann argues, do the obvious commercial constraints under which they were produced, as signalled here by the strained or seemingly arbitrary relations between print and poem. 'The ideas that seemed at first so delightful', Landon writes of the stages of literary creation, in her Introduction to the 1832 volume, 'are grown common, by passing through the familiarizing process of writing, printing, and correcting.' The gift-book format itself hints at this 'familiarization' process by drawing attention to the poem as product, the result less of inspiration than of the contingencies of commerce and labour. **Extracts 14–15**, which reproduce material from the 1832 and 1833 editions of *Fisher's Scrap-Book*, highlight these contingencies.

Extract 1: from John Taylor's Introduction to John Clare, *Poems Descriptive of Rural Life and Scenery* (London: Taylor and Hessey, 1820), pp. i–ii, iv, xx–xxi

The following Poems will probably attract some notice by their intrinsic merit; but they are also entitled to attention from the circumstances under which they were written. They are the genuine productions of a young Peasant, a day-labourer in husbandry, who has had no advantages of education beyond others of his class; and though Poets in this country have seldom been fortunate men, yet he is, perhaps, the least favoured by circumstances, and the most destitute of friends, of any that ever existed.

JOHN CLARE, the author of this Volume, was born at Helpstone, near Peterborough, Northamptonshire, on the 13th of July, 1793. He is the only son of Parker and Ann Clare, who are also natives of the same village, where they have always resided in extreme poverty; nor are they aware that any of their ancestors have been in better circumstances. Parker Clare is a farmer's labourer, and latterly he was employed in threshing; but violent colds brought on the rheumatism to such a degree that he was at length unable to work, or even to move without assistance. . . .

While such was the destitute condition of his parents, it may seem extraordinary that CLARE should have found the means to acquire any learning whatever, but by extra work as a ploughboy, and by helping his father morning and evening at threshing, he earned the money which paid for his education. From the labour of eight weeks he generally acquired as many pence as would pay for a month's schooling; and thus in the course of three years he received, at different times, so much instruction that he could read very well in the Bible. . . .

It was an accident which led to the publication of these Poems. In December 1818, Mr. Edward Drury, Bookseller, of Stamford, met by chance with the Sonnet to the Setting Sun, written on a piece of paper in which a letter had been wrapped up, and signed J. C.[33] Having ascertained the name and residence of the writer, he went to Helpstone, where he saw some other poems with which he was much pleased. At his request, CLARE made a collection of the pieces he had written, and added some others to them. They were then sent to London, for the opinion of the publishers, and they selected those which form the present volume. They have been printed with the usual corrections only of orthography and grammar, in such instances as allowed of its being done without changing the words: the proofs were then revised by CLARE, and a few alterations were made at his desire. The original MSS. may be seen at Messrs. Taylor and Hessey's.

The Author and his Poems are now before the public; and its decision will speedily fix the fate of the one, and, ultimately, that of the other: but whatever be the result to either, this will at least be granted, that no Poet of our country has shewn greater ability, under circumstances so hostile to its developement. . . .

Extract 2: John Clare to John Taylor (11 May 1820), in Mark Storey, ed., *The Letters of John Clare* (Oxford: Clarendon Press, 1985), p. 64[34]

Helpstone May 1820

Dear Taylor

Having little more then nothing to do this day I must do mischief by robbing you of 8d for this letter[35] be as it will I will cheapen it to you as much as I can by sending most of it in rhyme – I have been trying songs & want your judgment only either to stop me or to set me off at full gallop which your disaproval or applause has as much power to effect as if spoken by a majician and the rod of critiscism in your hand has as much power over your poor sinful ryhmer as the rod of Aaron in the Land of Egypt[36] – understand also by the by that Hilton is nearly done the 'Phiz'[37] when you send it send a good long Letter as long as ever you are able to send & as much as you are able to say forgive your idle corespondent I forgot I was writing to a man of business–

Farwell J. Clare

Extract 3: Eliza L. Emmerson to John Clare (11 May 1820), MS Eg. 2245, fols 118–20[38]

4 Berners Street
11 May 1820
My Dear Clare –
That my letters are at best, but sorry visitants – is, I fear, but too certain: how, or what, am I to expect in the present case? I have this consolation to cheer me, in the event of losing your future esteem, and friendship. tis this – I have perform'd my *duty*! a duty required of me by One,[39] whom you have the honor and happiness to call your friend! One, who values you – who is pleased to say in his letters to me – 'How truly dear Clare is to me, let my every days exertions in his favor tell' – to which he adds – 'If you are determind to serve poor Clare – you *must do your duty*! You must tell him to expunge certain highly objectionable passages in his 1st Volm – before the 3rd Edition appears – passages, wherein, his then depressed state hurried him not only into error, but into the most flagrant acts of injustice; by accusing those of pride, cruelty, vices, and ill directed passions – who, are the very persons, by whose truly generous and noble exertions he has been raised from misery and despondency.' – This is painful to me, my dear Clare, to tell you – because I feel assured, how sensible your heart *now* is, of the benefits and comforts you enjoy: – but, '*I must do my duty*' – for have I not been the cause of much being done for you? And can I deny to perform that, which is certainly due to the noble, and generous persons, who have so generously served you? but I will hasten to conclude this, *to me* distressing subject, by giving you another extract from his Lordships letter –

It has been my anxious desire of late, to establish our poets character, as that, of an honest and upright man – as a man feeling the strongest sense of gratitude for the encouragement he has received – but how is it possible I can continue to do this if he suffers another Edition of his poems to appear with this vile, unjust, and now would be ungrateful passages in them? – no, he must cut them out, or I cannot be satisfied that Clare is really as honest & upright as I could wish him! – tell Clare if he has still a recollection of what I have done, and am still doing for him, he must give me unquestionable *proofs* of being that man I would have him to be – *he must expunge expunge*!

It grieves me that our noble friend should feel the necessity of making these remarks *to me* – & still more so that it is my *duty* to communicate them immediately to you: – but, recollect for one moment, on the *manner* in which this great, and good man, has taken up your cause, how he has condescended to identify himself with you, and espoused your principles and character: recollect also, that I have been the cause of his doing this (tho' believe me Clare, I wish to take no vain merit to myself) & you will instantly banish from your mind all unpleasant feelings that may have arisen from these communications – I have only done my duty to my honored friend! – and as he desires it – my duty to you!

Let me now entreat you, as a true friend, as a Sister – to write immediately to Mr Taylor, and desire him *from yourself*, to expunge the objectionable lines – you have them *marked* in the Volume I sent you – for alas! they were named to me but too soon after your poems were published – as conveying '*Radical* and *ungrateful* sentiments', & I in consequence ventured to *note* them so pointedly in the margin, hoping you would withdraw them of your own accord, after the 1st Edition: – It is *not* now too late, to undo all the mischief – and it will be honorable in you, now that you enjoy blessings before unknown to you, and the severe privation of which, alone induced you to exclaim against the higher classes of society! *freely* then, my friend, withdraw every offending line, it will be *worthy* of your *honest, noble nature*. There are 10 lines in the 'Helpstone' beginning with 'Accursed wealth' – and also one sadly disliked in your beautiful poem on 'Genius' – 'That necessary tool to wealth and pride'. I ventured to write a line in the margin to substitute this – & I thought it connected the subject very well[40] – if you will indulge me by adopting this line, no person can ever know it, or indeed any other alteration I presumed to suggest in my marginal notes....

Yr. Ever sincere friend –
Eliz L. Emmerson

P.S. I forget to tell you that Ld. R. will lend you 'Walkers dictionary'[41] – as, he is very desirous, you should be better acquainted with our Language – and he wishes you to study the principals – viz – spelling, pronunciation, and gramatical sense – these, are very essential to you as a poet – and indeed very little can be done without such means: – and as to improving your style of language that can readily be done by consulting those authors you possess

– 'Blair – Addison – Mason – Young'[42] &c. &c. – Study, *study*, my dear Clare! is the certain road to Knowledge and Genius! aided by information – and a good heart to direct the whole, will no doubt lead you on, to fame, and fortune!

Farewel!

Extract 4: John Clare to John Taylor (16 May 1820), in Storey, ed., *Letters*, pp. 68–70

Dear Taylor

Being very much botherd latley I must trouble you to leave out the 8 lines in 'helpstone' beginning 'Accursed wealth' & two under 'When ease & plenty' – & one in 'Dawnings of Genius' 'That necessary tool' leave it out & put ***** to fill up the blank this will let em see I do it as negligent as possible d—n that canting way of being forcd to please I say – I cant abide it & one day or other I will show my Independance more stron[g]ly then ever you know who's the promoter of the scheme I dare say – I have told you to order & therefore the fault rests not with me while you are left to act as you please

yours John Clare

Helpstone May 16 1820

Extract 5: John Taylor to John Clare (6 June 1820), MS. Eg. 2245, fol. 140

My dear Clare,

... A Strong Attempt is made to get those Passages expunged from the next Edition,[43] which you left it to me to do as I pleased about; but I am inclined to remain obstinate, and if any Objection is made to my Judgment for so doing I am willing to abide the consequences. – How is Patty?[44] – Your half year's Dividend from the Funds will be payable in a Week or two.[45] – I cannot write the next Introduction[46] till I see all the Poems.

I am, Dear Clare,
Your sincere Friend
John Taylor

Extract 6: J. G. Lockhart, from 'Extracts from Mr. Wastle's Diary', no. ii, in *Blackwood's Edinburgh Magazine* 7 (June 1820): 322[47]

When one thinks of Hogg,[48] and of the silent but sure progress of his fame – or of Allan Cunningham,[49] and of the hold he has taken of the heart of Scotland almost without being aware of it himself – one cannot help feeling some qualms concerning the late enormous puffing of the Northamptonshire peasant, John Clare. I have never seen Clare's book, but from all the extracts I have seen, and from all the private accounts I have heard, there can be no doubt Clare is a man of talents and a man of virtue; but as to poetical genius, in the higher and the only proper sense of that word, I fear it would be very difficult to shew that he deserves half the fuss that has been made. Smoothness of versification and simplicity of thought seem to be his chief merits; but alas! in these days these are not enough to command or to justify such a sounding of the trumpet. The Guardian takes by far the best view of this subject[50] – Clare has exhibited powers that not only justify but demand attention and kindness – but his generous and enlightened patrons ought to pause ere they advise him to become anything else than a peasant – for a respectable peasant is a much more comfortable man, and always will be so, than a mediocre poet. Let them pause and think of the fate of the far more highly-gifted Burns, and beware alike of the foolish zeal and the sinful neglect of *his* countrymen.

Extract 7: John Clare to James Augustus Hessey ([10?] July 1820), in Storey, ed., *Letters*, pp. 83–5

My Dear Hessey

I have seen the third Edition & am cursed mad about it[51] the judgment of T[aylor] is a button hole lower in my opinion – it is good – but too subject to be tainted by medlars *false delicasy* damn it I hate it beyond every thing those primpt up misses brought up in those seminaries of mysterious wicknedness (Boarding Schools) what will please em? why we well know – but while their heart & soul loves to extravagance (what we dare not mention) false delicasy's seriousness muscles[52] up the mouth & condemns it – what in the name of delicasy doth poor Dolly say to incur such malice as to have her artless lamentations shut out[53] – they blush to read what they go nightly to balls for & love to practice   alas false delicasy – I fear thou art worse than dolly   say nothing to T. – he is left to do as he likes you know – & if we controul him he will give us up – but I think I shall soon be qualified to be my own editor – pride once rooted grows very fast you percieve – I expect Drury is in London – he will tell you my eagerness of having a new vol I hope you will be as eager & then 'tween us all three we shall get Taylor to work – I hope he will come home from bath a new man & be so far recoverd as to master his puzzling job with pleasure I have a great many more old & new things which I shall muster up for a third Vol if its ever calld for – the people round here are very anxious of a New Vols appearance – send me a letter by Drury tell me your opinions & intentions how you will proceed with the new vol wether the '*head*' (vanity agen you percieve) will be engraven–I have made out '*Scriven*'   he is historical

Engraver to his present majesty[54] – as to the cottage[55] for the sake of my young friend I must insist on thats being inserted so T. must let me have my wish there – but in these matters false delicasy I think will not interupt him – I have felt long enough for poor T. I assure you I know his taste & I know his embaresments   I often picture him in the midst of a circle of 'blue stockings' offering this & that opinion for emprovement or omision   I think to please all & offend all we shoud put out 215 pages of blank leaves & call it 'Clare in fashion'. . . .

Extract 8: James Augustus Hessey to John Clare (11 July 1820), MS. Eg. 2245, fols 172–3

My dear Clare

I have but a few minutes to spare and can only reply very shortly to your Letter which I have received this morning. I am not at all surprised at your being vexed at the Omission of any part of your Volume of Poems, and you may be assured that it was not resolved upon without the most mature deliberation & a firm conviction that your own Interest would be most essentially served by the Omission. The circumstance of their having been inserted at first, and again in the second Edition notwithstanding the remonstrances of many of our friends & of yours, is sufficient Evidence of Taylor's feeling as to their merit, and having given such a pledge of his opinion you may be sure he would not idly retract it. But he perceived that objections were continually made to them & that the sale of the Volume would eventually be materially injured and therefore he determined on leaving them out. Whether it be false or true delicacy which raises the objection to these pieces it is perhaps hardly worth while to enquire. If we are satisfied that in the Society which we frequent certain subjects must not be even alluded to, we must either conform to the rules of that Society or quit it. An author in like manner is expected to concede something to the tone of moral feeling of the Age in which he lives, and if he expects or wishes his works to be popular, to afford amusement or convey instruction, he must avoid such subjects as are sure to excite a Prejudice against him and to prevent his works from being generally read. And, after all, there is no hardship in all this. There is plenty of room for a man of Genius, of Delicacy, of Taste, to exercise himself in, without touching upon such things as are by common consent now avoided in all good Society as repugnant to good Taste and real Delicacy. We make allowances for Shakespeare's little touches of indelicacy and Double meaning, because such conversation was common in Society in his Day – but it would not be tolerated now, or if admitted at all, must be much more delicately wrapped up – However, you need be under no apprehensions respecting your new M.S.S. You may rely on finding in

Taylor a sincere friend and a discreet adviser, and one who is well able to appreciate the merit of your poetry and well qualified to stand as you phrase it, 'between you and the Public'. . . .
– believe me Ever Yours J. A. Hessey.

Extract 9: from John Clare to John Taylor (*c.* 8 March 1820), in Storey, ed., *Letters*, pp. 162–4

My dear Taylor

I shall write little this time as theres little nessesity for it   you will see I approve of most of your alterations as usual – No 5 you left out in the letter so I coud not say[56] but be what it will do as you woud with my approval the Poem you wish to omit I agree too & think it right as there is plenty to pick out of the 2 verses in the Ramble   your reasons for omitting them is convinced me of my mistake in thinking them good so omit them & welcome[57] you know I urge nothing – I only suggest – & if you dont select them with the same judgment as you woud was they your own productions you do your self an injury by being cramp'd with opinions   was I to know that was the case I woud suggest no more   your taste is preferable to any I have witnessd & on that I rely – mines not worth twopence – & a critics is too severe for me – a man of feeling that looks on faults with indulgence & never willfuly passes by a blossom he may chance to find on his journey is a man to my mind & such a one (no flattery mind from me) I reckon John Taylor – 'Woodseers'[58] is inscets which I daresay you know very well wether it be the proper name I dont know   tis what we call them & that you know is sufficient for us – they lye in little white notts of spittle on the backs of leaves & flowers   how they come I dont know but they are always seen plentiful in moist weather – & are one of the shepherds weather glasses when the head of the inscet is seen turnd upward it is said to token fine weather   when downward on the contrary wet may be expected – which no doubt is as good signs as Moors Almanack[59] posseses – I think they turn to grasshoppers & am almost certain for I have watchd them minutely.[60] . . . Mr G[ilchrist] tells me of Scotts death[61] but I know all about it & about it & am as sorry for it as he can be tho I knew nothing more of the man then by his actions which tells me he had more honesty and honour then his enemey Lockhardt is a d—d knave & a coward & my insignificant self woud tell him so to his teeth – but Mr. G tells me to stick to a Cudgel when I quarrel – I also hear that Bowles[62] is at him again – Bowles will whine him out at last if he dont mind – I like your alteration of the bucket much in 'Rosey Jane'[63] & am glad your friends urged you to it for I never liked it myself as it stood

yours &c &c &c John Clare

I promisd you a short letter but have given you plenty about nothing excuse it

Extract 10: from John Taylor to John Clare (27, 29 September 1820), MS. Eg. 2250, fols 146–7

My dear Clare,

I don't know anyone whose Letters give me more Pleasure than yours, and this last was doubly welcome from its containing the very things I wanted to hear from you about. Lord R. has expressed his Intention of disowning you in such strong Terms, unless the radical Lines as he called them were left out, that I conceived it would be deemed improper in me as your Friend to hold out any longer; and all I wanted therefore was your Authority or Concurrence. – My opinion is fixed as to the Needlessness of these Omissions for the Reasons assigned, and there are no others that can weigh with me: but let them be expunged and welcome, since so decided. – a Set is to be made against you if they are not. When the Follies of the Day are past with all the Fears they have engendered we can restore the Poems according to the earlier Editions –

29 Sept. I am much occupied with Business previous to my going out of Town tomorrow, and this causes the postponement of my present attempt to write, till I have scarcely Time to do it in any way. – Though I am willing to leave out the Lines beginning 'accursed wealth' which it still grieves me to do, I can see no Reason so imperative for complying with Lord R's further Demand that the 3rd & 4th Lines of the following Paragraph should also be omitted, viz 'Where Ease and Plenty' &c for I am convinced this is at least no exaggeration. – As for the 2 Lines in the Dawnings of Genius I have cut them out altogether, & now it reads very well, in fact better than ever,

> 'The rough rude Ploughman, on his fallow Ground,
> 'Will often stoop &c. –'

By this amendment I avoid, what I am desirous to do, the Insertion of any Lines not absolutely yours. My province qualifies me to cut out but not to introduce anything. . . .

To make your property in the Funds more secure, I have taken Woodhouse[64] as a joint Trustee with me. I know you would have no fears of my acting roguishly, but some of the *Great* & *Good* are not so charitable, knowing the Ways of the World better than the Ways of a Village.[65] . . .

I am dear Clare your faithful Friend John Taylor

Extract 11: from [Anon.] *Nobility Run Mad, or Raymond and His Three Wives: A Novel: By the author of the sailor boy and soldier boy,* 4 vols (London: Minerva Press, 1802), 1: 1-6

STEPPING into a circulating library one Saturday evening with a friend, where the mistress, as is generally the case every where but in London, dealt in a variety of articles in the perfumery and stationary line, as well as in Romances, Tales and Novels, I was near expressing my wonder at the degeneracy of the age, upon finding her shop or literary repository absolutely crowded with females of every denomination waiting to have their marble covered, half bound tales changed. My friend, who had drawn me there, merely wanted a cake of Windsor Soap; she would therefore have pushed forward, if I had not caught her by the arm, and requested that she would wait till it came to her turn; not that I was actuated by so much politeness, but far more by a wish, which all female authors feel, to hear their works descanted upon in a mixed company to whom they are not personally known; for among those who are aware that a man or woman has any pretensions to literary fame, no one chuses to give their real opinion of their works, though they very possibly don't scruple to pronounce them detestable the moment the suspected author's back is turned; and I delight in even hearing myself criticised, so long as it is by strangers. My friend, knowing my propensity, took the hint, and remained in the background. While the ladies assembled were some passing judgment upon various unfortunate authors, who had had the misfortune not to write to their feelings, others were requesting Mrs— to recommend them something in Mrs. Ratcliffe's style,[66] as they were fond of horrors; others declared their aversion to ghost tales, as only fit for nurseries, and wished for something sentimental; a fourth set wanted something to laugh at; the whole party speaking at once, and praising or criticising very indiscriminately, and not always with the greatest judgment: but at last my attention was arrested by a very pretty girl, who inquired, whether the SOLDIER BOY was at home.

'No, Miss,' was the reply, 'but you shall have it very soon.'

'So you have told me for this month, I do believe; I am positively very angry with you.'

'I hope not, my dear ma'am, for I give you my word of honour you shall have the first set that comes in; but the Sailor Boy took so well, that this, being by the same author, is also in great repute.'

'Oh then, I am sure it is a good thing,' cried several, 'for I never like to read a book that is always at home.'

'Why, to be sure, ladies, good things will be read, but bad one's have sometimes a great run.'

'Why, fools are easily pleased,' observed a sententious lady, who had objected to ghost tales; 'but you ought to form your opinion of works from the judgment of other readers, not from their run; the Sailor Boy has great faults; had the author consulted me, I should have advised her to make great alterations in her plan.'

'What! is it the production of a female?' asked the other.

'I am sure I don't know,' replied the mistress of the shop, 'but gentlemen have left the trade very much to the ladies of late.'

I will not, however, recapitulate every thing that was said for and against these two bantlings of mine, though upon the whole I had the satisfaction to find they were rather generally liked. I therefore left the shop, convinced that it was a pity to bury my *superior literary talents* under a bushel, and firmly resolved once more to dirty a few quires of paper, in hopes of amusing, and in some respects of instructing, the rising generation.

Sunday intervening, I could not set about my allotted task till the Monday, when I began by reading over the very judicious criticisms which have been wrote of the Sailor and Soldier Boy, and for which I feel myself infinitely indebted to Messrs. the Reviewers,[67] as they candidly point out my errors, and at the same time acknowledge I have some degree of merit, which is flattering to a very young author. The only return I can make for their indulgence is, to endeavour to avoid those faults in my future writings, which they have so very kindly discriminated in my first, and for which trouble I beg leave thus publicly to return them thanks.

Having thus expressed my gratitude towards those leaders of the public opinion, I shall, without further preface, enter upon my tale.

Extract 12: an anonymous review of *Nobility Run Mad, or Raymond and His Three Wives*, from *The Annual Review* 1 (1802): 725

IN Raymond, there is a good deal to praise; and compared with the generality of novels, it certainly claims precedence. The invention, character, and language are, in many places above mediocrity, seldom below it. The plot is artfully contrived and the denouement shews great ingenuity. In old Filmore and his grandson, the operation of avarice is well displayed, and the contrast exhibited in the benevolent young marquis Raymond, appears more marked from so judicious a foil. If we except to any character in this work, it is to that of Lady Arpasia Ermington, the nobleman's infidel wife: pictures of conjugal indiscretion coloured so strongly as this is, we conceive improper subjects for young and innocent minds. We would likewise recommend to the author to be more attentive to style. We have observed a peculiarity of phraseology which frequently recurs, such as 'mentally ejaculated he,' & c. which she would do well in future to avoid. These are the only defects of any importance which we perceived, and they are counterbalanced by considerable beauties.

Extract 13: from John Wilson ('Christopher North'), 'Monologue, or Soliloquy on the Annuals', *Blackwood's Edinburgh Magazine* 26 (December 1829): 949–51

... We often pity our poor ancestors. How they contrived to make the ends meet, surpasses our conjectural powers. What a weary waste must have seemed expanding before their eyes between morning and night! Don't tell us that the human female never longs for other pastime than

'To suckle fools and chronicle small beer,'[68]

True, ladies sighed not then for periodicals – but there, in the depths of their ignorance, lay their utter wretchedness....

We shall not enter into any historical details - for this is not a Monologue for the Quarterly[69] – but we simply assert, that in the times we allude to (don't mention dates) there was little or no reading in England. There was neither the Reading Fly nor the Reading Public. What could this be owing to, but the non-existence of periodicals? What elderly-young lady could be expected to turn from house affairs, for example, to Spenser's Fairy Queen? It is a long, long, long poem, that Fairy Queen of Spenser's; nobody, of course, ever dreamt of getting through it; but though you may have given up all hope of getting through a poem or a wood, you expect to be able to find your way back again to the spot where you unluckily got in; not so, however, with the Fairy Queen. Beautiful it is indeed, most exquisitely and unapproachably beautiful in many passages, especially about ladies and ladies' love more than celestial, for Venus loses in comparison her lustre in the sky; but still people were afraid to get into it then as now; and 'heavenly Una, with her milk-white lamb,'[70] lay buried in dust. As to Shakespeare, we cannot find many traces of him in the domestic occupations of the English gentry during the times alluded to; nor do we believe that the character of Hamlet was at all relished in their halls, though perhaps an occasional squire chuckled at the humours of Sir John Falstaff.[71] We have Mr. Wordsworth's authority for believing that Paradise Lost was a dead letter, and John Milton virtually anonymous. We need say no more. Books like these, huge heavy vols. lay with other lumber in garrets and libraries. As yet, periodical literature was not; and the art of printing seems long to have preceded the art of reading. It did not occur to those generations that books were intended to be read by people in general, but only by the select few. Whereas now, reading is not only one of the luxuries, but absolutely one of the necessaries of life, and we no more think of going without our book than without our breakfast; lunch consists now of veal-pies and Venetian Bracelets[72] – we still dine on Roast-beef, but with it, instead of Yorkshire pudding, a Scotch novel – Thomas Campbell[73] and Thomas Moore sweeten tea for us – and in 'Course of Time' we sup on a Welsh rabbit and a Religious Poem.

We have not time – how can we? – to trace the history of the great revolution. But a great revolution there has been, from nobody's reading any thing, to every body's reading all things; and perhaps it began with that good old proser Richardson, the father of Pamela, Clarissa, and Sir Charles Grandison.[74] He seems to have been a sort of idiot, who had a strange insight into some parts of human nature, and a tolerable acquaintance with most parts of speech. He set the public a-reading, and Fielding and Smollett[75] shoved her on – till the Minerva Press took her in hand – and then – the Periodicals. But such Periodicals! The Gentleman's Magazine – God bless it then, now, and for ever! – the Monthly Review, the Critical and the British Critic! The age had been for some years literary, and was now fast becoming periodical. Magazines multiplied. Arose in glory the Edinburgh, and then the Quarterly Review – Maga, like a new sun, looked out from heaven[76] – from her golden urn a hundred satellites drew light – and last of all, 'the Planetary Five,'[77] the Annuals, hung their lamps on high; other similar luminous bodies emerged from the clouds, till the whole circumference was bespangled, and astronomy became the favourite study with all ranks of people, from the King upon the throne to the meanest of his subjects. Now, will any one presume to deny, that this has been a great change to the better, and that there is now something worth living for in the world? Look at our literature now, and it is all periodical together. A thousand daily, thrice-a-week, twice-a-week, weekly newspapers, a hundred monthlies, fifty quarterlies, and twenty-five annuals! No mouth looks up now and is not fed; on the contrary, we are in danger of being crammed; an empty head is as rare as an empty stomach; the whole day is one meal, one physical, moral and intellectual feast; the Public goes to bed with a Periodical in her hand, and falls asleep with it beneath her pillow.

What blockhead thinks now of reading Milton, or Pope, or Gray? Paradise Lost is lost; it has gone to the devil. Pope's Epistles[78] are returned to the dead-letter office; the age is too loyal for 'ruin seize thee, ruthless king,'[79] and the oldest inhabitant has forgotten 'the curfew tolls.'[80]...

But lo! arrayed in figure of a fan, and gorgeous as spread-peacock-tail – the Annuals! The sunshine strikes the intermingled glow, and it threatens to set the house on fire. But softly – they are cool to the touch, though to the sight burning; innocuous is the lambent flame that plays around the leaves; even as, in a dewy night of fading summer, the grass-brightening circle of the still glow-worm's light!

Singular! They have formed themselves into classes beneath our touch according to some fine affinities of name and nature; and behold in one Triad, the Forget-me-Not, the Souvenir, and the Keepsake.[81]...

Extract 14: title page, Introduction, plates 33, 35 and 41, and accompanying poems, from *Fisher's Drawing Room Scrap-Book; With Poetical Illustrations by L. E. L.* [Letitia Elizabeth Landon] (London: Fisher, Son and Jackson, 1832)

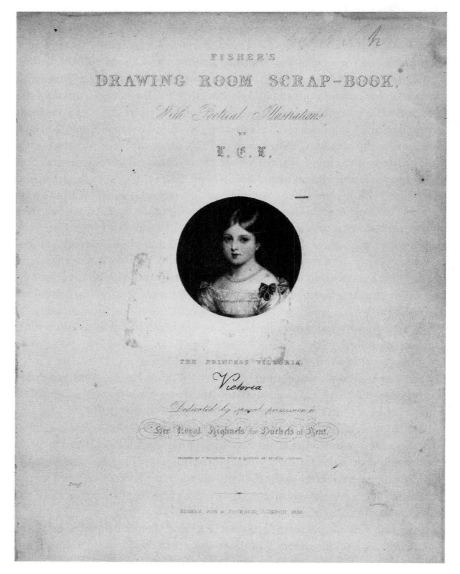

Plate 6

Introduction

THOUGH a preface be the first page seen in a volume, it is always the last page written. By that time, the golden age of hope has darkened into the iron age of fear. The ideas that seemed at first so delightful, are grown common, by passing through the familiarizing process of writing, printing, and correcting. A proof-sheet is a terrible reality: and you look upon your work with much the same feeling as people look upon the prospect to which they are accustomed – they are much more alive to its faults than its beauties.

For the Volume now offered to the public, I must plead for indulgence. It is not an easy thing to write illustrations to prints, selected rather for their pictorial excellence than their poetic capabilities: and mere description is certainly not the most popular species of composition. I have endeavoured to give as much variety as possible, by the adoption of any legend, train of reflection, &c. which the subject could possibly suggest: and, with the same view, have inserted the two poems marked 'C,' for which I am indebted to a friend, whose kindness I gratefully acknowledge. A book like this is a literary luxury, addressed chiefly to a young and gentler class of readers: may I therefore hope, that the judgement I seek to interest will err on the side of kindly allowance.

There are three portraits, to which only brief prose notices are affixed – the days of poetical flattery are as much in the past, as those of hoops and minuets. What the genius of Dryden could not redeem, I may be excused from even attempting.[82]

There is an old proverb, 'Leave well alone:' I shall, therefore, say little more of the embellishments than to mention, that the voluminous and expensive works from which they are selected, were 'fountains sealed'[83] to the many. I need not entreat for the Engravings that indulgence which myself required, but may trust them, as the Grecian orator did his client, to plead and win the cause by their own beauty.

L. E. L.

FURNESS ABBEY, IN THE VALE OF NIGHTSHADE, LANCASHIRE.

FISHER, SON, & C° LONDON, 1831.

Plate 7

Furness Abbey,
In the Vale of Nightshade, Lancashire

I WISH for the days of the olden time,
When the hours were told by the abbey chime,
When the glorious stars looked down through the midnight dim,
Like approving saints on the choir's sweet hymn:
    I think of the days we are living now,
    And I sigh for those of the veil and the vow.

    I would be content alone to dwell
    Where the ivy shut out the sun from my cell,
With the death's-head at my side, and the missal on my knee,
Praying to that heaven which was opening to me:
    Fevered and vain are the days I lead now,
    And I sigh for those of the veil and the vow.

    Silken broidery no more would I wear,
    Nor golden combs in my golden hair;
I wore them but for one, and in vain they were worn;
My robe should be of serge, my crown of the thorn:
    'Tis a cold false world we dwell in now,
    And I sigh for those of the veil and the vow.

    I would that the cloister's quiet were mine;
    In the silent depths of some holy shrine.
I would tell my blessed beads, and would weep away
From my inmost soul every stain of clay:
    My heart's young hopes they have left me now,
    And I sigh for those of the veil and the vow.

Plate 8

The African

IT was a king in Africa,
    He had an only son;
And none of Europe's crowned kings
    Could have a dearer one.

With good cane arrows five feet long,
    And with a shining bow,
When but a boy, to the palm woods
    Would that young hunter go.

And home he brought white ivory,
    And many a spotted hide;
When leopards fierce and beautiful
    Beneath his arrows died.

Around his arms, around his brow,
    A shining bar was rolled;
It was to mark his royal blood,
    He wore that bar of gold.

And often at his father's feet,
    The evening he would pass;
When, weary of the hunt, he lay
    Upon the scented grass.

Alas! it was an evil day,
    When such a thing could be;
When strangers, pale and terrible,
    Came o'er the distant sea.

They found the young prince mid the woods,
    The palm woods deep and dark:
That day his lion hunt was done,
    They bore him to their bark.

They bound him in a narrow hold,
    With others of his kind;
For weeks did that accursed ship
    Sail on before the wind.

Now shame upon the cruel wind,
    And on the cruel sea,
That did not with some mighty storm,
    Set those poor captives free:

Or, shame to those weak thoughts, so fain
    To have their wilful way:
God knoweth what is best for all –
    The winds and seas obey.

205

At length a lovely island rose
    From out the ocean wave,
They took him to the market-place,
    And sold him for a slave.

Some built them homes, and in the shade
    Of flowered and fragrant trees,
They half forgot the palm-hid huts
    They left far o'er the seas.

But he was born of nobler blood,
    And was of nobler kind;
And even unto his death, his heart
    For its own kindred pined.

There came to him a seraph child
    With eyes of gentlest blue:
If there are angels in high heaven,
    Earth has its angels too.

She cheered him with her holy words,
    She soothed him with her tears;
And pityingly she spoke with him
    Of home and early years.

And when his heart was all subdued
    By kindness into love,
She taught him from this weary earth
    To look in faith above.

She told him how the Saviour died
    For man upon the tree;
"He suffered," said the holy child,
    "For you as well as me."

Sorrow and death have need of faith –
    The African believed;
As rains fall fertile on the earth,
    Those words his soul received.

He died in hope, as only those
    Who die in Christ depart –
One blessed name within his lips,
    One hope within his heart.

Plate 9

The House in which Roscoe was Born[84]

A LOWLY roof, an English farm-house roof –
What is the train of thought that it should wake?
Why cheerful evenings, when the winter cold
Grows glad beside the hearth; or summer days,
When round the shady porch the woodbine clings;
Some aged man beneath, to hear whose words
The children leave off play; for he can tell
Of the wild sea, a sailor in his youth.
Yet here the mind's eye pictures other scenes –
A fair Italian city, in a vale,
The sanctuary of summer, where the air
Grows sweet in passing over myrtle groves.
Glides the blue Arno, in whose tide are glassed
Armed palaces, with marble battlements.
Forth ride a band of princely chivalry,
And at their head a gallant chieftain – he,
Lorenzo the magnificent.
Within this house was thy historian born,
Florence, thou pictured city; and his name
Calls up thy rich romance of history;
And this calm English dwelling fills the mind
With memories of Medici –

It is scarcely necessary to state, that Mr. Roscoe's principal work was the Life of Lorenzo di Medici.

207

Extract 15: Plates 42 and 49, and accompanying poems, from *Fisher's Drawing Room Scrap-Book; With Poetical Illustrations by L. E. L.* **(1833)**

MACAO.—CHINA.

Plate 10

Macao

Good Heaven! whatever shall I do?
I must write something for my readers:
What has become of my ideas?
Now, out upon them for seceders!
    Of all the places in the world,
To fix upon a port in China;
Celestial empire,[85] how I wish
I had been christened Celestina!
    The wish however's served for rhyme,
And here again invention falters:
Had it but been a town in Greece;
I might have raved about its altars,
    And talked of liberty and mass,
Of tyrants and Romaic dances,
Of Athens with a German king,[86]
And fifty thousand other chances:

Or had it only been in Spain;
A few night-stars the midnight gemming,
And a guitar, I might have scribbled
The rest from Contarini Flemming:[87]

Or Italy, the land of song;
Of myrtle, pictures, and of passion –
Ah! that was for mine earlier lute,
I write now in another fashion:

Or France, which, like an invalid,
Goes patching up a constitution;[88]
Those three most glorious days in June,[89]
Might have lain under contribution:

Or had it only been Madeira;
I might have made a charming fiction,
Of some young maiden crossed in love,
And dying of the contradiction.

I'm like a sailor sent to sea,
Sent with "no, nothing" for his sea-hoard;
What on earth can I find to say,
Of a pagoda or a tea-board?

No love, no murder, no description,
Their only "old association"
Is with the willow-pattern plates,
That on the dresser have their station.

I give it up in pure despair;
But well the muse may turn refractory,
When all her inspiration is –
A Chinese Town, and an English Factory.

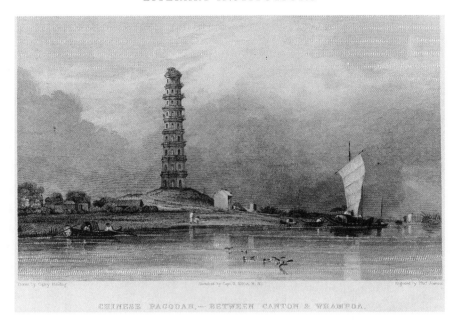

Plate 11

The Chinese Pagoda

Whene'er person is a poet,
No matter what the pang may be;
Does not at once the public know it?
Witness each newspaper we see.

"The parting look," "the bitter token,"
"The last despair," "he first distress;"
"The anguish of a heart that's broken –"
Do not these crowd the daily press?

If then our misnamed "heartless city,"
Can so much sympathy bestow;
If there is so much public pity
For every kind of private woe;

Why not for me? – my care's more real
Than that of all this rhyming band;
Whose hearts and tears are all ideal,
A sort of joint-stock kept on hand.

I'm one of those, I do confess,
Whom pity greatly can console;
To tell, is almost to redress,
Whate'er the "sorrow of my soul."

Now, I who thought the first[90] vexatious,
Despaired and knew not what to do,
Abused the stars, called fate ungracious –
Here is a second Chinese view!

I sent to Messrs. Fisher, saying
The simple fact – I could not write;
What was the use of my inveighing? –
Back came the fatal scroll that night.

"But, madam, such a fine engraving,
The country, too, so little known!"
One's publisher there is no braving –
The plate was work'd, "the dye was thrown."

But what's impossible, can never,
By any hazard come to be,
It is impossible that ever
This place can furnish hints to me.

O Captain Elliot,[91] what could make you
Forsake the Indian fanes of yore?
And what in mercy's name could take you
To this most stupid Chinese shore?

If in this world there is an object,
For pity which may stand alone,
It is a poet with no subject,
Or with a picture worse than none.

SELECT BIBLIOGRAPHY

Altick, Richard D., *The English Common Reader: A Social History of the Mass Reading Public, 1800–1900* (Chicago: University of Chicago Press, 1957). Still the standard work on the topic.

Blakey, Dorothy, *The Minerva Press 1790–1820* (Oxford: Bibliographic Society, 1939). A detailed account of the firm's history and significance.

Chilcott, Tim, *A Publisher and His Circle: The Life and Work of John Taylor, Keats's*

Publisher (London and Boston: Routledge and Kegan Paul, 1972). The best study of a publisher in the period.

Erikson, Lee, *The Economy of Literary Form: English Literature and the Industrialization of Publishing, 1800–1850* (Baltimore and London: Johns Hopkins University Press, 1996). Discusses of the role of a range of institutional and technological factors in literary creation.

Feather, John, *A History of British Publishing* (London: Croom Helm, 1988). Authoritative general survey (Parts 2 and 3 especially relevant to the period).

Klancher, Jon P., *The Making of English Reading Audiences, 1790–1832* (Madison: University of Wisconsin Press, 1987). Highly influential account of the growth and variety of reading publics in the period.

Leader, Zachary, *Revision and Romantic Authorship* (Oxford: Clarendon Press, 1996). Discusses the role of personal and institutional collaborators (friends, editors, publishers, patrons, reviewers, readers) in the revising process.

McGann, Jerome J., *The Beauty of Inflections: Literary Investigations in Historical Method and Theory* (Oxford: Clarendon Press, 1985). Ground-breaking essays on the social construction of literature.

Manning, Peter J., 'Wordsworth in the *Keepsake*, 1829', in John O. Jordan and Robert L. Patten, eds, *Literature in the Marketplace: Nineteenth-century British Publishing and Reading Practices* (Cambridge: Cambridge University Press, 1995). Contains useful information on Annuals in general.

Stephenson, Glennis, *Letitia Landon: The Woman Behind L. E. L.* (Manchester: Manchester University Press, 1995). Excellent chapters on L. E. L.'s relations with the Annuals, and on the role and character of Annuals in general.

Stillinger, Jack, *Multiple Authorship and the Myth of Solitary Genius* (New York: Oxford University Press, 1991). On collaborative authorship and the history and ideology of the 'myth' of solitary genius.

Tuchman, Gaye, *Edging Women Out* (London: Routledge, 1989). On the male invasion of traditionally female literary forms and markets.

NOTES

GENERAL INTRODUCTION

1   For the central documents of this debate, see Marilyn Butler, *Burke, Paine, Godwin and the Revolution Controversy* (Cambridge: Cambridge University Press, 1984).

2   The so-called 'Whig interpretation of history', most frequently associated with Thomas Babington Macaulay (1800–59), sees history as progressive and improving. It was classically identified and dissected by Herbert Butterfield in *The Whig Interpretation of History* (1931; London: G. Bell, 1951).

3   See, for example, Marilyn Butler, *Romantics, Rebels and Reactionaries* (Oxford: Oxford University Press, 1981), chapter 8. Marshall Brown reckons 'we may not be able to define either Enlightenment or Romanticism', though he plumps for seeing the latter as the 'fulfilment and awakening' of the former (see his essay 'Romanticism and Enlightenment' in Stuart Curran, ed., *The Cambridge Companion to British Romanticism* (Cambridge: Cambridge University Press, 1993), p. 25). Anne Janowitz reconfigures Romanticism in terms of the development of radical history from the late eighteenth century to the mid-Victorian period; she describes it as 'the literary form of a struggle taking place on many levels of society between the claims of individualism and the claims of communitarianism', in '"A Voice from Across the Sea": Communitarianism at the Limits of Romanticism', in Mary Favret and Nicola Watson, eds, *At the Limits of Romanticism: Essays in Cultural, Feminist and Materialist Criticism* (Bloomington and Indianapolis: University of Indiana Press, 1994), p. 84. Jerome McGann notes matter-of-factly in *The New Oxford Book of Romantic Period Verse* (Oxford: Oxford University Press, 1993), p. xxii, that 'some of the most impressive writing [of the period] is not romantic writing'. That McGann's anthology ends with poems by Tennyson is noteworthy. For historical accounts of the period's relation to 'Victorianism' see, for example, Ford Brown, *Fathers of the Victorians: The Age of Wilberforce* (Cambridge: Cambridge University Press, 1961) and Muriel Jaeger, *Before Victoria* (London: Chatto and Windus, 1956).

4   See Gareth Stedman-Jones, 'Rethinking Chartism', in *Languages of Class* (Cambridge: Cambridge University Press, 1983). The most prominent recent examples of labour historians who have taken the 'linguistic' or semiotic turn are probably Patrick Joyce, *Visions of the People: Industrial England and the Question of Class, 1848–1915* (Cambridge: Cambridge University Press, 1991) and James L. Epstein, *Radical Expression: Political Language, Ritual and Symbol in England, 1790–1850* (Oxford: Oxford University Press, 1994). The strength of feeling on both sides of this debate is registered in the

pages of the journal *Labour History Review*; see also Keith Jenkins, ed., *The Postmodern History Reader* (London: Routledge, 1997), pp. 289–383. It would be misleading, of course, to assume that historians have only recently awakened to the value of literary or aesthetic sources. It has been a feature of New Left historiography since the 1960s. E. P. Thompson, for example, saw class as a cultural institution with a strong subjective element; he regarded literature as both reflective and productive of class-consciousness and working-class aspirations. See the Preface to *The Making of the English Working Class* (1963; Harmondsworth: Penguin, 1977). Similarly, the History Workshop, based at Ruskin College, Oxford, has produced many studies of popular culture. See, for example, Raphael Samuel, *Theatres of Memory*, vol. 1, *Past and Present in Contemporary Culture* (London: Verso, 1994).

5 The impetus behind the 'return to history' of much recent criticism of the period can be seen as a reaction in the North American academy to the perceived dehistoricizing tendencies not only of New Criticism but of post-structuralism and deconstruction. The key text here is Jerome McGann's *The Romantic Ideology* (Chicago: University of Chicago Press, 1983), which argues for the restoration of 'an historical methodology' to counter the critical replication of Romantic notions of transcendence, spirituality, timelessness and indeterminacy. Following McGann's lead, New Historicist critics have ingeniously – if sometimes tortuously – sought to reconstruct an absent or displaced historical content in canonical Romantic texts. Two influential examples are Marjorie Levinson, *Wordsworth's Great Period Poems* (Cambridge: Cambridge University Press, 1986) and Alan Liu, *Wordsworth: The Sense of History* (Stanford: Stanford University Press, 1989). Nicholas Roe, in *The Politics of Nature: Wordsworth and Some Contemporaries* (London: Macmillan, 1992), p. 7, encapsulates a common misgiving about this New Historicist approach when he asks: 'What are the limits of displacement or denial within which the text can yield a credible historical or political interpretation?' A somewhat less contentious aspect of the New Historicism, its recovery of repressed voices (as opposed to themes or content), is obviously forwarded by this book, with its selections from women writers, working-class poets and polemicists, and black radicals. All historicist approaches to literature of this period owe a debt to the work of Raymond Williams, in particular *Culture and Society 1780–1850* (1958; Harmondsworth: Penguin, 1977). In this pioneering study of the evolution of the concept of culture over the last two centuries, Williams eroded the boundary between text and context, pushed the 'big six' poets to the margins of his discussion, and located the 'Romantic artist' as an aesthetic response to new modes of literary production – thus paving the way for more recent critical orthodoxies. For E. P. Thompson's importance to rethinking the formation of the British working class, see note 4.

6 The most comprehensive of the new anthologies are Anne K. Mellor and Richard E. Matlock, eds, *British Literature 1780–1830* (Fort Worth: Harcourt Brace College Publishers, 1995) and Duncan Wu, ed., *Romanticism: An Anthology* (Oxford: Basil Blackwell, 1994). Susan Wolfson and Peter Manning are preparing a comparably wide-ranging anthology entitled *The Romantics and Their Contemporaries* for the Longman's *Anthology of British Literature* series. More specialized anthologies include: McGann's *New Oxford Book of Romantic Period Verse*; Jennifer Breen, ed., *Women Romantics 1785–1832: Writings in Prose* (London: Everyman, 1996); Paula Feldman, ed., *British Women Poets of the Romantic Era: An Anthology* (Baltimore and London: Johns Hopkins University Press, 1997); and Duncan Wu, *Romantic Women Poets: An Anthology* (Oxford: Basil Blackwell, 1997).

7 Butler, *Burke, Paine, Godwin and the Revolution Controversy*, p. 1.

8 The founding documents of the controversy surrounding the term 'Romanticism' are Arthur

O. Lovejoy, 'On the Discrimination of Romanticisms' (1924), reprinted in *Essays on the History of Ideas* (New York: Columbia University Press, 1948), René Wellek, 'The Concept of Romanticism in Literary History' (1949), reprinted in *Concepts of Criticism* (New Haven: Yale University Press, 1963) and M. H. Abrams, 'English Romanticism: The Spirit of the Age', in Northrop Frye, ed., *Romanticism Reconsidered* (New York: Columbia University Press, 1963). In the wake of McGann's *The Romantic Ideology*, which influentially resurrected the controversy, a torrent of anti-Romanticist (i.e. Lovejoyian) recapitulations have followed. Among more recent examples are Jon P. Klancher, 'English Romanticism and Cultural Production', in H. Aram Veseer, ed., *The New Historicism* (London: Routledge, 1992), pp. 77–89; David Simpson, 'Romanticism, Criticism and Theory', in Curran, ed., *The Cambridge Companion to British Romanticism*, pp. 1–25; and the introductions to the following collections of essays: Philip W. Martin and Robin Jarvis, eds, *Reviewing Romanticism* (London: Macmillan, 1992); Joel Haefner and Carol Shiner Wilson, eds, *Re-visioning Romanticism: British Women Writers 1776–1837* (Philadelphia: University of Pennsylvania Press, 1994); and Favret and Watson, eds, *At the Limits of Romanticism*. For a suggestive, if somewhat densely argued, defence of Wellek and periodization in general, see Frances Ferguson, 'On the Numbers of Romanticisms', *English Literary History* 58 (1991): 471–98.

9   For relevant references see the Select Bibliography for Section 1.

10 Linda Colley, *Britons: Forging the Nation 1707–1837* (New Haven: Yale University Press, 1992). For reference to this book and a review of critical studies of regional and national fiction, see Section 5.

11 For the cult of Sensibility see Janet Todd, *Sensibility: An Introduction* (London: Methuen, 1986) and Jerome J. McGann, *The Poetics of Sensibility: A Revolution in Literary Style* (Oxford: Clarendon Press, 1996).

12 See, for example, Jon P. Klancher, *The Making of English Reading Audiences 1790–1832* (Madison: University of Wisconsin Press, 1987), Gary Kelly, 'Romantic Fiction' and Stuart Curran, 'Women Readers, Women Writers', both in Curran, ed., *The Cambridge Guide to British Romanticism*. See also Catherine Gallagher, *Nobody's Story: The Vanishing Acts of Women Writers in the Marketplace, 1670–1820* (Berkeley: University of California Press, 1994), Anne K. Mellor, *Romanticism and Gender* (London: Routledge, 1992), Donna Landry, *The Muses of Resistance: Laboring-Class Women's Poetry in Britain, 1739–1796* (Cambridge: Cambridge University Press, 1990), Marlon B. Ross, *The Contours of Masculine Desire: Romanticism and the Rise of Women's Poetry* (Oxford: Oxford University Press, 1989), Margaret Homans, *Women Writers and Poetic Identity* (Princeton: Princeton University Press, 1980), Sandra Gilbert and Susan Gubar, *The Madwoman in the Attic: The Woman Writer and the Nineteenth-Century Literary Imagination* (New Haven: Yale University Press, 1979), Nigel Leask, *British Romantic Writers and the East* (Cambridge: Cambridge University Press, 1992) and John Barrell, *The Infection of Thomas De Quincey: A Psychopathy of Imperialism* (New Haven: Yale University Press, 1991).

1 RADICAL JOURNALISM

1   William Cobbett, *Cobbett's Weekly Political Register* 31 (22) (1816): 573.

2   Robert Southey, *Essays Moral and Political*, 2 vols (London: John Murray, 1832), 1: 132–3; cited in Kevin Gilmartin, *Print Politics* (Cambridge: Cambridge University Press, 1996), p. 74.

3   E. P. Thompson, *The Making of the English Working Class* (Harmondsworth: Penguin, 1977), p. 660.

4   Thompson, *The Making of the English Working Class*, p. 661.

5　See Edward Royle and James Walvin, *English Radicals and Reformers 1760–1848* (Brighton: Harvester, 1982), chapter 2. For the idea that political reform would involve a restoration of customary rights, see E. P. Thompson, *Customs in Common* (London: Merlin, 1991).

6　See Olivia Smith, *The Politics of Language 1791–1819* (Oxford: Clarendon Press, 1984); James Epstein, *Radical Expression: Political Language, Ritual and Symbol in England, 1790–1830* (Oxford: Oxford University Press, 1994), chapters 1 and 3.

7　Royle and Walvin, *English Radicals and Reformers*, p. 98.

8　On Despard, see David Worrall, *Radical Culture: Discourse, Resistance and Surveillance, 1790–1820* (Hemel Hempstead: Harvester Wheatsheaf, 1992), chapter 2; for the Luddites as Jacobin plotters, see Thompson, *The Making of the English Working Class*, chapter 14.

9　For Cobbett, see George Spater, *William Cobbett: The Poor Man's Friend*, 2 vols (Cambridge: Cambridge University Press, 1982); Raymond Williams, *Cobbett* (Oxford: Oxford University Press, 1983); Leonora Nattrass, *William Cobbett: The Politics of Style* (Cambridge: Cambridge University Press, 1995); Gilmartin, *Print Politics*.

10　Gilmartin, *Print Politics*, p. 74. On the sales of the cheap issue of the *Political Register*, see also Spater, *William Cobbett*, 2: 347. Cobbett's other motive in producing a cheap radical paper was to combat the government's own cheap print offensive, a tactic first deployed by the state in the 1790s to combat the influence of cheap editions of Paine's *Rights of Man*. See Cobbett, *Political Register* 31 (20) (16 November 1820): 610–13. Cobbett also made the ironic point that parliamentary reform would abolish radical journalism at a stroke: 'This could knock us all up in the twinkling of an eye' (p. 613). On the growth of working-class readership in this period, see A. Aspinall, *Politics and the Press 1780–1850* (London: Home and Van Thel, 1949); R. K. Webb, *The British Working-Class Reader 1790–1848: Literacy and Social Tension* (London: George Allen and Unwin, 1955); Richard D. Altick, *The English Common Reader: A Social History of the Mass Reading Public 1800–1900* (Chicago and London: University of Chicago Press, 1957); Thompson, *The Making of the English Working Class*; Jon P. Klancher, *The Making of English Reading Audiences 1790–1832* (Madison: University of Wisconsin Press, 1987); David Vincent, *Literacy and Popular Culture in England 1750–1914* (Cambridge: Cambridge University Press, 1989).

11　Thompson, *The Making of the English Working Class*, p. 728.

12　Thompson, *The Making of the English Working Class*, p. 739; Gilmartin, *Print Politics*, p. 107. For Regency satire, see Edgell Rickword, *Radical Squibs and Loyal Ripostes: Satirical Pamphlets of the Regency Period, 1819–1821* (Bath: Adams and Dart, 1971) and Marcus Wood, *Radical Satire and Print Culture 1790–1822* (Oxford: Clarendon Press, 1994). Gilmartin's notion of the 'counterpublic sphere' (p. 53) is derived from Jürgen Habermas's influential *The Structural Transformation of the Public Sphere: An Inquiry into a Category of Bourgeois Society*, originally published in Germany in 1962 (Cambridge, Mass.: MIT Press, 1989). The thrust of Habermas's theory is that in the eighteenth century literature and culture took on the role of transmitting Enlightenment values to an increasingly literate and democratically-minded population. As the forces of commercialization became dominant in the early nineteenth century this bond between writer and reader began to break down and fragment. But Habermas's notion of literature as a social force for the advancement of civilizing values has been applied by critics to the burgeoning radical, dissenting and working-class culture of this period. See Terry Eagleton, *The Function of Criticism* (London: Verso, 1984). The Italian Marxist Antonio Gramsci also believed that intellectuals and writers had a key role to play in securing popular assent for a political ideology. While traditional political notions are expounded by 'traditional' intellectuals, radical ideas require 'organic' intellectuals from within the radical movement to put forward these views (the difference might be expressed, topically, as Burke against Paine). See David Forgacs, *A Gramsci Reader* (London: Lawrence and Wishart, 1988), chapter X.

13 For the popularity of *Black Dwarf*, see Klancher, *The Making of English Reading Audiences*, p. 101; Epstein, *Radical Expression*, p. 37; Malcolm Chase, 'Thomas Wooler', in Gary Kelly and E. Applegate, eds, *Dictionary of Literary Biography*, vol. 158, *British Reform Writers 1789–1832* (Detroit: Gale Research Publications, 1996). According to one contemporary, in the northeast of England the paper could be found 'in the hat crown of almost every pitman you meet' (cited in Epstein, *Radical Expression*, p. 37).

14 Gilmartin, *Print Politics*, pp 102–5.

15 Cited in Gilmartin, *Print Politics*, p. 99.

16 *Black Dwarf*, 30 June 1819. Wooler was influenced by Cartwright's *A Bill of Rights and Liberties* (1817).

17 This feature of Regency radical discourse is endemic, but see Thompson, *The Making of the English Working Class*, pp. 740–9, and Epstein, *Radical Expression*, chapter 1, for discussions of 'radicalized constitutionalism'.

18 See Epstein, *Radical Expression*, chapters 3 and 5. For the genesis of the English crowd's 'moral economy', see Thompson, *Customs in Common*, chapter IV.

19 R. J. White, *Waterloo to Peterloo* (Harmondsworth: Penguin, 1957), Donald Read, *Peterloo: The 'Massacre' and its Background* (Manchester: Manchester University Press, 1958), Joyce Marlow, *The Peterloo Massacre* (London: Rapp and Whiting, 1969), John Belchem, *'Orator' Hunt: Henry Hunt and English Working-Class Radicalism* (Oxford: Clarendon Press, 1985) and Robert Reid, *The Peterloo Massacre* (London: Heinemann, 1989) all absolve the government of direct responsibility for the massacre. Only Thompson, *The Making of the English Working Class*, claims that the arrest of Hunt was ordered by Sidmouth.

20 See the *Annual Register, or a View of the History, Politics and Literature for the Year 1819* (1820), Appendix to the Chronicle, p. 125.

21 For other poems from the radical press concerning Peterloo, see Michael Scrivener, ed., *Poetry and Reform: Periodical Verse from the English Democratic Press* (Detroit: Wayne State University Press, 1992). See also Scrivener's *Radical Shelley: The Philosophical Anarchism and Utopian Thought of Percy Bysshe Shelley* (Princeton: Princeton University Press, 1982), pp. 196–210 for a discussion of the iconography of Peterloo in popular prints, and the influence this imagery may have had on Shelley.

22 There is an interesting discussion of Hunt's procession in Gilmartin, *Print Politics*, pp. 128–39.

23 *Black Dwarf*, 15 September 1819, p. 608.

24 The Six Acts were analysed in detail in *Black Dwarf*, 5 January 1820.

25 For an even more apocalyptic assessment of the political mood of the time, see the series of 'Crisis' papers in Richard Carlile's *Republican*, from its launch on 27 August 1819 (the periodical can be seen as a direct product of Peterloo) to number 15 (15 December 1819). For Carlile see Joel Weiner, *Radicalism and Freethought in Nineteenth-century Britain: The Life of Richard Carlile* (London: Greenwood, 1983) and Epstein, *Radical Expression*, chapter 4.

26 See Patricia Hollis, *The Pauper Press: A Study in Working-Class Radicalism of the 1830s* (Oxford: Oxford University Press, 1970).

27 See Rickword, *Radical Squibs and Loyal Ripostes* and Wood, *Radical Satire and Print Culture*.

28 See Epstein, *Radical Expression*, pp. 156–7, for evidence of continuing commemorations of Peterloo into the 1850s.

NOTES TO PP. 12–19

29 Royle and Walvin, *English Radicals and Reformers*, p. 139.
30 The title of the periodical was probably taken from Walter Scott's novel of that title, published in 1816.
31 The motto: *Satire's my weapon, but I'm too discreet....* Alexander Pope, *The First Satire of the Second Book of Horace* (1733), ll. 69–72.
   Hectors: Bullies.
   supercargoes: Officers on ships with responsibility for the cargo; such men were renowned for their wealth.
   directors: Probably a reference to the directors of the disreputable South Sea Company.
32 *Sir John Byng*: (1772–1860), Earl of Stafford, commander of the northern district of the security forces 1819–22.
   Lord Grantham: Frederick John Robertson (1782–1859), Earl of Ripon. He introduced the Corn Law Bill in 1815.
   hussar-mustachios: Hussars were light cavalry regiments, originally from Hungary, renowned for their brilliantly-coloured uniforms and, presumably, dandyish appearance.
33 *church and king mobs*: Anti-Jacobin rioters. In 1791 a 'Church and King' mob burnt down the Birmingham home of the radical Joseph Priestley.
34 *the Regent*: The future George IV (1762–1830) was appointed Regent in 1811 when his father George III was declared insane. He succeeded to the throne in 1820. On 30 July 1819 he issued a proclamation which condemned the 'legislatorial attorney' system as unlawful and urged magistrates to 'use their best endeavours to bring to justice all persons who have been or may be guilty of uttering seditious speeches and harangues, and all persons concerned in any riots or unlawful assemblies'. See the *Annual Register for 1819*, Appendix to the Chronicle, pp. 123–4.
   proceedings at Birmingham: On 12 July 1819 Sir Charles Wolseley (1769–1846), a founder of the Hampden Club, was elected as 'legislatorial attorney' (or people's representative) for Birmingham. For his part in organizing an illegal event, Wooler was jailed for eighteen months in 1820.
35 *who warned all people, at their peril, to attend the meeting*: A reference to a handbill posted up by the Manchester magistrates on 31 July 1819, which declared: 'We, the undersigned magistrates, do hereby caution all persons to abstain, at their peril, from attending such illegal meeting.' As Donald Read points out, the faulty grammar 'reads as an instruction to *attend* the meeting: the Radicals immediately pounced on this error'. See Read, *Peterloo*, p. 117.
36 *Regent and his proclamation*: See note 34.
37 *septennial bill*: The Septennial Act was passed by the Whig government in 1716. It replaced the Triennial Act of 1694, and extended the term of office from three to seven years. It was repealed in 1911.
38 *Charles James Fox*: (1749–1806), Whig politician and leader of the parliamentary opposition in the 1780s and 1790s.
39 *Lord Cochrane*: Thomas, tenth Earl of Dundonald (1775–1860), admiral and radical, elected for Westminster 1807, expelled from the navy for exposing abuses, expelled from parliament on a trumped-up charge of fraud in 1814, re-elected but denied his seat. He was active in radical London politics 1814–17, when he took up the post of Admiral of the Chilean navy.
40 *Sir Francis Burdett*: (1770–1844), radical MP for Westminster 1807–37. He was sentenced to three months in jail for publishing this Address.
41 *King William*: William III (1650–1702), joint ruling monarch (with Queen Mary) from 1689, was formerly the Prince of Orange in the Dutch republic.
42 *Switzers*: Swiss.

218

Hessians, Hanoverians: Germans (Hesse and Hanover are regions of Germany).

43 *bloody Neroes*: Nero (37–68), Roman Emperor 54–68, murdered his second wife Poppaea by kicking her to death while she was pregnant.

44 *James the Second*: (1633–1701), King of Britain (1685–8).

    the seven bishops were tried for a libel: James II imprisoned seven bishops in May 1688 for their opposition to his pro-Catholic religious policies. They were acquitted in June 1688, shortly before the King abdicated. Hounslow Heath near London was the base for James's army.

45 *England expects every man to do his duty*: A famous rallying-cry attributed to Lord Nelson at the battle of Trafalgar (1805).

46 *Murder most foul, as at the best it is*: Shakespeare, *Hamlet*, I.v. 27–8 (slightly misquoted).

47 *Juggernaut*: In Hindu mythology, the followers of Krishna ritualistically threw themselves under his processional chariot, called the Juggernaut.

48 *Joseph Surface*: Thomas Barnes (1785–1841) was editor of *The Times* from 1817 to 1841.

49 *Ellenborough*: Edward Law, first Baron of Ellenborough (1750–1818). As Lord Chancellor (1802–18), he presided over the trials of many radicals, including Colonel Despard (1803), the Hunts (1812) and William Hone (1817). He resigned when Hone was acquitted.

50 *Let the gall'd jade wince, my withers are unwrung*: Shakespeare, *Hamlet*, III.ii.255.

51 *Smithfield*: In the build-up to Peterloo, Hunt chaired an important meeting at Smithfield, in the City of London, on 21 July 1819, attended by up to 80,000 supporters.

52 *Mr. Johnson*: Joseph Johnson (1791–1872), a Manchester brushmaker and part-owner of the radical *Manchester Observer*.

53 *the STATESMAN*: A London paper edited at different times by Cobbett and Wooler.

54 *Major Cartwright*: John Cartwright (1740–1824), the 'Father of Reform', whose career stretched back to the 1770s. In 1820 he was fined £100 for using seditious language. Byron unkindly called him 'Antient Pistol'.

55 *Mr. Hobhouse*: John Cam Hobhouse (1786–1869), reforming politician and friend of Byron, elected MP for Westminster in 1820.

56 *Wooler's British Gazette*: This was the London title of the *Manchester Observer* (Malcolm Chase, 'Thomas Wooler', p. 381).

57 *Trotter*: Thomas Trotter (1760–1832), physician to the fleet and medical writer. The works referred to are *A View of the Nervous Temperament* (1807) and 'An Essay, Medical, Philosophical and Chemical, on Drunkenness and its Effects on the Human Body' (1804).

58 *Every inordinate cup is unblessed, and the ingredient is a devil*: Shakespeare, *Othello*, II.ii. 298–9.

59 *Mr. Gale Jones*: John Gale Jones (1769–1838), London radical and veteran of the London Corresponding Society.

    Mr. Waddington: A London radical leader.

60 *audi alteram partem*: 'hear the other side' (no one should be condemned unheard, Latin).

61 *revolutions of the Peninsula, of France, and of Belgium*: A reference to the French Revolution of 1789, and nationalist resistance to Napoleonic rule in Spain and the Netherlands.

62 *Sydney, Hampden, Russell*: Seventeenth-century radicals. John Hampden (1594–1643) famously refused to pay the ship money tax in 1635, which made him a symbol of resistance to the power of the crown. He died of a bullet wound in the early stages of the Civil war. Algernon Sydney (1622–83) and Lord William Russell (1639–83) were executed for their part in the 'Rye House Plot', a conspiracy to murder King Charles II and his brother the Duke of York.

63 *Brandreth*: In June 1817 Jeremiah Brandreth (*d.* 1817) led an abortive uprising at Pentridge, near Nottingham. The authorities were alerted to the plot by the spy 'Oliver'. Though

Brandreth was executed for treason, the trial at Derby led to widespread revulsion at the government's use of spies and *agents provocateurs*.

64 *Edward II*: (1284–1327), King of England (1307–27).

65 *Lord Sidmouth*: Henry Addington (1757–1844), Home Secretary (1812–22). The 'jesuistical circular' was issued on 27 March 1817, advising magistrates promptly to arrest the 'vendors of blasphemous and seditious pamphlets and writings'. The legality of the circular was debated in parliament. See the *Annual Register, or a View of the History, Politics and Literature For the Year 1817* (1818), chapter V.

66 *Jeremy Bentham*: (1748–1832), utilitarian philosopher and member of the radical Westminster Committee. His *Plan of Parliamentary Reform* was issued in the form of a catechism in 1817.

67 *Messrs. Johnson, Knight, Saxton*: Manchester radicals. For Joseph Johnson, see note 52; John Knight (1763–1838) was a veteran of Lancashire radicalism and leader of the local Hampden Club; John Thaxter Saxton (*b*. 1776) was sub-editor of the *Manchester Observer*.

68 *expulsion of the Stuarts*: The defeat of Charles II's forces in the English Civil war (1642–9), and the deposing of James II in the 'Glorious Revolution' of 1689.
Habeas Corpus: The legal right to trial by jury has its roots in medieval law but was codified by Acts in 1679 and 1816.

69 *Dr Watson*: James Watson, London ultra-radical and Spencean. He was acquitted of treason for his part in the Spa Fields riot of 1816.
Mr. Blandford: E. J. Blandford, hairdresser, Spencean poet and chair of the 'Committee of 200 formed out of the great body of the NON-REPRESENTED PEOPLE of the British Metropolis' which organized the Smithfield meeting of 21 July 1819 at which Hunt spoke. For the Spenceans, see Malcolm Chase, *The People's Farm: English Radical Agrarianism 1775–1840* (Oxford: Clarendon Press, 1988) and Iain McCalman, *Radical Underworld: Prophets, Revolutionaries and Pornographers in London, 1795–1840* (Cambridge: Cambridge University Press, 1988).

70 *Dr. Hay-down-derry*: William Robert Hay (1761–1839), a cleric and the leading Manchester magistrate.

71 *three times three*: A popular toast to the highly honoured.

72 *Seagirtonians*: A sardonic reference to Britons: a 'sea-girt' is an area surrounded by sea.

73 *Let the gall'd jade wince...*: See note 50.

74 *Philippic*: A bitter invective. The term derives from Cicero's attacks on Mark Antony, 44–43BC.

75 *Preston, Thistlewood*: Thomas Preston and Arthur Thistlewood (1770–1820) were Spencean ultra-radicals who helped to organize Hunt's procession. Thistlewood was executed in 1820 for his part in the Cato Street conspiracy.

76 *Magna Charta*: The Magna Carta was a document agreed between King John and rebellious barons in June 1215. The charter guaranteed various feudal rights and put a brake on the monarch's power, but in radical legend it was the source of 'no taxation without representation' and trial by jury.
Bill of Rights: A statement of constitutional principles of government passed by Parliament in 1689. In addition to limiting the power of the monarch, it enshrined certain liberties dear to the hearts of later radicals, such as the right to petition the monarch, and the right to bear arms for defensive use.

77 *Birnan wood to Dunsinane*: Macbeth, IV.i.93–4.

2 POLITICAL ECONOMY

1   [Thomas Malthus], *An Essay on the Principle of Population, as it Affects the Future Improvement of Society, with Remarks on the Speculations of Mr. Godwin, M. Condorcet, and Other Writers* (London: Joseph Johnson, 1798), p. 204.

2   Adam Smith, *An Inquiry into the Nature and Causes of the Wealth of Nations*, ed. E. R. A. Seligman, 2 vols (1776; London: Everyman, 1910), 1: 375.

3   For the parliamentary influence of political economy in this period see B. Gordon, *Political Economy in Parliament, 1818–1823* (London: Macmillan, 1976). For political economy as fiction, see Harriet Martineau, *Poor Laws and Paupers Illustrated, I: The Parish: A Tale, II: The Hamlets: A Tale* (London: Charles Fox, 1833).

4   See, for instance: David Hume, 'Of the Populousness of Ancient Nations' (1777) in *Selected Essays*, ed. S. Copley and A. Edgar (Oxford: Oxford University Press, 1993), pp. 223–74; Smith, *The Wealth of Nations*, 1: 62–73; Adam Ferguson, *An Essay on the History of Civil Society*, ed. D. Forbes (1767; Edinburgh: Edinburgh University Press, 1966), pp. 137–45.

5   See, for instance: [Joseph Townsend], *A Dissertation on the Poor Laws: By a Well-Wisher to Mankind* (1786; Berkeley: University of California Press, 1971); F. M. Eden, *The State of the Poor; or an History of the Labouring Classes in England, from the Conquest to the Present Period*, 3 vols (London: J. Davis, 1797). See also A. W. Coats, 'Relief of Poverty, Attitudes to Labour, and Economic Change in England 1660–1782', *International Review of Social History* 21 (1976): 98–115.

6   I have used the original Joseph Johnson edition of 1798 here. See the Select Bibliography for an outline of modern editions of Malthus.

7   These two editions are in effect two distinct books. The first is a brisk political polemic of not much more than 50,000 words. The second, almost four times the length and freighted with empirical data, is more in the nature of a learned treatise.

8   An appendix to the 1817 edition of the *Essay on Population* included a brief and flustered passing comment: 'I should always particularly reprobate any artificial and unnatural modes of checking population, both on account of their immorality and their tendency to remove a necessary stimulus to industry.' See T. R. Malthus, *An Essay on the Principle of Population*, ed. D. Winch (Cambridge: Cambridge University Press, 1992), p. 393.

9   *The Annals of Agriculture*, edited by Arthur Young, were published in forty-seven substantial volumes between 1784 and 1809. Essential reading for the agricultural interest, they consisted of articles and correspondence on every aspect of farming and rural society, including the problems of the labouring poor.

10 There are five pieces on Malthus in Hazlitt's *Political Essays with Sketches of Public Characters* (1819) and an excellent summary in his *The Spirit of the Age: or Contemporary Portraits* (1825).

11 See H. J. M. Johnson, *British Emigration Policy 1815–1830* (Oxford: Clarendon Press, 1972).

12 Hansard's *Parliamentary Debates*, first series, 39, 1158–9, 25 March 1819.

13 The most detailed account of Cobbett is George Spater, *William Cobbett: The Poor Man's Friend*, 2 vols (Cambridge: Cambridge University Press, 1982). There is, however, no substitute for reading Cobbett himself.

14 William Hazlitt, 'Character of Cobbett', in *Table Talk: Essays on Men and Manners* (1821; Oxford: Oxford University Press, 1910), p. 65. There is a useful discussion of the contrasting radical styles of Cobbett and Hazlitt in E. P. Thompson, *The Making of the English Working Class*, second edition (Harmondsworth: Penguin, 1968), pp. 820–3.

15   J. L. and B. Hammond, *The Village Labourer* (1911; London: Longman, Green and Co., 1966), p. 180.

16   The best account of the Swing riots is Eric Hobsbawm and George Rudé, *Captain Swing* (Harmondsworth: Penguin, 1973).

17   See, for instance, David Jones, 'Thomas Campbell Foster and the Rural Labourer: Incendiarism in East Anglia in the 1840s', *Social History* 1 (January 1976): 5–43.

18   See Hazlitt, *A Reply to Malthus*, p. 16.

19   *cover*: A place at the dinner table.

20   *combination*: This was a contemporary term for a trade union. Hazlitt is specifically referring to the Combination Acts of 1799 and 1800 which used the law to suppress trade unionism. For a succinct account of the Combination Acts and their effects see John Rule, *The Labouring Classes in Early Industrial England, 1750–1850* (London: Longman, 1986), pp. 266–81.

21   Torrens is here referring to the rival systems of elementary educational provision recently established in England. Joseph Lancaster was influential in the setting up of the largely non-conformist British and Foreign Schools Society in 1808. Andrew Bell was the key figure in the rival National Society for Promoting Education of the Poor, set up by the Church of England in 1811. With minimal financial support from the state, these voluntary bodies had a limited impact in providing education for the working class in this period. Not until after the 1870 Education Act was there a national state education system with at least the aspiration to reach all working-class children. See Eric Hopkins, *Childhood Transformed: Working-Class Children in Nineteenth-Century England* (Manchester: Manchester University Press, 1994).

22   Ricardo produced revised editions of *The Principles* in 1819 and 1821. Apart from minor changes in punctuation and a single correction this passage remained unchanged. The standard edition of Ricardo is *The Works and Correspondence of David Ricardo*, ed. P. Sraffa and M. Dobb, 11 vols (Cambridge: Cambridge University Press, 1951–73).

23   In subsequent editions 'neat' was corrected to 'net'.

24   Ricardo argued that the rate of profit would ultimately decline to zero and hence capital accumulation and economic growth would, eventually, reach a 'stationary state'. According to his view, both the corn laws, which restricted the import of cheap food, and the poor laws kept wage costs artificially high. Their repeal would boost profits and thus postpone the stationary state. For a thorough account of Ricardo, see chapter 6 of Walter Eltis, *The Classical Theory of Economic Growth* (London: Macmillan, 1986).

25   *stock-jobbers*: A term referring to dealers in stocks and shares in the Stock Exchange. By the mid-eighteenth century, however, jobber had connotations of political corruption and chicanery. Cobbett detested everything to do with the City of London, regarding all forms of financial dealing as unproductive and thus parasitic upon the labour of the productive majority of the population.

26   *roundsmen*: The system of roundsmen was one of the devices parishes used to get labour out of able-bodied men receiving poor relief. There were different versions of the system. A pauper applying for poor relief might be sent from house to house ('doing the rounds'), receiving some wages for work done with the rest being made up by the parish. Or a farmer might receive a certain number of paupers on a weekly basis according to the size of his farm or the amount of his poor-rate contribution. In some places labourers were actually put up for auction! See W. E. Tate, *The Parish Chest: A Study of the Records of Parochial Administration in England* (Cambridge: Cambridge University Press, 1960).

27   William Sturges Bourne (1769–1845) and James Scarlett (1769–1844) were two MPs who made prominent parliamentary attacks on the traditional poor laws during the 1820s. Cobbett had a low opinion of parsons, wherever they were from.

28 *Hodge* and *Jobson* are, of course, imaginary farmers. But 'Hodge', a traditional abbreviation of the Christian name Roger, became the archetype of the silent, patient and impoverished rural labourer in Victorian England. See for instance Richard Jefferies, *Hodge and His Masters* (1880; Stroud: Alan Sutton, 1992). There is a wonderful short poem of 1899 by Thomas Hardy, 'Drummer Hodge', which transmutes the unknown farm labourer into the unknown soldier.

29 *vestry resolution*: A vestry meeting was a gathering of parishioners in the local Anglican church, a body which had managed ecclesiastical business of the parish from at least the fourteenth century. Under the old Poor Law it also had the power to assess and levy the poor rate and to distribute poor relief. Here Senior is specifically referring to the way a 'vestry resolution' can send a labourer on poor relief to work for a particular farmer on a temporary basis (see note 26). The new Poor Law of 1834 removed these powers from the vestry. See Tate, *The Parish Chest*, pp. 188–239.

3 ATHEISM

1 See David Berman, *A History of Atheism in Britain from Hobbes to Russell* (London and New York: Routledge, 1990), chapter 1.

2 *Answer to Dr. Priestley's Letters to a Philosophical Unbeliever* (1782) was chiefly anonymous but 'edited' by William Hammon, who made his declaration of atheism under his own name. Samuel Francis's *Watson Refuted* (1796) confirms the points made above: 'The world has too long been imposed upon by ridiculous attempts to vilify atheists and show their non-existence' (see David Berman, *A History of Atheism in Britain*, p. 122).

3 David Hume (1711–76); see especially 'Of Miracles' (1748) in *The Age of Enlightenment*, ed. Simon Eliot and Beverley Stern (London: Ward Lock Educational with Open University Press, 1979) and the posthumously published *Dialogues concerning Natural Religion* (1779) in *Dialogues and Natural History of Religion*, ed. J. C. A. Gaskin (Oxford: Oxford University Press, 1993).

4 Francis Bacon (1561–1626) was Lord Chancellor, a philosopher and scientific theorist; John Locke (1632–1704) was a philosopher; Isaac Newton (1642–1727) was a physicist; Anthony Ashley Cooper, Third Earl of Shaftesbury (1671–1713), was a philosopher.

5 John Toland (1669–1722); Thomas Woolston (1670–1733); Peter Annet (1693–1769); see Nicolas Walter, *Blasphemy Ancient and Modern* (London: Rationalist Press Association, 1990), p. 34.

6 For a good account of these cross-currents, see Knud Haakonssen, ed., *Enlightenment and Religion: Rational Dissent in Eighteenth-Century Britain* (Cambridge: Cambridge University Press, 1996).

7 See Simon Schama, *Citizens: A Chronicle of the French Revolution* (London: Penguin, 1989), p. 778.

8 Jean-Jacques Rousseau's educational treatise *Émile* (1762) was banned, and its author exiled from France, largely because of the deistic 'Creed of a Savoyard Priest' in Book 4. Claude-Adrien Helvétius's materialist *De l'esprit* (1758) was published only through court influence and Baron D'Holbach's more outspokenly atheistic *Système de la nature* was published under the pseudonym 'Mirabaud'. Both drew on the Epicurean arguments most widely known through Lucretius' poem *De Rerum Natura* (c. 55BC).

9 See Samuel Taylor Coleridge, 'Fears in Solitude' (1798), ll. 129–46; and Simon Schama, *Citizens*, pp. 829–36.

10 Letter to John Thelwall, 6 February 1797, quoted in Maureen McNeil, *Under the Banner of Science: Erasmus Darwin and his Age* (Manchester: Manchester University Press, 1987), p. 3.

11 Richard Carlile, *An Address to Men of Science* (London: R. Carlile, 1821), p. 20.

12 See Berman, *A History of Atheism in Britain*, p. 191.

13 See especially chapter 1.

14 *The Isis* (London: David France, 1832), pp. 292, 296.

15 See G. D. H. Cole, *Richard Carlile, 1790–1834* (London: Victor Gollancz, 1943), p. 25.

16 See Mary Wollstonecraft and William Godwin, *A Short Residence in Sweden* and *Memoirs of the Author of 'The Rights of Woman'* (1796 and 1798; London: Penguin, 1987), pp. 215, 270; Mary Hays, *Memoirs of Emma Courtney* (1796; Oxford: Oxford University Press, 1996), pp. 49–50.

17 See *Isis* 20–9 (23 June–25 August 1832).

18 Robert Owen (1771–1858) was arguably the founder of British socialism and an influential anti-religious thinker; see especially Robert Owen, *A New View of Society and Other Writings* (London: Penguin, 1991), pp. 309–22.

19 Erasmus Darwin, *The Temple of Nature; or, The Origin of Society* (London: Joseph Johnson, 1803). The extracts here are taken from *The Poetical Works of Erasmus Darwin*, vol. 3 (London: Joseph Johnson, 1806). The verse passage is from canto I ('Production of Life'), ll. 223–314 (pp. 20–30), and the prose 'Note on Spontaneous Vitality' is from the first of the sometimes essay-length 'Additional Notes' which follow the poem (pp. 191–204). Darwin's many detailed notes on the verse passage are too full to have included, but where useful I paraphrase or reproduce parts of them below. The 'Note on Spontaneous Vitality' is based on the false premise that microscopic organisms are constantly being generated from scratch: none the less it demonstrates the breadth and meticulousness of Darwin's research, and is of interest as a stepping-stone to evolutionary conclusions which are still broadly accepted today.

20 In a lengthy note, Darwin gives geological evidence that the earth is still 'young', i.e. evolving from an earlier state, and concludes: 'The Juvenility of the earth shows that it has had a beginning or birth, and is a strong natural argument evincing the existence of a cause of its production, that is of the Deity.' While it is true that many atheists such as Baron d'Holbach argued that the world had existed for ever, Darwin would be well aware of the Epicurean argument that it had come about through a fortuitous conglomeration of atoms, and would eventually disintegrate in the same way – a point Darwin himself makes more than once. In the present passage, as elsewhere, Darwin is making the simple notion of caused change stand in for that of God.

21 In these seven lines, Darwin gives us the now-accepted 'big bang' theory of the start of the universe, and the notion of a marine 'primal soup' from which emerged the life-forms that were to evolve into all the later forms of 'organic life'.

22 This last couplet gives rise to the note on 'Spontaneous Vitality of Microscopic Animals' extracted in the main text, on pp. 73–4. Darwin's note on the three key words 'Repulsion', 'Attraction' and 'Contraction' runs in part as follows:

The power of gravity may . . . be called the general attractive ether, and the matter of heat may be called the general repulsive ether; which constitute the two great agents in the changes of inanimate matter. . . . [T]he contractive ether requires at first the contact of a goad or stimulus . . . to excite the sensorial power of irritation.

23 In his note, Darwin argues that the aquatic origin of life is echoed in the need of mammalian embryos for a placenta, from which they extract oxygen through something like the gills of fish. Later in the poem and notes, he will elaborate on the idea that the growth of the embryo recapitulates the evolution of its species from others, as Charles Darwin would also argue.

24   *ens*: Being, entity. For this final staggering claim, Darwin's note simply points us to his scientific prose work *Zoonomia* (1794, revised in a more evolutionary direction 1801): 'The arguments showing that all vegetables and animals arose from such a small beginning, as a living point or living fibre, are detailed in Zoonomia, Sect. XXXIX. 4.8. on Generation.'

25   In canto I, ll. 401–17, Darwin tackles this myth (from Ovid's *Metamorphoses*, I), which his note describes as

of Egyptian origin, and ... probably a poetical account of the opinions of the magi or priests of that country; showing that the simplest animations were spontaneously produced like chemical combinations, but were distinguished from the latter by their perpetual improvement.

Darwin's belief that most classical myths derived ultimately from an Egyptian scientific wisdom lost with the invention of writing was strongly held and recurs throughout his work. It has clear links with the arguments of C. F. C. Volney, whose *Ruins, or Revolutions of Empires* (1791, translated 1792) became a major influence on British atheist and radical thought.

26   *animalcules*: Tiny animals.

27   By 'want of analogy', Darwin means the lack of anything similar being observable in the present.

28   *animalcula infusoria*: A class of protozoa found in infusions of decaying animal or vegetable matter.

29   *acescent*: sour.
     vibrio anguillula: A genus of minute nematode worms.
     viviparous: Bringing forth young in a live state.
     The references to Ellis, Shaw and Nodder do not perhaps need further tracing in this note on a note. But in this passage the miniature eels ('little worms'?) suddenly appearing in flour-paste may be the source of the reanimated 'vermicelli' uncertainly remembered by Mary Shelley from the conversations leading up to her composition of *Frankenstein*, in which Darwin was supposed to have 'preserved a piece of vermicelli in a glass case, till by some means it began to move with voluntary motion'. See her Introduction to the 1831 edition in Mary Shelley, *Frankenstein, or The Modern Prometheus: The 1818 Text*, ed. Marilyn Butler (Oxford: Oxford University Press, 1994), p. 193, and Butler's note, p. 260.

30   Titled 'Of Religion' and dated 'May 7, 1818' in dep. b 227/1 in the Abinger collection in the Bodleian Library, Oxford, but unpublished until its appearance in the 1993 edition cited, pp. 63–73. This extract is taken from pp. 63–7, p. 69.

31   Godwin was born in 1756 in Wisbech, Cambridgeshire, the son of a Calvinist Dissenting minister. In 1773 he entered the leading Dissenting academy at Hoxton near London, and from 1777 to 1783 he was a minister at various Dissenting churches.

32   Jeremiah 17:9.

33   *Socinianism*: Unitarianism: the belief that God is a single being and hence that Jesus, though inspired, was fully human. While many leading Unitarians of the day, such as Joseph Priestley, were fervently religious, for some, Unitarianism's emphasis on rationality and its close links with deism could be seen as the 'last stop' on the road towards abandoning Christianity altogether. It was a route taken by a great many former Presbyterians, in flight from the doctrinal intolerance of Calvinism.

34   He was expelled by his Suffolk congregation for his unacceptable views.

35   Jeremy Bentham (1748–1832), legal theorist and a founding figure of the social philosophy known as Utilitarianism. For more information see **extract 6**. Though Godwin shared many of Bentham's ideas, he disagreed with the coercive aspects of his plans for

maximizing human happiness, most graphically symbolized in the circular 'Panopticon' prisons he designed which allowed prisoners to be observed by their warders at all times.

36   John 1: 46.

37   This concern over how far to go in disabusing the common people constitutes Godwin's main difference from most of the other writers in this section. While he finally concludes that it would be wrong to leave them their illusions, he is clearly in no hurry for this to happen. In his later and fuller anti-religious work, *The Genius of Christianity Unveiled* (published 1873, though he wished on his daughter Mary Shelley the thankless task of publishing it on his death), he begins by considering how

The Ancient Egyptians, the Pythagoreans, the leaders of the Hindoo religion in India, the Druids, and a number of speculative men in all ages, have been of opinion, that there is one set of doctrines that it is convenient should be recommended to and imposed upon the vulgar, and another that should be communicated only to such as were found unquestionably worthy of that favour and distinction.
(Preliminary Essay 'On the Exoteric and Esoteric in Philosophy and Theology', in Mark Philp, ed., *Political and Philosophical Writings of William Godwin*, vol. 7, p. 99)

While concluding that 'there are not two castes of human creatures' deserving of different kinds of knowledge, Godwin's reluctance to publish his more outspoken writings in his lifetime, and the generally mandarin style which ensured that he was never prosecuted along with fellow radicals such as Thomas Paine and John Thelwall, suggests that he sometimes accepted such a distinction of 'castes' in practice.

38   This event happened in Paris on 20 June 1791: the crossing by thousands of armed demonstrators of the symbolic ribbon separating the area round the king's palace from the public part of the Tuileries Gardens signalled the final downfall of royal authority in revolutionary France. Though clearly a supporter of its principles, Godwin increasingly distanced himself from the 'mob'-led violence of the French Revolution.

39   In the previous paragraph, Godwin defines God as 'that principle that has made us what we are'. *Claude (Lorrain)*: (1600–82), French landscape painter.
      Michael Angelo (Buonarroti): (1475–1564), Italian sculptor and painter.

40   (*Georg Friedrich*) *Handel*: (1685–1759), German composer.

41   Published to be 'sold in London and Oxford', though its availability was very brief since the Oxford University authorities had all copies removed from bookshops and burnt. Shelley and T. J. Hogg were both expelled for its publication, but David Lee Clark argues that it was Shelley's work alone – see David Lee Clark, ed., *Shelley's Prose, or The Trumpet of a Prophecy* (1954; London: Fourth Estate, 1988), p. 37. It subsequently appeared almost verbatim in the note to the words 'There is no God' in Shelley's poem *Queen Mab* (1813). This extract is copied from Harry Buxton Forman, ed., *The Prose Works of Percy Bysshe Shelley* (London: Reeves and Turner, 1880), 1: 301–9, which reproduces the first edition scrupulously.

42   'The human mind cannot in any way accept as true that which lacks a clear and obvious demonstration', Sir Francis Bacon, *De Augmentis Scientiarum* (1623).

43   First published privately by Shelley through Schulze and Dean, and then in two parts in *The Theological Inquirer*, ed. Erasmus Perkins (London: M. Jones, 1815), pp. 6–24, 121–31 in the bound British Library collected edition. 'Perkins' (i.e. George Cannon) was a significant disseminator of atheistic material: see Iain McCalman, *Radical Underworld: Prophets, Revolutionaries and Pornographers in London, 1795–1838* (Cambridge:

Cambridge University Press, 1988). This extract is taken from Forman, ed., *The Prose Works of Percy Bysshe Shelley*, 2: 63–79. The speaker of this extract, Eusebes, is a believer in Christian revelation who none the less uses a battery of atheistic arguments to undermine the 'arguments from design' of his opponent Theosophus, whose name connotes 'theosophy'.

44 The idea that the universe needed order 'for its establishment ... not for its maintenance' is specifically deist. Using arguments from Godwin and Hume, 'Eusebes' argues that ideas of order and harmony, like those of good and evil, are purely human and relative constructs: this allows Shelley to politicize the argument by showing how certain ideas of harmony favour the interests of tyrants and – significantly for the vegetarian Shelley – meat-eaters.

45 Shelley's note: 'See Godwin's Political Justice, Vol. 1. p. 449.'

46 'By Richard Carlile. London: Printed and Published by R. Carlile, 55, Fleet Street. 1821. Price One Shilling.' The repetition of Carlile's name as currently-imprisoned author and unrepentant publisher at popular prices tells its own story. This extract is from pp. 6–10, 18–19.

47 Generally seen as fathers of the seventeenth-century scientific enlightenment, Francis Bacon, Isaac Newton and John Locke were all nominal Christians, despite much ongoing speculation as to their real views. Bacon as Lord Chancellor and Newton as President of the Royal Society and Master of the Mint were arguably government employees.

48 The physiologist William Lawrence (1783–1867) fell foul of the medical establishment for *An Introduction to Comparative Anatomy* (1816) and *Lectures on Physiology, Zoology, and the Natural History of Man* (1819), where he argued that life was a result of physical organization rather than an extraneously introduced soul. He was suspended from the Royal College of Surgeons and refused the copyright of the offending books, which ironically added to their circulation in pirated editions by radical publishers, including Carlile. For Lawrence's views on racial issues, see Section 4. By 'Neapolitans', Carlile means Italians who submit tamely to occupation by the Austrian Empire.

49 Taken from pp. 99, 106–9. 'Philip Beauchamp' is a pseudonym of the classical scholar George Grote (1794–1871), working over Jeremy Bentham's papers on the subject. In the phrase 'natural religion' the title continues the attack on eighteenth-century deism seen elsewhere in these extracts, though not all deists would agree that 'natural religion' includes the idea of an interventionist God pilloried here.

50 Grote is referring to the proverb 'God helps them that help themselves' (collected in George Herbert, *Outlandish Proverbs*, 1640), much revived in the religious self-help culture of the nineteenth century.

51 'God never sends mouths but he sends meat': proverb collected by W. C. Hazlitt, *English Proverbs and Proverbial Phrases* (1869).

52 Here Grote repeats some of the ideas of Thomas Malthus's *An Essay on the Principle of Population* (1798) and anticipates those of Samuel Smiles's *Self-Help* (1859). Such advocacy of restraint to the poor in the name of economic individualism is part of the anti-communalist tendency which attracted criticism of utilitarianism from more left-wing positions.

53 Published weekly, then as a collected edition, from which this excerpt is taken (pp. 1–4). The Rotunda was a lecture theatre in Blackfriars, leased by Carlile and Robert Taylor.

54 Richard Carlile, who became Sharples's common-law husband in 1833, and Robert Taylor, author of *Diegesis* (1829) and *The Devil's Pulpit* (1830). *Diegesis* argued that Christianity was an amalgam of elements from older mythologies such as the Egyptian and Indian, following in the steps of such earlier atheistic comparative mythographers as C. F. C. Volney and Georges Dupuis. Taylor was currently in prison for blasphemy, and Carlile for political involvement in the Swing riots.

55 In the Dedication to the collected *Isis*, Sharples recommends atheism as an aid to beauty:

the truth of knowledge blands the cheek, while it expands the mind and gives to the eye such a glowing, intellectual fire as no other grace can bestow. A superstitious woman is never beautiful; while expanding knowledge will put smiles and charms on any face.

56 In the context of agitation for the 1832 Reform Bill, this imagery of 'coming storm' denotes an expectation of possibly imminent revolution.

57 Genesis 2: 18: 'It is not good that the man should be alone; I will make him an help meet for him.'

4 EMPIRE AND RACE

1 See David Brion Davis, *The Problem of Slavery in the Age of Revolution* (Ithaca: Cornell University Press, 1975), pp. 447–9.

2 See James Walvin and Paul Edwards, eds, *Black Personalities in the Era of the Slave Trade* (London: Macmillan, 1983), pp. 171–81; Seymour Drescher, *Capitalism and Antislavery: British Mobilization in Comparative Perspective* (London: Macmillan, 1986), pp. 43–5; Sander L. Gilman, 'Black Bodies, White Bodies: Toward an Iconography of Female Sexuality in Late Nineteenth-Century Art, Medicine, and Literature', in Henry Louis Gates, ed., *'Race', Writing, and Difference* (Chicago: University of Chicago Press, 1985), pp. 232–8.

3 Robert Wedderburn, *The Horrors of Slavery and Other Writings*, ed. Iain McCalman (Edinburgh: Edinburgh University Press, 1991), pp. 16–17.

4 Nancy Stepan, *The Idea of Race in Science: Great Britain 1800–1900* (London: Macmillan, 1982), p. 1.

5 See p. 227, n. 48.

6 See Introduction to Mary Shelley, *Frankenstein, or The Modern Prometheus: The 1818 Text*, ed. Marilyn Butler (Oxford: Oxford University Press, 1994).

7 See Charles Grant, 'Observations on the State of Society among the Asiatic Subjects of Great Britain, Particularly with Respect to Morals; and on the Means of Improving it', *Parliamentary Papers* 10 (1812–13), paper 282.

8 For a discussion of the official British response to *sati* in India see Lata Mani, 'Contentious Traditions: The Debate on *Sati* in Colonial India', *Cultural Critique* 7 (1987): 119–56 and V. N. Datta, *Sati: A Historical, Social and Philosophical Enquiry into the Hindu Rite of Widow Burning* (Delhi: Manohar, 1988).

9 See Javed Majeed, *Ungoverned Imaginings: James Mill's The History of British India and Orientalism* (Oxford: Oxford University Press, 1992), p. 85 and Nigel Leask, *British Romantic Writers and the East: Anxieties of Empire* (Cambridge: Cambridge University Press, 1992), p. 96.

10 Abu Talib Ibn Muhammad Khan, *Travels of Mirza Abu Taleb Khan in Asia, Africa, and Europe, during the years 1799, 1800, 1801, 1802, and 1803, written by himself in the Persian Language*, trans. Charles Stewart, 3 vols (1810; London: Longman, 1814), 1: x; the Advertisement to the second edition also notes that the Bengal government,

convinced of the policy of disseminating such a work among the Natives of the British Dominions in the East, ordered the Original in the Persian language to be printed. Forty Copies of the Book arrived in England; and it may be seen either in the East-India Company's Library in London, or at their College in Hertfordshire.

(pp. xi–xii)

The Persian text was published in Calcutta in 1812, followed by two editions of an abridged Persian version in 1827 and 1836.

11 Ibid., 1: 196–267, 284.

12 The following four pieces come from the collection of newspaper reports and printed ephemera compiled by Daniel Lysons.

13 *Hottentot*: A person from South Africa; and in a derogatory sense, a person of inferior intellect or culture.

14 The African Institution, founded in 1807 to the acclamation of the Evangelical press, aimed to 'redeem' Africa and prepare West Indian slaves for eventual freedom.

15 The slave rebellion of 1791 in St Domingue led by Toussaint L'Ouverture was unprecedented in size and violence. The following twelve years saw the military involvement and massive losses of the French, British and Spanish; the independent state of Haiti was declared in 1804.

16 Maroon communities of runaway slaves in Jamaica employed guerrilla tactics against the British. In the Second Maroon War of 1795–6 the British used Cuban hunting dogs to search out the Maroons.

17 The Irish Rebellion of 1798.

18 Boswell was one of the many slave-holders who purchased Wedderburn's mother.

19 Andrew Bell (1753–1832) and Joseph Lancaster (1778–1838) both promoted schools for the poor based on a system of mutual instruction. Controversy over their respective methods arose between 1805 and 1811 when Bell was identified with the established church and Lancaster with non-conformism; the central issue was whether the Church of England should control popular education.

20 (*George*) *Washington*: (1732–99), American general and first president of the United States (1789–97).

21 *Joshua Steele*: (1700–1791), established a liberal regime on his Barbados plantations which promoted 'voluntary' labour through the payment of low wages to slaves. He turned his estates into manors and his slaves into copyholders who paid him in terms of their labour. His letters to Thomas Clarkson on the management of his estates were published in 1814.

22 *Van Diemen's Land*: Tasmania.

23 *New Holland*: Australia.

24 (*François*) PÉRON: (1775–1810), a French naturalist and traveller; author of *Voyage de Découvertes aux Terres Australes pendant les années 1800–1804* (1817).

25 (*Jean-Jacques*) *Rousseau*: (1712–78), the French political philosopher, novelist and educationalist. In the *Discourse on Inequality* (1755), Rousseau argues that man in a 'state of nature' is content and innocent, but that modern society and the institution of private property bring unhappiness and servitude.

26 *ATTILA*: (*c.* 406–53), King of the Huns.
     ZINGIS: Genghis Khan (*c.* 1162–1227), Mongol conqueror.
     TAMERLANE: (1336–1404), Timur/central Asia, conqueror.

27 *ZOROASTER*: (*c.* 630–553 BC), Iranian religious leader, prophet and founder of Zoroastrianism.

28 *the religion of BRAMAH*: Hinduism.

29 *palankeen*: A covered litter.

30 From François Bernier, *History of the Late Revolution of the Empire of the Great Mogul* (1671). A French doctor and intellectual, Bernier (1620–88) was employed for twelve years at the Mughal court as a physician and adviser on developments in European science and philosophy. He published a highly influential account of contemporary Mughal history.

31 *Pietro Della Valle*: (1586–1652), an Italian aristocrat who travelled in India from 1623 to 1626. On his return to Rome he became honorary chamberlain to the pope. An English translation of his travel account appeared as *The Travels of Pietro della Valle, a noble Roman, into East India and Arabia Deserta* (1664).

32 Affonso da Albuquerque, *Commentarios de Afonso Dalboquerque*: (1557). Albuquerque (1453–1515) established the Portuguese presence in India through his conquests; he was Viceroy of India from 1509 to 1515.

33 *Mark Wilks*: (c. 1760–1831), Lieutenant Colonel in the Madras army and political resident at the court of Mysore from 1803 to 1808. He published *Historical Sketches of the South of India, In an Attempt to Trace the History of Mysore* (1810–17).

34 *Pundits*: Hindu scholars; the Pundits attached to British courts were employed to inform the British judges on issues of Hindu law.

35 *Shasters*: The law books or sacred texts of the Hindus.

36 *Zemindar*: Landholder.

37 *Alexander the Great*: (356–323BC), Greek conqueror.

38 *Claudius Buchanan*: (1766–1815), an East India Company chaplain in India from 1797 to 1808, backed by the Clapham Sect. He toured Hindu temples in south and west India in an attempt to discover how best to promote Evangelism; his findings were published as *Christian Researches in Asia*. On his return to Britain, he continued to campaign for the Evangelical cause.

39 Pierre François Xavier de Charlevoix (1682–1761), French Jesuit, traveller and historian of the French colonies of North America, published *Histoire et description générale de la Nouvelle France* (1744), cited in *An Essay on the History of Civil Society* (1767) by Adam Ferguson (1723–1816), professor of philosophy and mathematics at Edinburgh.

40 William Jones, 'Charge to the Grand Jury at Calcutta, June 10, 1787' and 'Charge to the Grand Jury at Calcutta, June 10, 1785', in William Jones, *The Works of Sir William Jones*, 6 vols (London: G. G. and J. Robinson and R. H. Evans, 1799), 3: 21, 14. Sir William Jones (1746–94), Supreme Court Judge in Calcutta and founder of the Asiatic Society of Bengal, was a renowned orientalist scholar, jurist, translator and poet.

41 Francis Buchanan (1762–1829) worked for the East India Company as a medical officer. He was also a naturalist and historian who published *A Journey from Madras Through the Countries of Mysore, Canara and Malabar* in 1807.

42 (William) Tennant: A chaplain in India, published *Indian Recreations: Consisting Chiefly of Strictures on the Domestic and Rural Economy of the Mahometans & Hindoos* (1802).

43 From Jan Splinter Stavorinus, *Voyages to the East Indies* (1798). Stavorinus (1739–88) was a Dutch naval officer who put down a slave revolt in Berbice (1763) and undertook several voyages to the East Indies. He ended his career as Rear Admiral in the Zeeland Admiralty and accounts of his voyages were published posthumously by his son.

44 From John Le Couteur, *Letters Chiefly from India* (1790). Le Couteur (1761–1835) was an army officer in India involved in the campaigns against Mysore; he ended his career as a Lieutenant-General.

45 Buchanan, *A Journey from Madras*.

46 *Hetopadesa*: A Sanskrit collection of fables, translated into English by Charles Wilkins in 1787.

47 *Jug*: Ritual sacrifice.

48 From Nathaniel Brassey Halhed, *Code of Gentoo Laws* (1776); Halhed (1751–1830) was an East India Company servant and orientalist who translated legal texts from Persian and published a Bengali grammar.
    cowries: Small shells used as currency.
    pun: A certain number of cowries, usually eighty.

49 From John Zephaniah Holwell, *Interesting Historical Events, Relative to the Provinces of Bengal and the Empire of Indostan*, 2nd edition (1766). Holwell (1711–98) was a medical officer with the East India Company, best known for his account of the capture of Calcutta by Siraj-ud Daula in 1756, the *Genuine Narrative of the Deplorable Deaths of the English Gentlemen, and Others, who were Suffocated in the Black-Hole in Fort-william, at Calcutta*, which was the source of the long-lived story of the Black Hole of Calcutta.

50 Louis XVI (1754–93), guillotined in 1793 for repeated acts of treason against the Republic.

51 Oliver Goldsmith, *The Vicar of Wakefield* (1766), chapter 8, 'A Ballad', ll. 30–1. Goldsmith (*c.* 1730–74) was a writer, dramatist and poet, whose most renowned work of fiction was *The Vicar of Wakefield*.

52 *William Jones: A Grammar of the Persian Language* (1771).

53 *bagnios*: Brothels.

54 *Mary-la-bonne*: Marylebone, in west-central London.

5 NATION AND STATE

1 See Peter Garside, 'Popular Fiction and the National Tale: Hidden Origins of Scott's *Waverley*', in *Nineteenth Century Literature* 40 (1) (June 1991): 30–53.

2 For the continuities between nineteenth-century and contemporary Irish politics and culture see David Cairns and Shaun Richards, *Writing Ireland: Colonialism, Nationalism and Culture* (Manchester: Manchester University Press, 1988) and Terry Eagleton, *Heathcliff and the Great Hunger: Studies in Irish Culture* (London: Verso, 1995).

3 Theobald Wolfe Tone (1763–98), leader of the United Irishmen, an organization influenced by French revolutionary thought and active in both Protestant and Catholic circles throughout the 1790s. The rising he led in May 1798 failed to receive French support and was put down with savage reprisals. See R. F. Foster, *Modern Ireland: 1600–1972* (Harmondsworth: Allen Lane, 1988), p. 280: 'The 1798 rising was probably the most concentrated episode of violence in Irish history.' Tone committed suicide after his capture.

4 Irish Catholics were denied access to most forms of public office, and, indeed, many other forms of civil liberty, following the abdication of James II in 1688. Much anti-Catholic legislation applied to both kingdoms of England and Ireland, although following the abortive rising against King William in 1691, Irish Catholics were subject to even greater restrictions, affecting both their property rights and marriage arrangements. Some limited modifications to Catholic disabilities had been made by the end of the eighteenth century.

5 Robert Emmet (1778–1803) had been active in the United Irishmen. He sought French help for Irish independence. He was tried and executed in 1803, and was reputed to have declared from the dock: 'Let no man write my epitaph until my country takes her place among the nations of the earth.'

6 The Ribbonmen were perhaps the most politically conscious of a large number of rural protest groups active in early nineteenth-century Ireland. Eagleton, in *Heathcliff and the Great Hunger*, p. 84, suggests: 'The secret societies practised a kind of preservative violence. Their goal was less revolution than the restoration of a customary moral economy which the forces of capitalist modernization were gravely jeopardizing.' Thus the analogy with Luddism and the Swing riots. The Luddites were active in the Midlands and North of England between 1811 and 1813, breaking machinery, particularly in the textile industry, which they saw as the source of lowering wages, unemployment and a more

general disruption of the rural craft economy. 'Captain Swing' was the name given to the mythic leader of the riots that took place throughout southern England in the winter of 1830. The rural Defenders provided popular support among the Catholic peasantry for the United Irishmen during the 1790s, and were similarly influenced by French revolutionary ideas. The term Fenian is used to describe the various organizations active in the struggle for national independence from the 1850s onwards, the most important of which was the Irish Republican Brotherhood (IRB) founded in 1858.

7 Thomas Davis (1814–45) was a Dublin lawyer and popular author. Together with John Blake Dillon (1816–66) and Charles Gavan Duffy (1816–1903), he founded *The Nation* in 1842, a periodical committed to formulating a programme for national liberation.

8 See, for example, Eric Hobsbawm, *Nations and Nationalism since 1780: Programme, Myth, Reality* (Cambridge: Cambridge University Press, 1990). Also Hugh Seton-Watson, *Nations and States: An Enquiry into the Origins of Nations and the Politics of Nationalism* (London: Methuen Press, 1977).

9 Sydney Owenson (?1776–1859) was a novelist and travel writer, born in Galway, and known as Lady Morgan after her 1812 marriage to Sir Thomas Morgan. She wrote a series of novels with Irish settings and themes: *O'Donnel* (1814); *Florence Macarthy* (1818); *The O'Briens and the O'Flahertys* (1827). Maria Edgeworth (1767–1849) was a novelist and educational writer, who was born in England but from 1792 lived on her father's estate at Edgeworthstown in County Longford, Ireland. Her later novels dealing with Irish material include *Ennui* (1809), *The Absentee* (1812) and *Ormond* (1817).

10 The best critical discussion of Owenson's fiction stressing this point occurs in Eagleton, *Heathcliff and the Great Hunger*, pp. 177–87.

11 Historically, Ireland consisted of four separate provinces (Connaught, Leinster, Munster and Ulster) reflecting the old Gaelic kingships. After 1600, by the process known as 'plantation', Ulster, the north-eastern province, was actively settled by Protestant land-owners and tenant farmers, frequently from southern Scotland. This demographic trans-formation has continued to determine Irish history.

12 At this time Gaelic was entering a process of sharp decline, but the Scottish dialect would have been even more distinctive in comparison with native Irish uses of English.

13 Jonathan Swift (1667–1745) was a satirist and poet, who was born and died in Ireland. He was the author of *Gulliver's Travels* (1726) and numerous essays and pamphlets on Irish affairs. His 'patriotic' defence of Irish interests is invariably mediated by a deeper misanthropy. William Butler Yeats (1865–1939), poet and playwright, was born into an Anglo-Irish family in Dublin. He was active in the revival of Irish culture at the end of the century, helping to found the Abbey Theatre in 1904. He brought a characteristically 'modernist' scepticism to the aspirations of Irish nationalist politics, with which he was only guardedly involved.

14 James MacPherson (1736–96) published 'translations' of two ancient Gaelic epics, supposedly by the poet Ossian. Although almost wholly invented they enjoyed extremely wide circulation and popularity throughout Britain and Europe in the latter half of the eighteenth century. They contributed significantly to a wider revival of interest in ancient Scottish culture and a more general revaluation of European folklore and popular poetry.

15 Bruce P. Lenman, *Integration and Enlightenment: Scotland 1746–1832* (London: Edward Arnold, 1981), p. vi.

16 Henry Dundas (1742–1811) was MP for Midlothian, Home Secretary, Secretary of State for War and First Lord of the Admiralty. As a lawyer descended from an old aristocratic family he had access to most of the leading landed interests in Scotland, through whom he normally secured the election of pro-government candidates.

17 The eighteenth century saw an extraordinary flowering of intellectual life and activity in

Scotland, associated largely with the universities of Edinburgh, St Andrews, Glasgow and Aberdeen. Key figures include David Hume (1711–76), author of the *Treatise on Human Nature* (1739–40), *Political Discourses* (1752) and *A History of Great Britain* (1754–61), and Adam Smith (1723–90), author of *The Wealth of Nations* (1776). These, and other writers, were widely influential throughout Britain, Europe and America and contributed much of our modern vocabulary for discussing questions of historical change, economic development and the relations between state and society. On this phase of Scottish intellectual history see Istvan Hvont and Michael Ignatieff, eds, *Wealth and Virtue: The Shaping of Political Economy in the Scottish Enlightenment* (Cambridge: Cambridge University Press, 1983). For an extremely suggestive account of the relations between Scottish Enlightenment thought and the success of the Union see Tom Nairn, *The Break-up of Britain* (London: New Left Books, 1977), pp. 126–95.

18   The rapid conquest of continental Europe by French armies served not only to export revolutionary political ideas, but also involved the destruction of the old imperial state systems in central, southern and eastern Europe. These included the Austro-Hungarian and Russian empires. This had the effect of generating both the possibility of national liberation and unification among, for example, Italian, German and Hungarian speakers, and patriotic sentiments directed against Napoleonic France. The reimposition of old imperial boundaries and dynasties at the Congress of Vienna (1814–15) inevitably placed the national question at the centre of the political stage which it would dominate until, at least, 1848. For a general history of the period see Eric Hobsbawm, *The Age of Revolution, 1789–1848* (London: Weidenfeld, 1962). For the many contradictory developments within nationalist theories and politics see Martin Thom, *Republics, Nations and Tribes* (London: Verso, 1995).

19   Francis Jeffrey (1773–1850) was a lawyer, journalist and editor. For the circulation figures of the *Edinburgh* see Lenman, *Integration and Enlightenment*, p. 111. The *Quarterly Review*, founded in 1809, was edited by Archibald Constable (1776–1827). John Wilson (1785–1854) wrote for *Blackwood's* under the name of 'Christopher North'. *Blackwood's* took its name from the bookseller/publisher William Blackwood (1776–1834), who was its first editor.

20   James Hogg (1770–1835) was a poet and novelist, whose best-known work is now *The Confessions of a Justified Sinner* (1824). A character based on Hogg called 'The Ettrick Shepherd' first appeared in a series of satiric dialogues, the 'Noctes Ambrosianae', by John Wilson, published in *Blackwood's* from 1822.

21   John Galt (1779–1839) was a writer and failed entrepreneur. His novels, which he preferred to call 'philosophical histories', include *Annals of the Parish* (1821), *The Ayrshire Legatees* (1821), *The Provost* (1822), *The Entail* (1823), *Ringan Gilhaize* (1823) and *The Last of the Lairds* (1826). *Annals of the Parish* may well have been written in 1813, thus predating *Waverley* (1814).

22   Thomas Carlyle (1795–1881) was an essayist, translator and historian, whose reputation as a writer was established in the 1830s, at which time he left Scotland for London.

23   See Garside, 'Popular Fiction and the National Tale'. Garside identifies a number of novelists, both Irish and Scottish, who seem to have anticipated, or at least complemented, Scott in his treatment of 'national' themes.

24   See Thom, *Republics, Nations and Tribes*. Also Benedict Anderson, *Imagined Communities: Reflections on the Origin and Spread of Nationalism* (London: Verso, 1983). The literature on the theory and development of modern nationalism has grown enormously. While Thom's work is one of the most suggestive and wide-ranging, certainly for this period, it contains passages and arguments of real obscurity.

25   For an extremely hostile account of the state visit of 1822 and Scott's diverse politicking

see John Sutherland, *The Life of Walter Scott* (Oxford: Blackwell, 1995).

26 Friedrich Von Schlegel (1772–1829) was a poet and philosopher, who, together with his older brother August Wilhelm, translated Shakespeare into German. Schlegel's early revolutionary sympathies underwent significant transformation, a shift characteristic perhaps of some of the contradictions that lay within nationalist thought at the time.

27 Details of the financial crisis of 1825/6 can be found in D. Simpson and A. Wood, *Sir Walter Scott, 'Thoughts on the Proposed Change of Currency'* and John Wilson Croker, *'Two Letters on Scottish Affairs'* (Shannon: Irish University Press, 1972), pp. v–xxv.

28 For Scott's influence see, for example, Donald Davie, *The Heyday of Sir Walter Scott* (London: Routledge and Kegan Paul, 1961) and J. H. Alexander and David Hewitt, eds, *Scott and His Influence* (Aberdeen: Association for Scottish Literary Studies, 1983).

29 *To J. D. Esq. M.P.*: The novel is in the form of a series of letters addressed from Ireland by the hero Mortimer to an English friend.

30 *chiefs of Ireland*: Following the Reformation the late sixteenth century saw a concerted effort by the Tudor monarchy under Elizabeth I to subdue the leadership of Catholic Ireland which was seen as representing a threat to the English Protestant settlement. The last province to resist was Ulster whose chieftains were Hugh O'Neill (1540–1616) and Rory O'Donnell (1575–1608). Pursuing a campaign against English military garrisons (1598–1603), they finally surrendered six days after Elizabeth's death. O'Neill was reconfirmed in his title of Earl of Tyrone and O'Donnell was created Earl of Tyrconnell. Their expectation that they would be regranted their hereditary lands by James I seems to have been partly thwarted and in 1607, believing themselves about to be charged with conspiracy to rebellion, they fled the country. This 'Flight of the Earls' meant that all their land was forfeit to the Crown and thus available for 'plantation'.

six entire counties: The counties referred to here are not identical with the six counties of contemporary Northern Ireland. They are Armagh, Cavan, Coleraine (renamed Londonderry), Donegal and Fermanagh, where O'Neill and O'Donnell held most of their estates.

favourites: Since so many of the planters in Ulster were Scottish it is assumed that they were 'favourites' of James I who was originally king of Scotland.

31 *cead-mile failta*: 'a hundred thousand welcomes' (Irish).

32 *Milesian*: Meaning 'Irish'. The name is taken from that of a fabulous Spanish king, Milesius, whose sons were reputed to have conquered Ireland around 1300BC.

33 *bleach green*: The place where flax is washed and blanched prior to being made into linen.

34 *palladium*: Originally a statue of Pallas Athene (the Greek goddess of wisdom) which conferred security on the city which contained it. A giant statue of this kind was in Troy, and its capture by the Greeks anticipated the fall of the city. Used here in the more general sense of 'safeguard'.

35 *staple commodity*: Linen. See note 33.

36 *species of agriculture*: Presumably stock-raising, as less labour-intensive than arable farming for crops and thus a source of rural unemployment. Simultaneously, the Irish population was growing rapidly in the eighteenth century as the potato became increasingly the staple diet.

37 Owenson's note:

Belfast cannot be deemed the *metropolis* of Ulster, but may almost be said to be the *Athens* of Ireland. It is at least the CYNOSURE of the province in which it stands; and those beams of genius, which are there concentrated, send to the extremest point of the hemisphere in which they shine, no faint ray of illumination.

Belfast as the 'Athens of Ireland' suggests an analogy with Edinburgh's reputation as the Athens of the North. 'Cynosure' refers literally to the constellation of Ursa Minor, in whose tail appears the Pole Star, and thus a source of direction as well as illumination.

38 *fane*: Temple, here used ironically.

39 *bards*: Poets and musicians enjoyed high social status in Gaelic cultures generally.

40 *mon wi the twa heads*: 'man with the two heads' (Scottish).

41 *gang*: 'go' (Scottish).

42 *Kearn*: 'cairn' (Scottish).

43 *wains*: 'children' (Scottish).

44 *kanie chiel*: 'canny fellow' (Scottish).

45 *Hibernian*: Irish, derived from Roman name for Ireland.

46 *morgue*: A false sense of superiority.

47 *laws of exception*: Anti-Catholic legislation.

48 *sbirri*: 'police informers, spies' (Italian).

49 *proconsular*: Delegated rather than direct authority.

50 Owenson's note:

These half measures are, however, in the present state of affairs almost inevitable. – A divided cabinet founded upon a divided state of public opinion, opposes an insuperable barrier to a frank and honest reform: and oscillations of principle and of practice must attend the effort to manage factions so nicely balanced.

51 *divide et impera*: 'divide and rule' (Latin).

52 *Ube bene, ibi patria*: 'where there is happiness, there is my country' (Latin).

53 *Irish airs*: Moore's first volume of *Irish Airs and Melodies* appeared in 1807.

54 *Bruce or a Wallace*: Robert Bruce (1274–1329), King of Scotland, and William Wallace (1272–1305), legendary Scottish patriot.

55 *Rinaldo*: One of the heroes of *Orlando Furioso* (1516), an epic poetic allegory by the Italian poet, Ludovico Ariosto (1474–1533).

56 *errando etc.*: 'Wandering in those forests / In search of many wonderful adventures / But as the places and the events are so obscure / Very few of them have received recognition.' Ariosto, *Orlando Furioso*, canto iv.

57 *six hundred years*: The obscurity of Irish history begins, for Moore, with the arrival of the English, under Henry II, in the twelfth century.

58 Moore's note: 'See Warner's History of Ireland, vol. I. Book ix.' Malachi is a recurring name among ancient Irish chieftains who flourished in the ninth and tenth centuries. Ferdinando Warner published one volume of *The History of Ireland* in 1763.
    Briens: Brian Boru (c. 941–1014), King of Munster and All Ireland, is perhaps the best known of these ancient kings.

59 Moore's note: 'Statius, Thebaid. lib. xii.' Statius was a Roman poet whose epic *Thebaid* was produced AD90–1.

60 *Antiochians*: Inhabitants of Antioch, in Syria, one of the major cities of the eastern part of the Roman Empire.
    Theodosius: Roman Emperor, AD388–95.

61 Moore gives here a long note from Gibbon:

A sort of civil excommunication (says Gibbon) which separated them from their fellow-citizens by a peculiar brand of infamy; and this declaration of the supreme magistrate tended to justify, or at least to excuse, the insults of a fanatic populace. The secretaries were gradually disqualified for the possession of honourable or lucrative employments, and Theodosius was satisfied with his own justice when he decreed, that, as the Eunomians distinguished the nature of the son from that of the Father, they should be incapable of making their wills, or of receiving any advantage from testamentary donations.

The irony of laws 'by Christians against Christians' is, of course, highly pointed in the Irish context. Edward Gibbon (1737–94) published *The Decline and Fall of the Roman Empire* (1776–88). The Eunomians followed what was known as the Arian heresy, which denied that Christ shared the same divine nature as his father, God.

62 Moore gives a long note:

Nicephor. lib. xii. cap. 43. – This story is also in Sozomen, lib. vii. cap. 23; but unfortunately Chrysostom says nothing whatever about it, and he not only had the best opportunities of information, but was too fond of music, as appears by his praises of psalmody (Exposit. in Psalm. xli.), to omit such a flattering illustration of its powers. He imputes their reconciliation to the interference of the Antiochian solitaries, while Zozimus attributes it to the remonstrances of the sophist Libanius. – Gibbon, I think, does not even allude to the story of the musicians.

Nicephorus, Sozomen and Zozimus are all Greek historians of the early Christian church. Chrysostom and Libanius are Latin writers of the same period – fourth and fifth centuries BC.

63 *Williams*: The Reverend David Williams is the putative recipient of Peter's letters.
64 *Weimar*: Capital of a small duchy of the same name, whose enlightened Duke had, from the 1770s, patronized large numbers of German writers.
65 *Wieland*: Christoph Martin Wieland (1733–1813), poet, novelist, playwright and translator.
Schiller: Friedrich Von Schiller (1759–1805), dramatist and poet.
Goethe: Johann Wolfgang von Goëthe (1749–1832), poet, essayist, novelist, critic and scientist.
66 *Leipsick*: Leipzig, the nearest large city to Weimar.
67 *Row*: Generic term for London's publishing industry centred originally on Paternoster Row (cf. modern 'Fleet Street').
68 *Bibliopoles*: Booksellers.
69 *Robertson*: William Robertson (1721–93), author of *History of Scotland* (1759).
70 *Creeches*: William Creech (1745–1815), head of a family of Edinburgh booksellers.
71 *Memphis or Palmyra*: Types of fabulous 'oriental' city. Memphis was the capital of the Egyptian Old Kingdom, Palmyra a Syrian city under the Roman Empire.
72 *videlicet*: 'that is to say' (Latin).
73 *Ballantyne*: James Ballantyne (1772–1833), an Edinburgh printer who worked for Blackwood and Constable.
74 *The Lay of the Last Minstrel*: (1805), Scott's first best-selling narrative poem.
75 *Marmion*: (1808), Scott's second best-selling narrative poem.
76 *Waverley*: (1814), Scott's first novel.
Old Mortality: (1816), novel set during the late seventeenth-century Scottish religious wars.
Scott, in 1819, was still publishing fiction anonymously, as 'The Author of Waverley'.
77 *Clarendon*: Edward Hyde, 1st Earl of Clarendon (1609–74), author of *History of the Rebellion and Civil Wars in England* (begun 1641, published posthumously 1702–4).
78 *'Cachinno monstrarier'*: 'grotesque mocking laughter' (Italian).
79 *Thomson*: James Thomson (1700–48), a poet born in Scotland, which he left in 1725. Author of *The Seasons* (1730).

80 *quoad*: 'as regards' (Latin).

81 *ne pars sincera trahatur*: 'in order that the truth is not betrayed' (Latin).

82 *Colonel Harrison*: (1616–60), English parliamentary general, executed as a regicide at the Restoration.

83 *Facillime Princeps*: 'easily the first' (Latin).

84 *'Brother near the throne'*: From Pope, *Epistle to Dr Arbuthnot* (1735), l. 198.

85 *former Letter*: The letters were originally published in the *Edinburgh Weekly Journal* in March 1826.

86 *Revenue Boards and Stamp-Office*: Government departments responsible for taxation. There were numerous discrepancies between Scottish and English tax laws at the time of the Union (1707), which were largely resolved in favour of England.

87 *Caledonian Canal*: A project for a canal to be built through the Highlands of the north of Scotland.

88 *Deus ex machina*: Literally 'god from a machine' (Latin), conventionally used to refer to any providential intervention as at the end of stage drama.

89 Shakespeare, *Henry IV Part 1*, I. iii.1–3.

90 The quotations in this passage are from Shakespeare, *King Lear*, II.iv, where Lear's daughters Goneril and Regan argue that their father no longer has need of his courtiers and household servants. 'Patrick' is a generic term for Irishmen and Scott ironically suggests that the Irish MPs should support the Scots on these matters.

91 *absit omen!*: 'God forbid!' (Latin).

92 *Bacon*: Francis Bacon (1561–1626), author of *Essays* (1597–1625) dealing in such maxims.

93 *chests of tea*: Alludes to the 'Boston Tea Party', an incident just prior to the American Revolution when citizens threw chests of tea into Boston harbour as a protest against high import duties.

6 GENDER

1 Hannah More (1745–1833) and William Wilberforce (1759–1833) belonged to the Clapham Sect, the first recognizable Evangelical grouping. Hannah More's books were seen as excellent gifts for young women, and from the late 1780s to early 1830s she was an extremely popular author, widely known and quoted. There were thirty editions of her only novel, *Coelebs in Search of a Wife* (1809), in her lifetime, and 21,000 copies sold. See Leonore Davidoff and Catherine Hall, *Family Fortunes: Men and Women of the English Middle Class 1780–1850* (London: Hutchinson, 1987).

2 See Barbara Taylor, *Eve and the New Jerusalem: Socialism and Feminism in the Nineteenth Century* (London: Virago, 1983). Taylor writes of the analogy between feminism and the popular campaign for the abolition of the British slave trade: 'The campaign, which was led by the Evangelicals, involved large numbers of women who were, however, consigned to an auxiliary position and even banned from direct participation in the 1840 World Anti-Slavery Congress held in London' (p. 35).

3 William St Clair, *The Godwins and the Shelleys* (London: Faber and Faber, 1989), p. 509, argues that the quantity of conduct literature aimed at women can be related directly to levels of social anxiety sparked off by other forms of conflict:

The biggest rush comes after 1793 with the outbreak of war, the Terror in France, the treason trials, and the anti-Jacobin panic. There is a dip in the early 1800s when the short-lived Peace of Amiens (1801–1803) seemed to imply a return to normality, but numbers pick up again with the resumption of war. After Waterloo they fall rapidly back to pre-war levels. By the 1830s although a few continued to be published or reprinted, they had become obsolete.

4 John Gregory (1724–73) was professor of medicine at the University of Edinburgh.
5 Davidoff and Hall, *Family Fortunes*, p. 110.
6 Gisborne's collection of *Poems Sacred and Moral* (1798) was issued in later editions with an ode to the memory of William Cowper, published separately in 1800.
7 See Davidoff and Hall, *Family Fortunes*, p. 112.
8 See John Barrell's discussion in *The Political Theory of Painting from Reynolds to Hazlitt: 'The Body of the Public'* (New Haven and London: Yale University Press, 1986), p. 279.
9 Rejecting the advice of his friend Richard Woodhouse, Keats revised a key stanza of 'The Eve of St Agnes', making the action more sexually explicit. In a letter to John Taylor of 19 September 1819, reprinted in Hyder Rollins, ed., *The Letters of John Keats*, 2 vols (Cambridge, Mass.: Harvard University Press, 1958), 2: 162–3, Woodhouse wrote:

though there are no improper expressions, but all is left to inference; and though, profanely speaking, the interest on the reader's imagination is greatly heightened – yet I do apprehend it will render the poem unfit for ladies, and indeed scarcely to be mentioned to them among the 'things that are'. He says he does not want ladies to read his poetry; that he writes for men.

10 See Roger Sales, *Jane Austen and Representations of Regency England* (London: Routledge, 1996), pp. 57–80.
11 This account derives from an article by Marie F. Busco, 'The "Achilles" in Hyde Park', *Burlington Magazine* 130 (1988): 920–4. The sculptor, Sir Richard Westmacott (1775–1856), trained in Rome under Canova (who had created a monumental nude sculpture of Napoleon which did not find favour with its subject and is now in Apsley House, the London home of the Duke of Wellington). Westmacott was professor of sculpture at the Royal Academy from 1827 to 1857 and created the pediment of the British Museum portico in 1847.
12 Quoted in Busco, 'Achilles', 922. Elizabeth Vassall Fox (1770–1845) married Henry Richard Vassall Fox, 3rd Baron Holland in 1797 and presided over the Whig circle at Holland House. She sent a message to Napoleon at Elba and books to St Helena. She received from Napoleon the bequest of a snuff box given to him by Pius XI.
13 Sales, *Jane Austen and Representations of Regency England*, p. 72, writes that Beau Brummell, like the Prince Regent, 'enjoyed dressing up and playing at soldiers in Brighton but, according to the legend, resigned his commission in 1798 when the regiment was ordered to go to Manchester'.
14 See Alan Richardson, *Literature, Education and Romanticism: Reading as Social Practice 1780–1832* (Cambridge: Cambridge University Press, 1994), pp. 183–4, for a helpful discussion of the position of Maria Edgeworth in relation to the debate about gender and education.
15 See **extract 2** and Allardyce Nicoll, *A History of English Drama 1660–1900*, 3 vols (Cambridge: Cambridge University Press, 1952), 3: 61–7.
16 William Godwin, *Memoirs of the Author of a Vindication of the Rights of Woman*, first edition (London: Joseph Johnson, 1798), pp. 1–2.
17 John Evans (1767–1827) was born in Monmouthshire and went to Edinburgh University. In 1791 he accepted an invitation from the morning congregation of general baptists to

preach at their church in Worship St, London. He was chosen as pastor the following year and stayed until his death.

18 As T. W. Laqueur writes in 'The Queen Caroline Affair: Politics as Art in the Reign of George IV', *Journal of Modern History* 54 (1982): 429: 'On one Sunday in 1820, Wilberforce bought nineteen different metropolitan newspapers to follow the early stages of the queen's case.'

19 See Linda Colley, *Britons: Forging the Nation 1707–1837* (1992; London: Pimlico Press, 1994), p. 271.

20 For excellent discussions of the Queen Caroline affair and the death of Princess Charlotte, see Davidoff and Hall, *Family Fortunes*, p. 150, Colley, *Britons*, p. 265 and Laqueur, 'The Queen Caroline Affair'.

21 'Commonplaces' 73 (15 November 1823), in *Complete Works*, ed. P. P. Howe, 21 vols (London and Toronto: J. M. Dent, 1930–54), 20: 136.

22 Milton, *Paradise Lost*, VIII, 601–2. Adam is discussing with Raphael the place of women in marriage.

23 *Machiavel*: Niccolò Machiavelli, Renaissance political writer and statesman of Florence, best known for *The Prince* (written 1513), a treatise on statecraft.
Thalestris: Legendary Amazon queen. The name is given to 'the fierce Virago' who urges Belinda to arms in Alexander Pope's 1714 version of *The Rape of the Lock* (canto 5, l. 36).

24 See Acts 10: 35: 'he that … worketh righteousness, is accepted with him.'

25 This passage refers to Jean-Jacques Rousseau's novel, *Julie, ou La Nouvelle Héloïse* (1761), which was Rousseau's greatest popular success. This epistolary novel tells the story of the love of the tutor St Preux for his pupil, Julie, and of the marriage, despite this love, of Julie to Baron Wolmar.

26 The focus on passion and feeling as destructive of virtue suggests an attack on some aspects of the literature of Sensibility. For a helpful account of the literature of Sensibility see Janet Todd, *Sensibility: An Introduction* (London and New York: Methuen, 1986).

27 See Milton, *Paradise Lost*, I, 543–5: 'at which the universal Host upsent / A shout that tore Hells Concave, and beyond / Frighted the Reign of Chaos and old Night.'

28 *Bagshot*: In John Gay's *The Beggar's Opera* (1728), Robin of Bagshot is one of Peachum's gang. Bagshot suggests a place notorious for criminals and highwaymen. More's note here reads: 'The newspapers announce that Schiller's Tragedy of the Robbers, which inflamed the young nobility of Germany to inlist themselves into a band of highwaymen to rob in the forests of Bohemia, is *now acting in England by persons of quality!*'
Johann Christoph Friedrich von Schiller, with his first play *Die Rauber* (1781), became the chief figure of the *Sturm und Drang* (Storm and Stress) movement. In the play, Karl von Moor, the heroic robber, takes to the woods to right the wrongs of his father's court, in contrast to his wicked brother Franz. The theme of resistance to corrupt authority gave the play a topical force in England in the early 1790s and it was read with approval by Wordsworth and Coleridge. *Die Rauber* was translated by Alexander Fraser Tytler in 1792 as *The Robbers*. This translation was adapted for private performance by Hon. Keppel Craven and produced at Brandenburgh House in 1798. Altered again, it appeared at the Haymarket in 1799. More's attack in this passage on the German dramatists August von Kotzebue (1761–1819), Schiller and Johann Wolfgang von Goethe (1749–1832) was the most influential of a series of attacks on the translations of German literature. A postscript to the second edition of Tytler's translation of *The Robbers* declares that after reading Hannah More's work the translator wished 'earnestly … that he had *left undone* what he has *done*'.

29 Milton, *Paradise Lost*, II, 678. From the passage in which Satan and the fallen angels explore the 'Universe of death' which is Hell.

30 *French infidels*: A reference to the *philosophes*: Voltaire, Diderot, Rousseau.

31 More's references to German literature suggest the works of the *Sturm und Drang* movement. Inspired in Germany in the late eighteenth century by Rousseau's idealism and characterized by a rejection of literary conventions, it focused on the figure of the artist as rebel or outsider, on the cult of genius and on nature. Key writers were the young Goethe (particularly in his novel *The Sorrows of Young Werther* (1774) which was seen by some as advocating suicide), Schiller and Johann Gottfried Herder (1744-1803), the philosopher and critic. Many of the plays of this movement were translated and adapted for the English stage in the 1790s.

32 *Illuminatism*: The *Illuminatenorden* were a society of freemason-like character, founded in 1776 by Adam Weishaupt of Ingolstadt. The group held deistic and republican views and was strongly anti-Jesuit; it was suppressed in 1784 by the Elector Karl Theodor of Bavaria on the instructions of the Society of Jesus.

33 *the* Stranger: A translation of a play by Kotzebue. Two versions of Kotzebue's *Menschenhass und Reue* (1789) appeared under this title and it became a popular success on the stage. Enthusiasm for German drama reached a peak in the years 1798-1800, culminating in the publication of Benjamin Thompson's *The German Theatre* (1800). Kotzebue was overwhelmingly the most popular German playwright. His *Der Kind der Liebe* (1790) appeared in an English translation as *The Natural Son* in 1798, was published in the same year as *Lover's Vows*, altered by the novelist and actress Elizabeth Inchbald and acted under the same title at Covent Garden in the same year. This is the play acted in Jane Austen's *Mansfield Park* (1815).

34 A reference to Mary Wollstonecraft. Describing Mary's relationship with Gilbert Imlay, Godwin writes:

we not unfrequently meet with persons, endowed with the most exquisite and delicious sensibility, whose minds seem almost of too fine a texture to encounter the vicissitudes of human affairs, to whom pleasure is transport, and disappointment is agony indescribable. This character is finely portrayed by the author of *The Sorrows of Werter*. Mary was in this respect a female Werter. (*Memoirs*, pp. 111-12)

35 Wollstonecraft's second novel *Maria or the Wrongs of Woman* was published after her death in 1798.

36 Cowper, *The Task* (1784), III, 61-3. William Cowper (1731-1800) was a favourite poet amongst Evangelicals.

37 See 1 Corinthians 4: 7. St Paul's epistles were much quoted by Evangelicals writing on gender.

38 Henry Fuseli (1741-1825) was born in Zurich, and encouraged by Sir Joshua Reynolds in 1767 to become an artist. He studied Michelangelo and other artists at Rome 1770-8, and became Professor of Painting at the Royal Academy in 1799.

39 Fuseli's note here reads: 'Vel duo vel nemo – turpe et miserabile!' ('Either both or none – disgracefully and wretchedly').

40 *Medea*: A figure from Greek myth, who in Euripides' play (431BC) murders her children to take revenge on her unfaithful husband.

41 *M. Agnolo*: Michelangelo Buonarroti (1475-1564), Italian sculptor, painter, architect and poet. Important precursors included Giotto, Masaccio and Donatello.
    Raffaello: Raphael, properly Raffaello Sanzio (1483-1520), one of the most famous painters of the High Renaissance in Italy.

42 *Osymandias*: Rameses II of Egypt. The subject of a sonnet by Shelley, composed 1817.
    Pericles: (*c.* 495-429BC), Athenian statesman.
    Constantine: (*c.* 285-337), Roman Emperor from 329 who founded Constantinople (324)

on the site of Byzantium, was sympathetic to Christianity and converted on his deathbed. The three figures mark the transition from Egypt to Greece to Rome and to Christianity as centres of power.

43   Princess Charlotte Augusta (1796–1817), the daughter of Queen Caroline and the Prince Regent. She was ignored by her father during her childhood but angered him in 1814 by breaking off her engagement to William, Prince of Orange. She married Prince Leopold of Saxe-Coburg in May 1816 and died in childbirth, 19 November 1817.

44   Evans's note here reads: 'The above work proceeded from the pen of the celebrated Mrs. HANNAH MORE, and it is reported that much was suggested by this publication to aid and finish the Royal education.'

45   From Thomas Gray, 'Elegy written in a Country Churchyard' (1750), l. 14.

46   *Dr. Porteus*: Beilby Porteus (1731–1818), successively bishop of Chester and London, chaplain to George III, 1769. Supported the Evangelical party in both sees.

47   Psalms 128: 3: 'thy wife shall be as a fruitful vine.'

48   From the First Epistle of Peter I: 24–5.

49   Princess Charlotte, who died in childbirth in 1817. Caroline had been denied access to her in 1812.

50   George III, who had arranged the ill-fated marriage between Caroline and the Prince of Wales.

51   Alluding to Burke's famous defence of Marie Antoinette in his 1791 *Reflections on the Revolution in France*: 'I thought ten thousand swords must have leaped from their scabbards to avenge even a look that threatened her with insult. – But the age of chivalry is gone.' See Edmund Burke, *Reflections on the Revolution in France* (Harmondsworth: Penguin, 1969), p. 170.

52   *Madame D'Arblay*: The novelist Frances or Fanny Burney (1752–1840). The success of her first novel *Evelina* in 1778 brought her widespread recognition in literary and other circles. She married General D'Arblay, a French refugee in England, in 1793.

53   Thursday was the day of the resumption of the hearing in the House of Lords of the Bill of Pains and Penalties against the Queen. This bill, depriving Caroline of her privileges and based on charges of misconduct, was introduced into the House of Lords by Lord Liverpool on 5 July 1820 and abandoned on 10 November. This amounted to an acquittal.

54   *Lady Ann*: Lady Anne Hamilton (1766–1846), a lady-in-waiting to the Queen.
      Alderman Wood: Queen Caroline was living at the house of her friend, Matthew Wood, 77 South Audley Street, Grosvenor Square.

55   *Lord John Russell*: (1792–1878), Whig MP, advocate of parliamentary reform, introduced Reform Bill 1832.
      Castlereagh: Robert Stewart, second Marquis of Londonderry (1769–1822), better known as Viscount Castlereagh, politician. Chief Secretary for Ireland 1799–1801, Foreign Secretary 1812–22. Led House of Commons after Perceval's death. Active in the case against Queen Caroline.

56   Dr Samuel Parr: (1747–1825), perpetual curate at Hatton, Warwickshire from 1785. Latin scholar and political writer, often involved in literary quarrels. Parr had protested in the parish prayer-book at Hatton against the omission of Queen Caroline's name from the liturgy.

57   Charles Burney, who died in 1817.

58   From Act 1 of Goldsmith's *The Good Natur'd Man* (1768). Croaker: 'To be sure, if this weather continues – I say nothing – But God send we be all better this day three months.'

59   Wellington defeated Marmont at the Arapiles Hills, near Salamanca in 1812, Soult at Toulouse in 1814 and King Joseph at Vittoria in 1813. The battle of Waterloo was on 17 June 1815.

7 LITERARY INSTITUTIONS

1 See Lee Erikson, *The Economy of Literary Form: English Literature and the Industrialization of Publishing, 1800–1850* (Baltimore and London: Johns Hopkins University Press, 1996), p. 20:

> After the French Revolution and throughout the Napoleonic Wars, the importation of rags from France was curtailed. The reduction in the supply of the raw material for making paper, coupled with a gradually increasing demand for paper in England, caused the price of demy (the kind of paper most commonly used in printing books) to rise from 20 shillings a ream in 1797 to thirty-two shillings a ream in 1810, an increase of over 50 per-cent. Because the cost of paper was one-half to two-thirds of the cost of printing a book, books became more expensive.

2 For a wide-ranging and influential theoretical account of the literary 'market' in the period see Jon P. Klancher, *The Making of English Reading Audiences, 1790–1832* (Madison: University of Wisconsin Press, 1987).

3 For an historical account of the image of the author as single and autonomous and of recent theoretical challenges to this image, see Jack Stillinger, *Multiple Authorship and the Myth of Solitary Genius* (New York: Oxford University Press, 1991).

4 See Jan Fergus and Janice Farrar Thaddeus, 'Women Publishers and Money, 1790–1820', in *Studies in Eighteenth-Century Culture*, vol. 17 (East Lansing, Mich.: Colleagues Press, 1987), pp. 191–207.

5 Philip Gaskell, *A New Introduction to Bibliography* (Oxford: Clarendon Press, 1972), p. 298.

6 Archibald Constable (1774–1827) was Scott's Edinburgh publisher. His fall, a product in part of the failure of his London agents, in part of the heavy investment required for large first editions, brought Scott down and broke his health, while also terrifying the whole of the British publishing trade.

7 For example, Wordsworth and Coleridge's *Lyrical Ballads* was first published by the Bristol bookseller Joseph Cottle in 1798 in an edition of 500 copies and retailed at five shillings. It brought its authors thirty guineas, and its publisher made Wordsworth a gift of the copyright, which was valued at nothing. When the volume was favourably reviewed (it received ten notices, seven of them positive) it sold steadily enough for Longman to publish an expanded, two-volume second edition in 1800, again of 500 copies, retailed at ten shillings. This second edition brought the authors £100. Erikson, *The Economy of Literary Form*, p. 5, likens the profits made by literary publishers in the period to those of 'recent modern academic publishers of literary criticism'.

8 For Keats's determination to gain a living as a poet see Hyder Rollins, ed., *The Keats Circle: Letters and Papers 1816–1878*, 2 vols (1948; Cambridge, Mass.: Harvard University Press, 1965), 1: 307–8. John Barnard, in *John Keats* (Cambridge: Cambridge University Press, 1987), pp. 7–8, 11–13, argues for the reasonableness of Keats's aim of supporting himself as a poet and/or man of letters.

9 See G. M. Matthews, ed., *Keats: The Critical Heritage* (London: Routledge and Kegan Paul, 1971), p. 109.

10 The most thorough history of the firm is provided by Tim Chilcott, *A Publisher and His Circle: The Life and Work of John Taylor, Keats's Publisher* (London: Routledge and Kegan Paul, 1972). Walter Savage Landor (1775–1864) was a poet and prose writer best known for *Imaginary Conversations*, a prose work published between 1824 and 1829; Thomas De Quincey (1785–1859) was a prolific journalist and the author of *Confessions of an English Opium Eater*, first published in the *London Magazine* (1821–4); George Darley

(1795–1846) was a poet and editor on the staff of the *London Magazine*; Thomas Hood (1790–1845) was a poet, sub-editor of the *London Magazine*, and a friend of the essayist Charles Lamb (1775–1834); Francis Cary (1772–1844) was a translator of Dante; and Thomas Carlyle (1795–1881) was a prominent prose writer, historian and Victorian sage. For Hunt and Hazlitt see note 12.

11 Ann Taylor's *Maternal Solicitude for a Daughter's Best Interests* was published in 1813 in an edition of 750 copies and went through twelve editions in twelve years. Its author received sixty guineas for the copyright, and a further ten guineas for each subsequent edition over 1,000 copies. Chilcott calls this arrangement with Ann Taylor 'probably the most profitable investment they [Taylor and Hessey] ever made' (*A Publisher and His Circle*, p. 67). During 1815 another of Ann Taylor's books, *Practical Hints to Young Females*, sold 4,000 copies in eight months, while Jane Taylor's *Display, a Tale for Young People*, sold 3,000 copies in seven months. Chilcott estimates that the Taylors' conduct books earned Taylor and Hessey a total profit of over £10,000 between 1814 and 1831 (ibid., p. 68).

12 Leigh Hunt (1784–1859), editor of the radical *Examiner*, had been imprisoned from 1813 to 1815 for an article attacking the Prince Regent. His political stance in the *Examiner*, which he edited from 1808 to 1821, was consistently reformist. Association with Hunt, as with the radical journalist and essayist William Hazlitt (1778–1830), brought instant enmity from the Tory periodicals, in particular *Blackwood's* and the *Quarterly Review*. Keats's poor sales were affected by this association, even before *Blackwood's* infamous attack on him in April 1818 as a member of 'the Cockney School of Poetry'.

13 For 'institutional relations and pressures' in general (also in the period) see four books by Jerome J. McGann: *A Critique of Modern Textual Criticism* (Chicago: University of Chicago Press, 1983); *The Beauty of Inflections: Literary Investigations in Historical Method and Theory* (Oxford: Clarendon Press, 1985); *Social Values and Poetic Acts: The Historical Judgement of Literary Works* (Cambridge, Mass.: Harvard University Press, 1988); and *The Textual Condition* (Princeton: Princeton University Press, 1991). For Byron's relations with the market see Jerome Christensen, *Lord Byron's Strength: Romantic Writing and Commercial Society* (Baltimore and London: Johns Hopkins University Press, 1993) and Peter J. Manning, *Reading Romantics: Texts and Contexts* (New York: Oxford University Press, 1990).

14 It was *Poems Descriptive* for which Clare sent Taylor more than twice as many poems as any publisher could afford to print; for his next collection, *The Village Minstrel* (1821), even a two-volume format (some 420 pages) required omissions. As for *The Shepherd's Calendar* (1827), Clare sent Taylor what Taylor estimated as enough material to fill 440 pages. See John Taylor to John Clare, 15 June 1825, in Mark Storey, ed., *The Letters of John Clare* (Oxford: Clarendon Press, 1985), p. 331. For imperfect or illegible manuscripts see John Taylor to John Clare, 6 January 1821, ibid., p. 135.

15 Andrew Motion, 'Watchful Heart: The Poetics and Politics of John Clare', review of Hugh Haughton, Adam Phillips and Geoffrey Summerfield, eds, *John Clare in Context* (Cambridge: Cambridge University Press, 1994), in *Times Literary Supplement*, 8 July 1994, p. 6.

16 Marilyn Butler, 'Culture's Medium: The Role of the Review', in Stuart Curran, ed., *The Cambridge Companion to British Romanticism* (Cambridge: Cambridge University Press, 1993), p. 121.

17 Octavius Gilchrist (1779–1823) was a Stamford grocer, a critic and the editor of *Drakford's Stamford News*. He was an early friend and correspondent of Clare, and wrote the first article about him to appear in a national publication, in the January 1820 edition of the *London Magazine*.

18   See Mark Storey, 'Clare and the Critics', in Haughton, Phillips and Summerfield, eds., *John Clare in Context*, p. 28.

19   John Taylor to James Hessey, 18 January 1814, quoted in Chilcott, *A Publisher and His Circle*, p. 22. Maria Edgeworth (1767–1849) was an influential educationalist as well as a successful novelist. Her best-known novels are *Castle Rackrent* (1800), *Belinda* (1801) and *The Absentee* (1812).

20   See Erikson, *The Economy of Literary Form*, p. 131.

21   These and other facts about circulating libraries derive from Alison Adburgham, *Women in Print* (London: George Allen and Unwin, 1972); Erikson, *The Economy of Literary Form*, pp. 124–46; Hilda M. Hamlyn, 'Eighteenth-century Circulating Libraries in England', *Library*, 5th ser., 1 (1946–7): 197–222; Edward Jacobs, 'Anonymous Signatures: Circulating Libraries, Conventionality, and the Production of Gothic Romances', *English Literary History* 62 (1995): 603–29; Q. D. Leavis, *Fiction and the Reading Public* (London: Chatto and Windus, 1932), pp. 3–18; and Alan Dugald McKillop, 'English Circulating Libraries, 1725–50', *Library*, 4th ser., 14 (1934): 477–85.

22   For a history of the firm see Dorothy Blakey, *The Minerva Press 1790–1820* (Oxford: Bibliographic Society, 1939).

23   Gaye Tuchman, *Edging Women Out* (London: Routledge, 1989).

24   The quote about skimming comes from the popular Irish novelist John Banim, in a novel entitled *Revelations of the Dead-Alive* (London: W. Simpkin and R. Marshall, 1824), p. 114, quoted in Erikson, *The Economy of Literary Form*, p. 28; Erikson is also the source for the statistic from *Poole's Index to Periodical Literature*.

25   For literary Annuals see Bradford Booth, *A Cabinet of Gems* (Berkeley: University of California Press, 1938); Erikson, *The Economy of Literary Form*, pp. 29–32; Peter J. Manning, 'Wordsworth in the *Keepsake*, 1829', in John O. Jordan and Robert L. Patten, eds, *Literature in the Marketplace: Nineteenth-century British Publishing and Reading Practices* (Cambridge: Cambridge University Press, 1995), pp. 44–73; and Anne Renier, *Friendship's Offering* (London: Private Libraries Association, 1964).

26   Robert Southey to Allan Cunningham, 21 December 1828, in Charles Cuthbert Southey, ed., *The Life and Correspondence of Robert Southey*, 6 vols (London: Longman, Brown, Green and Longmans, 1849–50), 5: 339, quoted in Erikson, *The Economy of Literary Form*, pp. 30–1.

27   Felicia Hemans (1793–1835) and Letitia Landon (1802–38) were the most popular and influential women poets of the early nineteenth century; Charlotte Smith (1749–1806) was a successful novelist as well as poet; Thomas Moore (1779–1852) was the author of *Irish Melodies* (1807–35) and other best-selling collections of poems and lyrics; Robert Southey (1774–1843) and Samuel Rogers (1763–1855) were among the age's best-known and most prolific poets.

28   Quoted in Manning, 'Wordsworth in the *Keepsake*, 1829', p. 52.

29   Ibid., p. 55.

30   John Clare to John Taylor, 19 December 1825, in Mark Storey, ed., *The Letters of John Clare*, p. 351.

31   The best study of Landon, and of her work for the Annuals, is Glennis Stephenson, *Letitia Landon: The Woman Behind L. E. L.* (Manchester: Manchester University Press, 1995).

32   Jerome McGann, *The Poetics of Sensibility: A Revolution in Literary Style* (Oxford: Clarendon Press, 1996), pp. 165–70.

33   *Edward Drury*: (1797–1843), bookseller, John Taylor's cousin. Drury hoped to benefit from the publication of Clare's poems and soon quarrelled with his cousin, earning Clare's distrust, while also seeding the poet's distrust in Taylor.

34   Storey prints Clare's letters without editorial emendation, but leaves a space 'where a

sentence might be supposed to have ended' (p. xxxiii). I have followed his practice.

35   *robbing you of 8d for this letter*: Postage was paid by recipients, not senders, in the early nineteenth century.

36   *the rod of Aaron in the Land of Egypt*: Aaron's rod had miraculous powers and was used by him to force the Pharaoh of Egypt to grant him and his brother Moses their wish to worship God in the wilderness. See Exodus vii–ix.

37   *the 'Phiz'*: An idiomatic word for physiognomy or portrait. On 20 May 1820 Clare received a sketch of himself by William Hilton R. A. (1786–1839). Clare was displeased with the sketch.

38   The Egerton MSS in the British Library consist of six volumes of letters to Clare, abbreviated 'MS Eg. 2245–50'. Eliza Louise Emmerson (1742–1847), Clare's most frequent and fervent correspondent, was a friend of Lord Radstock and a fellow Evangelical.

39   *One*: Lord Radstock, Clare's most important patron.

40   The ten lines Lord Radstock had marked in 'Helpstone' are 111–18 and 121–2:

> Accursed Wealth! o'er-bounding human laws
> Of every evil thou remain'st the cause:
> Victims of want, those wretches such as me,
> Too truly lay their wretchedness to thee:
> Thou art the bar that keeps from being fed
> And thine our loss of labour and of bread;
> Thou art the cause that levels every tree,
> And woods bow down to clear a way for thee.
> . . .
> When ease and plenty, known but now to few,
> Were known to all and labour had its due.

In the fourth edition of *Poems Descriptive* Taylor and Clare finally acceded to the removal of lines 111–18 plus the two preceding lines: 'Oh! who could see my dear green willows fall /What feeling heart, but dropt a tear for all.' Lines 121–2 were retained. The offending line in 'Dawnings of Genius' is line 15 from the passage: 'That rough rude ploughman, off his fallow grounds /(That necessary tool of wealth and pride,)/While moil'd and sweating by some pasture's side' (14–16). Mrs Emmerson's proposed alternative to line 15 was 'With Nature! simple Nature! for his guide'.

41   *Walkers dictionary*: Clare was sent a number of grammar books and dictionaries by friends and well-wishers. For discussion of his knowledge of grammar see James McKusick, 'John Clare and the Tyranny of Grammar', *Studies in Romanticism* 33 (Summer 1994): 255–77.

42   *Blair – Addison – Mason – Young*: With the exception of Joseph Addison (1672–1719), poet and essayist, Mrs Emmerson is here suggesting that Clare emulate the 'graveyard poets' who specialized in melancholy reflections on mortality: Robert Blair (1699–1746), best known for his poem *The Grave* (1743); Edward Young (1683–1765), known for *Night Thoughts* (1742–5); and William Mason (1724–97), imitator, friend and literary executor of Thomas Gray, and author of a series of Gray-inspired *Elegies* (1762).

43   *the next Edition*: The second edition; cuts were not made until the fourth edition.

44   *Patty*: Clare's wife, Martha Turner Clare (1799–1871). They were married on 16 March 1820.

45   *the Funds*: The money Clare received from the subscription Lord Radstock organized amounted to nearly £200:

To this was added £100 from Earl Fitzwilliam and an advance from Taylor and Hessey of a further £100.... The money was then invested in Navy Five Per Cents with the intention of providing Clare with a regular, and safe, half-yearly dividend – to be paid through his publishers.

(Edward Storey, *A Right to Song: The Life of John Clare* (London: Methuen, 1982), p. 160)

46   *the next Introduction*: To Clare's second volume, *The Village Minstrel* (1821).

47   J. G. (John Gibson) Lockhart (1794–1854) was editor of the *Quarterly Review* from 1826 to 1853, a regular contributor to *Blackwood's Edinburgh Magazine* (not only as the diarist 'Mr Wastle'), and Sir Walter Scott's son-in-law and biographer.

48   *Hogg*: James Hogg (1770–1835), Scottish writer who, like Clare, was known as a 'peasant poet'; his literary nickname was 'the Ettrick Shepherd'; author of the novel *The Private Memoirs and Confessions of a Justified Sinner* (1824).

49   *Allan Cunningham*: (1784–1842), Scottish poet whose collections of verse, *Traditional Tales of the English and Scottish Peasant* (1822) and *The Songs of Scotland* (1825), were published by Taylor and Hessey.

50   *The Guardian*: Lockhart is referring to an unsigned article in the *Guardian* of 28 May 1820, p. i, describing Clare as 'simply a tolerable versifier' and deriding the panegyrics of his 'bustling friends' as 'ridiculous'.

51   *the third Edition*: Clare's objection is to the omission of two poems from the third edition of *Poems Descriptive*, 'Dolly's Mistake' and 'My Mary', on the grounds of indelicacy.

52   *muscles*: Muzzles.

53   *poor Dolly*: What Dolly says in 'Dolly's Mistake' is not the problem; the problem is her 'mistake' or seduction, especially when treated so lightly – at least according to the parents and guardians who pressured Taylor for cuts.

54   *'Scriven'*: Edward Scriven (1775–1841) engraved the Hilton portrait of Clare, which was used as the frontispiece to *The Village Minstrel*.

55   *cottage*: A drawing of Clare's cottage (or 'hut') by Francis Simpson, the nephew of his friend Octavius Gilchrist. Clare wanted the drawing included in the fourth edition of *Poems Descriptive*.

56   Taylor numbered his proof corrections sequentially but seems to have omitted No. 5.

57   Storey, ed., *Letters*, p. 162n., quotes Taylor's comment: 'I remembered the additions to the *Ramble* but thought and still think that the Poem is better as it is, without them – The Circumstances they notice will be useful in some future poem.'

58   *'Woodseers'*: Insects of great leaping ability, hence the more common name of 'froghoppers'.

59   *Moors Almanack*: An almanack is a calendar of days and months with astronomical and other data. Francis Moore's Almanack was published from 1698 to 1713.

60   Taylor includes this description verbatim – properly punctuated, spelled and initialled ('J. C.') – in the glossary to *The Village Minstrel*.

61   *Scotts death*: John Scott (1782–1821), the first editor of the *London Magazine*, was killed in a duel with Jonathan Christie, a friend of John Gibson Lockhart. The duel was a result of a literary quarrel between Scott and Lockhart, though Scott's death seems to have been an accident. Lockhart's notice of Clare's *Poems Descriptive* (**extract 6**) helps explain the latter's animus.

62   *Bowles*: William Lisle Bowles (1762–1850), author of *Fourteen Sonnets* (1789) and an important influence on Coleridge and Southey. Gilchrist had quarrelled with Bowles in *A Letter to the Rev. William Lisle Bowles* (1820) about Bowles's criticisms of Pope.

Gilchrist's letter mentions Clare several times and reprints a number of his sonnets from *Poems Descriptive*.

63 'Rosey Jane', published with Taylor's alterations in *The Village Minstrel* (1821).

64 *Woodhouse*: Richard Woodhouse (1788–1834), barrister and friend of Keats.

65 *Ways of a Village*: One of several titles Clare and Taylor considered for what eventually became *The Village Minstrel*.

66 *Mrs. Ratcliffe's style*: Ann Radcliffe (1764–1823), Gothic novelist. Her best-known novel, *The Mysteries of Udolpho* (1794), is much referred to by Jane Austen in *Northanger Abbey* (1818), which also discusses circulating libraries.

67 *Messrs. the Reviewers*: *The Soldier Boy* received a brief, broadly favourable notice in the *Critical Review*, April 1801. Neither *The Sailor Boy* (1800) nor *Diurnal Events* (1816), the author's other two novels aside from *Nobility Run Mad*, received reviews.

68 'To suckle fools and chronicle small beer': Shakespeare, *Othello*, II.i.160.

69 *the Quarterly*: The less lively rival Tory review to *Blackwood's*.

70 'heavenly Una, with her milk-white lamb': Una is the companion of Red Crosse Knight, the hero of Book One of *The Faerie Queene* (1590, books 1–3; 1596, books 4–6) by Edmund Spenser (1552?–99). See book 1, canto 1, stanza 4.

71 *Sir John Falstaff*: Old, fat, witty, corrupt comic character in Shakespeare's *Henry IV, Parts 1 and 2* and *The Merry Wives of Windsor*.

72 *Venetian Bracelets*: *The Venetian Bracelet* (1829), a poem by Letitia Landon (1802–38).

73 *Thomas Campbell*: (1777–1844); his most popular poem was *Pleasures of Hope* (1799).

74 *Richardson*: Samuel Richardson (1689–1761), novelist, author of *Pamela* (1740), *Clarissa* (1747) and *Sir Charles Grandison* (1753).

75 *Fielding and Smollett*: Henry Fielding (1707–54) and Tobias Smollett (1721–71), novelists.

76 *The Gentleman's Magazine*: Of the periodicals listed by Wilson, *The Gentleman's Magazine* was established in 1731, *The Monthly Review* in 1749, *The British Critic* in 1793, *The Edinburgh Review* in 1802, *The Quarterly Review* in 1809 and its Tory rival, 'Maga', or *Blackwood's Edinburgh Magazine*, in 1817.

77 'the Planetary Five': Only five of the planets, Earth excluded, were known to the Ancients: Mercury, Venus, Mars, Jupiter and Saturn.

78 *Pope's Epistles*: Alexander Pope (1688–1744), whose Epistles include those 'To a Young Lady [Miss Blount] with the Works of Voiture' (1712); the four Epistles of *An Essay on Man* (1733–4); and the five Epistles of *Moral Essays* (1731–5), the fifth of which was originally written in 1715.

79 'ruin seize thee, ruthless king': Line 7 of *The Bard*, a poem by Thomas Gray (1716–71).

80 'the curfew tolls': From the opening line of Gray's *Elegy Written in a Country Churchyard* (1751): 'The curfew tolls the knell of parting day.'

81 *the Forget-me-Not, the Souvenir, and the Keepsake*: The rest of Wilson's 'Monologue' is devoted to detailed accounts of these three Annuals and of a second 'triad' of publications: *Friendship's Offering*, *The Iris* and *The Amulet*.

82 *Dryden*: John Dryden (1631–1700), poet, critic and dramatist, a target of satire for extravagantly flattering his patrons.

83 'fountains sealed': See Song of Solomon, iv.12: 'A garden inclosed is my sister, my spouse; a spring shut up, a fountain sealed.'

84 *Roscoe*: William Roscoe (1753–1831), historian, poet, botanist, banker and Whig MP. His *Life of Lorenzo de' Medici* was published in 1795.

85 *Celestial empire*: That is, China; from a translation of the Chinese *tianchao*, literally 'heavenly dynasty'.

86 *Athens with a German king*: Otho I (1815–67), the first king of independent Greece,

reigned from 1832 to 1862. He was the son of King Ludwig I of Bavaria.

87 *Contarini Flemming*: The impetuous Byronic hero of *Contarini Fleming: A Psychological Romance* (1832), a novel by Benjamin Disraeli (1804–81).

88 *France ... Goes patching up a constitution*: The French rewrote their constitution in 1830, when Louis Philippe I, Duke of Orleans, came to the throne; he reigned until the 1848 revolution.

89 *Those three most glorious days in June*: Refers to a short-lived republican insurrection against the French government in June 1832.

90 *first*: That is, 'Macao', the first poem about China in the volume.

91 *Captain Elliot*: Robert Elliot (*fl.* 1822–33), RN, topographical draughtsman, produced the sketches from which this engraving and the 'Macao' plate were taken. A series of his sketches, *Views in the East*, were published in 1830–3.

INDEX